MznLnx

Missing Links Exam Preps

Exam Prep for

Thomas' Calculus

Thomas & Finney, 1st Edition

The MznLnx Exam Prep is your link from the texbook and lecture to your exams.
The MznLnx Exam Preps are unauthorized and comprehensive reviews of your textbooks.

All material provided by MznLnx and Rico Publications (c) 2010
Textbook publishers and textbook authors do not particpate in or contribute to these reviews.

MznLnx

Rico
Publications

Exam Prep for Thomas' Calculus
1st Edition
Thomas & Finney

Publisher: Raymond Houge
Assistant Editor: Michael Rouger
Text and Cover Designer: Lisa Buckner
Marketing Manager: Sara Swagger
Project Manager, Editorial Production: Jerry Emerson
Art Director: Vernon Lowerui

Product Manager: Dave Mason
Editorial Assitant: Rachel Guzmanji
Pedagogy: Debra Long
Cover Image: Jim Reed/Getty Images
Text and Cover Printer: City Printing, Inc.
Compositor: Media Mix, Inc.

(c) 2010 Rico Publications
ALL RIGHTS RESERVED. No part of this work covered by the copyright may be reproduced or used in any form or by an means--graphic, electronic, or mechanical, including photocopying, recording, taping, Web distribution, information storage, and retrieval systems, or in any other manner--without the written permission of the publisher.

Printed in the United States
ISBN:

For more information about our products, contact us at:
Dave.Mason@RicoPublications.com

For permission to use material from this text or product, submit a request online to:
Dave.Mason@RicoPublications.com

Contents

CHAPTER 1
Preliminaries — 1

CHAPTER 2
Limits and Continuity — 21

CHAPTER 3
Derivatives — 39

CHAPTER 4
Applications of Derivatives — 65

CHAPTER 5
Integration — 87

CHAPTER 6
Applications of Integrals — 108

CHAPTER 7
Transcendental Functions — 129

CHAPTER 8
Techniques of Integration — 156

CHAPTER 9
Infinite Series — 171

CHAPTER 10
Conic Sections, Parametrized Curves, and Polar Coordinates — 191

CHAPTER 11
Vectors and Analytic Geometry in Space — 194

CHAPTER 12
Vector-Valued Functions and Motion in Space — 197

CHAPTER 13
Multivariable Functions and Partial Dervatives — 200

CHAPTER 14
Multiple Integrals — 204

CHAPTER 15
Integration in Vector Fields — 207

ANSWER KEY — 210

TO THE STUDENT

COMPREHENSIVE

The *MznLnx* Exam Prep series is designed to help you pass your exams. Editors at MznLnx review your textbooks and then prepare these practice exams to help you master the textbook material. Unlike study guides, workbooks, and practice tests provided by the texbook publisher and textbook authors, *MznLnx* gives you **all** of the material in each chapter in exam form, not just samples, so you can be sure to nail your exam.

MECHANICAL

The MznLnx Exam Prep series creates exams that will help you learn the subject matter as well as test you on your understanding. Each question is designed to help you master the concept. Just working through the exams, you gain an understanding of the subject--its a simple mechanical process that produces success.

INTEGRATED STUDY GUIDE AND REVIEW

MznLnx is not just a set of exams designed to test you, its also a comprehensive review of the subject content. Each exam question is also a review of the concept, making sure that you will get the answer correct without having to go to other sources of material. You learn as you go! Its the easiest way to pass an exam.

HUMOR

Studying can be tedious and dry. MznLnx's instructional design includes moderate humor within the exam questions on occassion, to break the tedium and revitalize the brain

Chapter 1. Preliminaries

1. _____ is a branch of mathematics which deals with triangles, particularly triangles in a plane where one angle of the triangle is 90 degrees, and a variety of other topological relations such as spheres, in other branches, such as spherical _____.
   - a. Trigonometry0
   - b. Thing
   - c. Undefined
   - d. Undefined

2. In Euclidean geometry, a _____ is the set of all points in a plane at a fixed distance, called the radius, from a given point, the center.
   - a. Thing
   - b. Circle0
   - c. Undefined
   - d. Undefined

3. A _____ is a set of numbers that designate location in a given reference system, such as x,y in a planar _____ system or an x,y,z in a three-dimensional _____ system.
   - a. Thing
   - b. Coordinate0
   - c. Undefined
   - d. Undefined

4. _____ is a set of numbers, in the broadest sense of the word, together with one or more operations, such as addition or multiplication.
   - a. Number system0
   - b. Thing
   - c. Undefined
   - d. Undefined

5. In mathematics, a _____ may be described informally as a number that can be given by an infinite decimal representation.
   - a. Real number0
   - b. Thing
   - c. Undefined
   - d. Undefined

6. In mathematics, the _____ is a conic section generated by the intersection of a right circular conical surface and a plane parallel to a generating straight line of that surface. It can also be defined as locus of points in a plane which are equidistant from a given point.
   - a. Parabola0
   - b. Thing
   - c. Undefined
   - d. Undefined

7. In mathematics, a _____ is a two-dimensional manifold or surface that is perfectly flat.
   - a. Thing
   - b. Plane0
   - c. Undefined
   - d. Undefined

8. _____ means of or relating to the French philosopher and mathematician René Descartes.
   - a. Thing
   - b. Cartesian0
   - c. Undefined
   - d. Undefined

9. The mathematical concept of a _____ expresses the intuitive idea of deterministic dependence between two quantities, one of which is viewed as primary and the other as secondary. A _____ then is a way to associate a unique output for each input of a specified type, for example, a real number or an element of a given set.
   - a. Function0
   - b. Thing
   - c. Undefined
   - d. Undefined

10. _____ is a mathematical subject that includes the study of limits, derivatives, integrals, and power series and constitutes a major part of modern university curriculum.
   a. Thing
   b. Calculus0
   c. Undefined
   d. Undefined

11. In mathematics, a _____ is an ordered list of objects. Like a set, it contains members, also called elements or terms, and the number of terms is called the length of the _____. Unlike a set, order matters, and the exact same elements can appear multiple times at different positions in the _____.
   a. Sequence0
   b. Thing
   c. Undefined
   d. Undefined

12. A _____ is a one-dimensional picture in which the integers are shown as specially-marked points evenly spaced on a line.
   a. Number line0
   b. Thing
   c. Undefined
   d. Undefined

13. _____ or arithmetics is the oldest and most elementary branch of mathematics, used by almost everyone, for tasks ranging from simple daily counting to advanced science and business calculations.
   a. Arithmetic0
   b. Thing
   c. Undefined
   d. Undefined

14. A _____ is a number that is less than zero.
   a. Negative number0
   b. Thing
   c. Undefined
   d. Undefined

15. In mathematics, an _____ is a statement about the relative size or order of two objects.
   a. Thing
   b. Inequality0
   c. Undefined
   d. Undefined

16. _____ (Groups, Algorithms and Programming) is a computer algebra system for computational discrete algebra with particular emphasis on, but not restricted to, computational group theory.
   a. Gap0
   b. Thing
   c. Undefined
   d. Undefined

17. In mathematics, a _____ is a statement that can be proved on the basis of explicitly stated or previously agreed assumptions.
   a. Theorem0
   b. Thing
   c. Undefined
   d. Undefined

18. A _____ is a set whose members are members of another set or a set contained within another set.
   a. Subset0
   b. Thing
   c. Undefined
   d. Undefined

19. _____ are groups whose members are members of another set or a set contained within another set.

Chapter 1. Preliminaries

    a. Subsets0
    c. Undefined
    b. Thing
    d. Undefined

20. In mathematics, a _____ number is a number which can be expressed as a ratio of two integers. Non-integer _____ numbers (commonly called fractions) are usually written as the vulgar fraction a / b, where b is not zero.
    a. Thing
    b. Rational0
    c. Undefined
    d. Undefined

21. In mathematics, an _____ number is any real number that is not a rational number- that is, it is a number which cannot be expressed as a fraction m/n, where m and n are integers.
    a. Irrational0
    b. Thing
    c. Undefined
    d. Undefined

22. In mathematics, an _____ is any real number that is not a rational number ¡ª that is, it is a number which cannot be expressed as m/n, where m and n are integers.
    a. Thing
    b. Irrational number0
    c. Undefined
    d. Undefined

23. In mathematics, _____ are any real number that is not a rational number ¡ª that is, it is a number which cannot be expressed as m/n, where m and n are integers.
    a. Thing
    b. Irrational numbers0
    c. Undefined
    d. Undefined

24. In geometry, a line _____ is a part of a line that is bounded by two end points, and contains every point on the line between its end points.
    a. Segment0
    b. Concept
    c. Undefined
    d. Undefined

25. In geometry and physics, _____ are half-lines that continue forever in one direction.
    a. Thing
    b. Rays0
    c. Undefined
    d. Undefined

26. A _____ is a part of a line that is bounded by two end points, and contains every point on the line between its end points.
    a. Line segment0
    b. Thing
    c. Undefined
    d. Undefined

27. _____ is the state of being greater than any finite real or natural number, however large.
    a. Infinite0
    b. Thing
    c. Undefined
    d. Undefined

28. In mathematics, a set is called _____ if there is a bijection between the set and some set of the form {1, 2, ..., n} where n is a natural number.
    a. Finite0
    b. Thing
    c. Undefined
    d. Undefined

29. In elementary algebra, an _____ is a set that contains every real number between two indicated numbers and may contain the two numbers themselves.
   a. Interval0
   b. Thing
   c. Undefined
   d. Undefined

30. In geometry, an _____ is a point at which a line segment or ray terminates.
   a. Thing
   b. Endpoint0
   c. Undefined
   d. Undefined

31. A _____ is a set of possible values that a variable can take on in order to satisfy a given set of conditions, which may include equations and inequalities.
   a. Solution set0
   b. Thing
   c. Undefined
   d. Undefined

32. In mathematics, defined and _____ are used to explain whether or not expressions have meaningful, sensible, and unambiguous values.
   a. Thing
   b. Undefined0
   c. Undefined
   d. Undefined

33. In mathematics, the _____ (or modulus) of a real number is its numerical value without regard to its sign.
   a. Absolute value0
   b. Thing
   c. Undefined
   d. Undefined

34. An _____ is a combination of numbers, operators, grouping symbols and/or free variables and bound variables arranged in a meaningful way which can be evaluated..
   a. Thing
   b. Expression0
   c. Undefined
   d. Undefined

35. _____, either of the curved-bracket punctuation marks that together make a set of _____
   a. Parentheses0
   b. Thing
   c. Undefined
   d. Undefined

36. The _____ (symbol _____) and the millibar (symbol mbar, also mb) are units of pressure.
   a. Bar0
   b. Thing
   c. Undefined
   d. Undefined

37. The _____ integers are all the integers from zero on upwards.
   a. Nonnegative0
   b. Thing
   c. Undefined
   d. Undefined

38. In plane geometry, a _____ is a polygon with four equal sides, four right angles, and parallel opposite sides. In algebra, the _____ of a number is that number multiplied by itself.
   a. Square0
   b. Thing
   c. Undefined
   d. Undefined

Chapter 1. Preliminaries

39. In mathematics, a _____ of a number x is a number r such that r^2 = x, or in words, a number r whose square (the result of multiplying the number by itself) is x.
   a. Square root0
   b. Thing
   c. Undefined
   d. Undefined

40. In mathematics, the _____ of a coordinate system is the point where the axes of the system intersect.
   a. Thing
   b. Origin0
   c. Undefined
   d. Undefined

41. In mathematics, a _____ of a complex-valued function f is a member x of the domain of f such that f(x) vanishes at x, that is, x : f (x) = 0.
   a. Root0
   b. Thing
   c. Undefined
   d. Undefined

42. In mathematics, a _____ is the result of multiplying, or an expression that identifies factors to be multiplied.
   a. Product0
   b. Thing
   c. Undefined
   d. Undefined

43. In mathematics, a _____ is the end result of a division problem. It can also be expressed as the number of times the divisor divides into the dividend.
   a. Thing
   b. Quotient0
   c. Undefined
   d. Undefined

44. A _____ is one of the basic shapes of geometry: a polygon with three vertices and three sides which are straight line segments.
   a. Triangle0
   b. Thing
   c. Undefined
   d. Undefined

45. _____ is the theorem stating that for any triangle, the measure of a given side must be less than the sum of the other two sides but greater than the difference between the two sides.
   a. Triangle inequality0
   b. Thing
   c. Undefined
   d. Undefined

46. A _____ is the result of the addition of a set of numbers. The numbers may be natural numbers, complex numbers, matrices, or still more complicated objects. An infinite _____ is a subtle procedure known as a series.
   a. Thing
   b. Sum0
   c. Undefined
   d. Undefined

47. In financial mathematics, the _____ volatility of an option contract is the volatility _____ by the market price of the option based on an option pricing model.
   a. Implied0
   b. Thing
   c. Undefined
   d. Undefined

48. The _____, the average in everyday English, which is also called the arithmetic _____ (and is distinguished from the geometric _____ or harmonic _____). The average is also called the sample _____. The expected value of a random variable, which is also called the population _____.

a. Mean0
b. Thing
c. Undefined
d. Undefined

49. _____ are the basic objects of study in graph theory. Informally speaking, a graph is a set of objects called points, nodes, or vertices connected by links called lines or edges.
   a. Graphs0
   b. Thing
   c. Undefined
   d. Undefined

50. _____ usually refers to money in the form of liquid currency, such as banknotes or coins.
   a. Thing
   b. Cash0
   c. Undefined
   d. Undefined

51. In set theory and other branches of mathematics, the _____ of a collection of sets is the set that contains everything that belongs to any of the sets, but nothing else.
   a. Thing
   b. Union0
   c. Undefined
   d. Undefined

52. In mathematics, the _____ of two sets A and B is the set that contains all elements of A that also belong to B (or equivalently, all elements of B that also belong to A), but no other elements.
   a. Thing
   b. Intersection0
   c. Undefined
   d. Undefined

53. A _____ decimal is a number whose decimal representation eventually becomes periodic (i.e. the same number sequence _____ indefinitely).
   a. Repeating0
   b. Thing
   c. Undefined
   d. Undefined

54. Mathematical _____ are the wide variety of ways to capture an abstract mathematical concept or relationship.
   a. Thing
   b. Representations0
   c. Undefined
   d. Undefined

55. In mathematics, a _____ is a demonstration that, assuming certain axioms, some statement is necessarily true.
   a. Thing
   b. Proof0
   c. Undefined
   d. Undefined

56. In geometry, two lines or planes if one falls on the other in such a way as to create congruent adjacent angles. The term may be used as a noun or adjective. Thus, referring to Figure 1, the line AB is the _____ to CD through the point B.
   a. Perpendicular0
   b. Thing
   c. Undefined
   d. Undefined

57. In geometry, _____ lines are two lines that share one or more common points.
   a. Intersecting0
   b. Thing
   c. Undefined
   d. Undefined

58. An _____ is when two lines intersect somewhere on a plane creating a right angle at intersection

Chapter 1. Preliminaries

a. Thing
b. Axes0
c. Undefined
d. Undefined

59. In astronomy, geography, geometry and related sciences and contexts, a plane is said to be _____ at a given point if it is locally perpendicular to the gradient of the gravity field, i.e., with the direction of the gravitational force at that point.
   a. Thing
   b. Horizontal0
   c. Undefined
   d. Undefined

60. In mathematics and its applications, a _____ is a system for assigning an n-tuple of numbers or scalars to each point in an n-dimensional space.
   a. Concept
   b. Coordinate system0
   c. Undefined
   d. Undefined

61. An _____ is a collection of two not necessarily distinct objects, one of which is distinguished as the first coordinate and the other as the second coordinate.
   a. Ordered pair0
   b. Thing
   c. Undefined
   d. Undefined

62. A _____ consists of one quarter of the coordinate plane.
   a. Thing
   b. Quadrant0
   c. Undefined
   d. Undefined

63. The _____ of measurement are a globally standardized and modernized form of the metric system.
   a. Thing
   b. Units0
   c. Undefined
   d. Undefined

64. A _____ is a symbolic representation denoting a quantity or expression. It often represents an "unknown" quantity that has the potential to change.
   a. Thing
   b. Variable0
   c. Undefined
   d. Undefined

65. _____ is a synonym for information.
   a. Thing
   b. Data0
   c. Undefined
   d. Undefined

66. A _____ is a function that assigns a number to subsets of a given set.
   a. Thing
   b. Measure0
   c. Undefined
   d. Undefined

67. In Euclidean geometry, a uniform _____ is a linear transformation that enlargers or diminishes objects, and whose _____ factor is the same in all directions. This is also called homothethy.
   a. Thing
   b. Scale0
   c. Undefined
   d. Undefined

68. An _____ is a straight line around which a geometric figure can be rotated.

Chapter 1. Preliminaries

    a. Axis0   b. Thing
    c. Undefined   d. Undefined

69. A _____ is a vehicle, missile or aircraft which obtains thrust by the reaction to the ejection of fast moving fluid from within a _____ engine.
    a. Thing   b. Rocket0
    c. Undefined   d. Undefined

70. _____ is the estimation of a physical quantity such as distance, energy, temperature, or time.
    a. Thing   b. Measurement0
    c. Undefined   d. Undefined

71. In mathematics, the conjugate _____ or adjoint matrix of an m-by-n matrix A with complex entries is the n-by-m matrix A* obtained from A by taking the transpose and then taking the complex conjugate of each entry.
    a. Thing   b. Pairs0
    c. Undefined   d. Undefined

72. An _____ is an increase, either of some fixed amount, for example added regularly, or of a variable amount.
    a. Thing   b. Increment0
    c. Undefined   d. Undefined

73. _____ is often used to describe the measurement of the steepness, incline, gradient, or grade of a straight line. The _____ is defined as the ratio of the "rise" divided by the "run" between two points on a line, or in other words, the ratio of the altitude change to the horizontal distance between any two points on the line.
    a. Slope0   b. Thing
    c. Undefined   d. Undefined

74. In mathematics, an _____ .
    a. Ellipse0   b. Thing
    c. Undefined   d. Undefined

75. Any angle larger than 90 degrees and less than 180 degrees, is called an _____ angle.
    a. Concept   b. Obtuse0
    c. Undefined   d. Undefined

76. In geometry, a _____ is defined as a quadrilateral where all four of its angles are right angles.
    a. Thing   b. Rectangle0
    c. Undefined   d. Undefined

77. In geometry and trigonometry, a _____ is defined as an angle between two straight intersecting lines of ninety degrees, or one-quarter of a circle.
    a. Thing   b. Right angle0
    c. Undefined   d. Undefined

78. Angles smaller than a right angle are called _____ angles (less than 90 degrees).

Chapter 1. Preliminaries

a. Acute0
b. Concept
c. Undefined
d. Undefined

79. In mathematics, the _____ of a function is the set of all "output" values produced by that function. Given a function $f : A \to B$, the _____ of f, is defined to be the set $\{x \in B : x = f(a) \text{ for some } a \in A\}$.
   a. Range0
   b. Thing
   c. Undefined
   d. Undefined

80. A _____ is a quantity that denotes the proportional amount or magnitude of one quantity relative to another.
   a. Ratio0
   b. Thing
   c. Undefined
   d. Undefined

81. In topology and related areas of mathematics a _____ or Moore-Smith sequence is a generalization of a sequence, intended to unify the various notions of limit and generalize them to arbitrary topological spaces.
   a. Net0
   b. Thing
   c. Undefined
   d. Undefined

82. _____ is a relation in Euclidean geometry among the three sides of a right triangle.
   a. Pythagorean Theorem0
   b. Thing
   c. Undefined
   d. Undefined

83. In classical geometry, a _____ of a circle or sphere is any line segment from its center to its boundary. By extension, the _____ of a circle or sphere is the length of any such segment. The _____ is half the diameter. In science and engineering the term _____ of curvature is commonly used as a synonym for _____.
   a. Radius0
   b. Thing
   c. Undefined
   d. Undefined

84. _____ is a circle with a unit radius, i.e., a circle whose radius is 1.
   a. Thing
   b. Unit circle0
   c. Undefined
   d. Undefined

85. In mathematics, the concept of a _____ tries to capture the intuitive idea of a geometrical one-dimensional and continuous object. A simple example is the circle.
   a. Curve0
   b. Thing
   c. Undefined
   d. Undefined

86. In trigonometry, the _____ is a function defined as $\tan x = \sin x / \cos x$. The function is so-named because it can be defined as the length of a certain segment of a _____ (in the geometric sense) to the unit circle. In plane geometry, a line is _____ to a curve, at some point, if both line and curve pass through the point with the same direction.
   a. Thing
   b. Tangent0
   c. Undefined
   d. Undefined

87. Mathematical _____ is used to represent ideas.
   a. Notation0
   b. Thing
   c. Undefined
   d. Undefined

Chapter 1. Preliminaries

88. In mathematics, the multiplicative inverse of a number x, denoted 1/x or x^{-1}, is the number which, when multiplied by x, yields 1. The multiplicative inverse of x is also called the _____ of x.
    a. Thing
    b. Reciprocal0
    c. Undefined
    d. Undefined

89. In mathematics, science including computer science, linguistics and engineering, an _____ is, generally speaking, an independent variable or input to a function.
    a. Thing
    b. Argument0
    c. Undefined
    d. Undefined

90. The word _____ comes from the Latin word linearis, which means created by lines.
    a. Linear0
    b. Thing
    c. Undefined
    d. Undefined

91. A _____ is an equation in which each term is either a constant or the product of a constant times the first power of a variable.
    a. Thing
    b. Linear equation0
    c. Undefined
    d. Undefined

92. _____ is the transport of people on a trip/journey or the process or time involved in a person or object moving from one location to another.
    a. Travel0
    b. Thing
    c. Undefined
    d. Undefined

93. _____ is electromagnetic radiation with a wavelength that is visible to the eye (visible _____) or, in a technical or scientific context, electromagnetic radiation of any wavelength.
    a. Light0
    b. Thing
    c. Undefined
    d. Undefined

94. A _____, as defined by the International Astronomical Union, is a celestial body orbiting a star or stellar remnant that is massive enough to be rounded by its own gravity, not massive enough to cause thermonuclear fusion in its core, and has cleared its neighboring region of planetesimals.
    a. Planet0
    b. Thing
    c. Undefined
    d. Undefined

95. _____ is a temperature scale named after the German physicist Daniel Gabriel _____, who proposed it in 1724.
    a. Thing
    b. Fahrenheit0
    c. Undefined
    d. Undefined

96. _____ is, or relates to, the _____ temperature scale.
    a. Thing
    b. Celsius0
    c. Undefined
    d. Undefined

97. _____ is a physical property of a system that underlies the common notions of hot and cold; something that is hotter has the greater _____.

Chapter 1. Preliminaries

a. Temperature0
b. Thing
c. Undefined
d. Undefined

98. In mathematics, there are several meanings of _____ depending on the subject.
a. Degree0
b. Thing
c. Undefined
d. Undefined

99. Sir Isaac _____, was an English physicist, mathematician, astronomer, natural philosopher, and alchemist, regarded by many as the greatest figure in the history of science
a. Newton0
b. Person
c. Undefined
d. Undefined

100. In geometry, the _____ of an object is a point in some sense in the middle of the object.
a. Thing
b. Center0
c. Undefined
d. Undefined

101. _____ is the property of a physical object that quantifies the amount of matter and energy it is equivalent to.
a. Mass0
b. Thing
c. Undefined
d. Undefined

102. In mathematics, a _____ is a countable collection of open covers of a topological space that satisfies certain separation axioms.
a. Development0
b. Thing
c. Undefined
d. Undefined

103. _____, a field in mathematics, is the study of how functions change when their inputs change. The primary object of study in _____ is the derivative.
a. Thing
b. Differential calculus0
c. Undefined
d. Undefined

104. In mathematics and the mathematical sciences, a _____ is a fixed, but possibly unspecified, value. This is in contrast to a variable, which is not fixed.
a. Thing
b. Constant0
c. Undefined
d. Undefined

105. The metre (or _____, see spelling differences) is a measure of length. It is the basic unit of length in the metric system and in the International System of Units (SI), used around the world for general and scientific purposes.
a. Concept
b. Meter0
c. Undefined
d. Undefined

106. A _____ given two distinct points A and B on the _____, is the set of points C on the line containing points A and B such that A is not strictly between C and B.
a. Thing
b. Ray0
c. Undefined
d. Undefined

107. In mathematics, a _____ (also spelled reflexion) is a map that transforms an object into its mirror image.

a. Reflection0
b. Concept
c. Undefined
d. Undefined

108. In geometry, the relations of _____ are those such as 'lies on' between points and lines (as in 'point P lies on line L'), and 'intersects' (as in 'line L_1 intersects line L_2', in three-dimensional space). That is, they are the binary relations describing how subsets meet.
   a. Thing
   b. Incidence0
   c. Undefined
   d. Undefined

109. In geometry, a _____ is a special kind of point, usually a corner of a polygon, polyhedron, or higher dimensional polytope. In the geometry of curves a _____ is a point of where the first derivative of curvature is zero. In graph theory, a _____ is the fundamental unit out of which graphs are formed
   a. Vertex0
   b. Thing
   c. Undefined
   d. Undefined

110. In geometry, an _____ polygon is a polygon which has all sides of the same length.
   a. Equilateral0
   b. Thing
   c. Undefined
   d. Undefined

111. _____ is the distance around a given two-dimensional object. As a general rule, the _____ of a polygon can always be calculated by adding all the length of the sides together. So, the formula for triangles is P = a + b + c, where a, b and c stand for each side of it. For quadrilaterals the equation is P = a + b + c + d. For equilateral polygons, P = na, where n is the number of sides and a is the side length.
   a. Thing
   b. Perimeter0
   c. Undefined
   d. Undefined

112. _____ is the middle point of a line segment.
   a. Thing
   b. Midpoint0
   c. Undefined
   d. Undefined

113. The _____ of a geographic location is its height above a fixed reference point, often the mean sea level.
   a. Elevation0
   b. Thing
   c. Undefined
   d. Undefined

114. _____ is the fee paid on borrowed money.
   a. Thing
   b. Interest0
   c. Undefined
   d. Undefined

115. _____ or investing is a term with several closely-related meanings in business management, finance and economics, related to saving or deferring consumption.
   a. Investment0
   b. Thing
   c. Undefined
   d. Undefined

116. In mathematics, a _____ of a k-place relation $L \subseteq X_1 \times ... \times X_k$ is one of the sets X_j, $1 \leq j \leq k$. In the special case where k = 2 and $L \subseteq X_1 \times X_2$ is a function $L : X_1 \to X_2$, it is conventional to refer to X_1 as the _____ of the function and to refer to X_2 as the codomain of the function.

Chapter 1. Preliminaries 13

   a. Domain0   b. Thing
   c. Undefined   d. Undefined

117. Leonhard _____ was a pioneering Swiss mathematician and physicist, who spent most of his life in Russia and Germany.
   a. Euler0   b. Person
   c. Undefined   d. Undefined

118. An _____ or member of a set is an object that when collected together make up the set.
   a. Thing   b. Element0
   c. Undefined   d. Undefined

119. In a function the _____, is the variable which is the value, i.e. the "output", of the function.
   a. Thing   b. Dependent variable0
   c. Undefined   d. Undefined

120. The _____ of a solid object is the three-dimensional concept of how much space it occupies, often quantified numerically.
   a. Volume0   b. Thing
   c. Undefined   d. Undefined

121. In mathematics, _____ geometry was the traditional name for the geometry of three-dimensional Euclidean space — for practical purposes the kind of space we live in.
   a. Thing   b. Solid0
   c. Undefined   d. Undefined

122. In mathematics, a _____ is the set of all points in three-dimensional space (R^3) which are at distance r from a fixed point of that space, where r is a positive real number called the radius of the _____. The fixed point is called the center or centre, and is not part of the _____ itself.
   a. Thing   b. Sphere0
   c. Undefined   d. Undefined

123. _____ was a pioneering Swiss mathematician and physicist, who spent most of his life in Russia and Germany.
   a. Person   b. Leonhard Euler0
   c. Undefined   d. Undefined

124. In Euclidean geometry, a _____ is moving every point a constant distance in a specified direction.
   a. Concept   b. Translation0
   c. Undefined   d. Undefined

125. _____ is a branch of mathematics concerning the study of structure, relation and quantity.
   a. Concept   b. Algebra0
   c. Undefined   d. Undefined

126. In mathematics, an inequality is a statement about the relative size or order of two objects. For example 14 > 10, or 14 is _____ 10.
   a. Greater than0
   b. Thing
   c. Undefined
   d. Undefined

127. _____ are objects, characters, or other concrete representations of ideas, concepts, or other abstractions.
   a. Thing
   b. Symbols0
   c. Undefined
   d. Undefined

128. In mathematics, the _____ f is the collection of all ordered pairs. In particular, graph means the graphical representation of this collection, in the form of a curve or surface, together with axes, etc. Graphing on a Cartesian plane is sometimes referred to as curve sketching.
   a. Graph of a function0
   b. Thing
   c. Undefined
   d. Undefined

129. The _____ is a measurement of how a function changes when the values of its inputs change.
   a. Thing
   b. Derivative0
   c. Undefined
   d. Undefined

130. _____ are external two-dimensional outlines, with the appearance or configuration of some thing - in contrast to the matter or content or substance of which it is composed.
   a. Shapes0
   b. Thing
   c. Undefined
   d. Undefined

131. A _____ number is a positive integer which has a positive divisor other than one or itself.
   a. Composite0
   b. Thing
   c. Undefined
   d. Undefined

132. A _____, formed by the composition of one function on another, represents the application of the former to the result of the application of the latter to the argument of the composite.
   a. Composite function0
   b. Thing
   c. Undefined
   d. Undefined

133. In mathematics, a _____ of a positive integer n is a way of writing n as a sum of positive integers.
   a. Thing
   b. Composition0
   c. Undefined
   d. Undefined

134. _____ means "constancy", i.e. if something retains a certain feature even after we change a way of looking at it, then it is symmetric.
   a. Symmetry0
   b. Thing
   c. Undefined
   d. Undefined

135. _____ are functions which satisfy particular symmetry relations, with respect to taking additive inverses.
   a. Thing
   b. Even function0
   c. Undefined
   d. Undefined

Chapter 1. Preliminaries

136. In mathematics, _____ and odd functions are functions which satisfy particular symmetry relations, with respect to taking additive inverses.
 a. Even functions0
 b. Thing
 c. Undefined
 d. Undefined

137. A _____ defined function f(x) of a real variable x is a function whose definition is given differently on disjoint subsets of its domain.
 a. Piecewise0
 b. Thing
 c. Undefined
 d. Undefined

138. An _____ is a triangle in which all sides are of equal length.
 a. Equilateral triangle0
 b. Thing
 c. Undefined
 d. Undefined

139. A _____ can refer to a line joining two nonadjacent vertices of a polygon or polyhedron, or in some contexts any upward or downward sloping line. .
 a. Thing
 b. Diagonal0
 c. Undefined
 d. Undefined

140. A _____ is a three-dimensional solid object bounded by six square faces, facets, or sides, with three meeting at each vertex.
 a. Cube0
 b. Thing
 c. Undefined
 d. Undefined

141. A _____ is a deliberate process for transforming one or more inputs into one or more results.
 a. Calculation0
 b. Thing
 c. Undefined
 d. Undefined

142. _____ is a notation for writing numbers that is often used by scientists and mathematicians to make it easier to write large and small numbers.
 a. Scientific notation0
 b. Thing
 c. Undefined
 d. Undefined

143. _____ is a technique used in algebra to solve quadratic equations, in analytic geometry for determining the shapes of graphs, and in calculus for computing integrals, including, but hardly limited to, the integrals that define Laplace transforms. The essential objective is to reduce a quadratic polynomial in a variable in an equation or expression to a squared polynomial of linear order. This can reduce an equation or integral to one that is more easily solved or evaluated.
 a. Thing
 b. Completing the square0
 c. Undefined
 d. Undefined

144. _____ of a two-dimensional figure is a line such that, if a perpendicular is constructed, any two points lying on the perpendicular at equal distances from the _____ are identical.
 a. Thing
 b. Axis of symmetry0
 c. Undefined
 d. Undefined

Chapter 1. Preliminaries

145. _____ the expected value of a random variable displays the average or central value of the variable. It is a summary value of the distribution of the variable.
- a. Thing
- b. Determining0
- c. Undefined
- d. Undefined

146. In mathematics, a _____ is a polynomial equation of the second degree. The general form is $ax^2 + bx + c = 0$.
- a. Quadratic equation0
- b. Thing
- c. Undefined
- d. Undefined

147. In mathematics, an _____ on a real vector space is a choice of which ordered bases are "positively" oriented, or right-handed, and which are "negatively" oriented, or left-handed.
- a. Orientation0
- b. Thing
- c. Undefined
- d. Undefined

148. A _____ is 360° or 2δ radians.
- a. Turn0
- b. Thing
- c. Undefined
- d. Undefined

149. Any point where a graph makes contact with an coordinate axis is called an _____ of the graph
- a. Intercept0
- b. Thing
- c. Undefined
- d. Undefined

150. The _____ is a unit of plane angle. It is represented by the symbol "rad" or, more rarely, by the superscript c (for "circular measure"). For example, an angle of 1.2 radians would be written "1.2 rad" or "1.2c" (second symbol can produce confusion with centigrads).
- a. Radian0
- b. Thing
- c. Undefined
- d. Undefined

151. In geometry, _____, or general position for a set of points, or other configuration, means the general case situation, as opposed to some more special or coincidental cases that are possible.
- a. Standard position0
- b. Thing
- c. Undefined
- d. Undefined

152. Initial objects are also called _____, and terminal objects are also called final.
- a. Coterminal0
- b. Thing
- c. Undefined
- d. Undefined

153. _____ is a unit of plane angle, equal to 180/δ degrees, or about 57.2958 degrees
- a. Thing
- b. Radian measure0
- c. Undefined
- d. Undefined

154. In Euclidean geometry, an _____ is a closed segment of a differentiable curve in the two-dimensional plane; for example, a circular _____ is a segment of a circle.
- a. Arc0
- b. Concept
- c. Undefined
- d. Undefined

Chapter 1. Preliminaries

155. A circular _____ or circle _____ also known as a pie piece is the portion of a circle enclosed by two radii and an arc.
   a. Thing
   b. Sector0
   c. Undefined
   d. Undefined

156. In mathematics, the _____ functions are functions of an angle; they are important when studying triangles and modeling periodic phenomena, among many other applications.
   a. Thing
   b. Trigonometric0
   c. Undefined
   d. Undefined

157. The _____ are functions of an angle; they are important when studying triangles and modeling periodic phenomena, among many other applications.
   a. Trigonometric functions0
   b. Thing
   c. Undefined
   d. Undefined

158. Two mathematical objects are equal if and only if they are precisely the same in every way. This defines a binary relation, _____, denoted by the sign of _____ "=" in such a way that the statement "x = y" means that x and y are equal.
   a. Equality0
   b. Thing
   c. Undefined
   d. Undefined

159. In mathematics, the additive inverse, or _____ of a number n is the number that, when added to n, yields zero. The additive inverse of n is denoted −n. For example, 7 is −7, because 7 + (−7) = 0, and the additive inverse of −0.3 is 0.3, because −0.3 + 0.3 = 0.
   a. Thing
   b. Opposite0
   c. Undefined
   d. Undefined

160. In mathematics, the _____ of a number n is the number that, when added to n, yields zero. The _____ of n is denoted −n. For example, 7 is −7, because 7 + (−7) = 0, and the _____ of −0.3 is 0.3, because −0.3 + 0.3 = 0.
   a. Thing
   b. Additive inverse0
   c. Undefined
   d. Undefined

161. In geometry, _____ angles are angles that have a common ray coming out of the vertex going between two other rays.
   a. Concept
   b. Adjacent0
   c. Undefined
   d. Undefined

162. In statistics, _____ means the most frequent value assumed by a random variable, or occurring in a sampling of a random variable.
   a. Concept
   b. Mode0
   c. Undefined
   d. Undefined

163. _____ is an adjective usually refering to being in the centre.
   a. Central0
   b. Thing
   c. Undefined
   d. Undefined

Chapter 1. Preliminaries

164. _____ has one 90° internal angle a right angle.
   a. Right triangle0
   b. Thing
   c. Undefined
   d. Undefined

165. _____ is a trigonemtric function that is important when studying triangles and modeling periodic phenomena, among other applications.
   a. Sine0
   b. Thing
   c. Undefined
   d. Undefined

166. _____ is a term in Trigonometry used to describe the secant of the complement of a cirlce.
   a. Cosecant0
   b. Thing
   c. Undefined
   d. Undefined

167. The _____ of an angle is the ratio of the length of the adjacent side to the length of the hypotenuse.
   a. Cosine0
   b. Concept
   c. Undefined
   d. Undefined

168. _____ is a trigonometric function that is the reciprocal of cosine.
   a. Thing
   b. Secant0
   c. Undefined
   d. Undefined

169. A frame of _____ is a particular perspective from which the universe is observed.
   a. Thing
   b. Reference0
   c. Undefined
   d. Undefined

170. The _____ of a mathematical object is its size: a property by which it can be larger or smaller than other objects of the same kind; in technical terms, an ordering of the class of objects to which it belongs.
   a. Magnitude0
   b. Thing
   c. Undefined
   d. Undefined

171. In mathematics, an _____ is any of the arguments, i.e. "inputs", to a function. Thus if we have a function f(x), then x is a _____.
   a. Thing
   b. Independent variable0
   c. Undefined
   d. Undefined

172. In mathematics, a _____ function in the sense of algebraic geometry is an everywhere-defined, polynomial function on an algebraic variety V with values in the field K over which V is defined.
   a. Thing
   b. Regular0
   c. Undefined
   d. Undefined

173. In business, particularly accounting, a _____ is the time intervals that the accounts, statement, payments, or other calculations cover.
   a. Period0
   b. Thing
   c. Undefined
   d. Undefined

174. _____ is the ratio of the adjacent to the opposite side of a right-angeled triangle

Chapter 1. Preliminaries

a. Thing
b. Cotangent0
c. Undefined
d. Undefined

175. In statistics the _____ of an event i is the number n_i of times the event occurred in the experiment or the study. These frequencies are often graphically represented in histograms.

a. Frequency0
b. Concept
c. Undefined
d. Undefined

176. A _____ is a function that repeats its values after some definite period has been added to its independent variable.

a. Thing
b. Periodic function0
c. Undefined
d. Undefined

177. _____ is the difference of electrical potential between two points of an electrical or electronic circuit, expressed in volts

a. Voltage0
b. Thing
c. Undefined
d. Undefined

178. In linear algebra and geometry, a rotation (_____) is a type of transformation from one system of coordinates to another system of coordinates such that distance between any two points remains invariant under the transformation.

a. Rotational0
b. Thing
c. Undefined
d. Undefined

179. In combinatorial mathematics, a _____ is an un-ordered collection of unique elements.

a. Combination0
b. Concept
c. Undefined
d. Undefined

180. An _____ is an equality that remains true regardless of the values of any variables that appear within it, to distinguish it from an equality which is true under more particular conditions.

a. Thing
b. Identity0
c. Undefined
d. Undefined

181. The _____ is a statement about a general triangle which relates the lengths of its sides to the cosine of one of its angles.

a. Law of cosines0
b. Thing
c. Undefined
d. Undefined

182. If the sides of the triangle are a, b and c and the angles opposite those sides are A, B and C, then the _____ states: a/sin A=b/sin B=c/sin C=2R where R is the radius of the triangle's circumcircle.

a. Thing
b. Law of sines0
c. Undefined
d. Undefined

183. In the mathematical field of numerical analysis, the _____ in some data is the discrepancy between an exact value and some approximation to it.

a. Approximation Error0
b. Thing
c. Undefined
d. Undefined

184. The _____ is a nonnegative scalar measure of a wave's magnitude of oscillation, that is, the magnitude of the maximum disturbance in the medium during one wave cycle.
   a. Amplitude0
   b. Thing
   c. Undefined
   d. Undefined

185. _____ is the mathematical action of repeatedly adding or subtracting one, usually to find out how many objects there are or to set aside a desired number of objects.
   a. Counting0
   b. Thing
   c. Undefined
   d. Undefined

186. The _____ is the distance around a closed curve. _____ is a kind of perimeter.
   a. Thing
   b. Circumference0
   c. Undefined
   d. Undefined

187. In physics, the _____ of a system of particles is a specific point at which, for many purposes, the system's mass behaves as if it were concentrated.
   a. Thing
   b. Center of mass0
   c. Undefined
   d. Undefined

Chapter 2. Limits and Continuity

1. _____ is a branch of mathematics which deals with triangles, particularly triangles in a plane where one angle of the triangle is 90 degrees, and a variety of other topological relations such as spheres, in other branches, such as spherical _____.
   a. Thing
   b. Trigonometry0
   c. Undefined
   d. Undefined

2. An _____ in policy debate is part of a speech which is flagged as not responding to the line-by-line arguments on the flow.
   a. Thing
   b. Overview0
   c. Undefined
   d. Undefined

3. The _____ is a fundamental concept in analysis. Informally, a function f can be made as close to L as desired, by making x close enough to p.
   a. Thing
   b. Limit of a function0
   c. Undefined
   d. Undefined

4. _____ is a branch of mathematics concerning the study of structure, relation and quantity.
   a. Algebra0
   b. Concept
   c. Undefined
   d. Undefined

5. _____ is a mathematical subject that includes the study of limits, derivatives, integrals, and power series and constitutes a major part of modern university curriculum.
   a. Calculus0
   b. Thing
   c. Undefined
   d. Undefined

6. The mathematical concept of a _____ expresses the intuitive idea of deterministic dependence between two quantities, one of which is viewed as primary and the other as secondary. A _____ then is a way to associate a unique output for each input of a specified type, for example, a real number or an element of a given set.
   a. Thing
   b. Function0
   c. Undefined
   d. Undefined

7. In mathematics, an _____, mean, or central tendency of a data set refers to a measure of the "middle" or "expected" value of the data set.
   a. Concept
   b. Average0
   c. Undefined
   d. Undefined

8. _____ is a kind of property which exists as magnitude or multitude. It is among the basic classes of things along with quality, substance, change, and relation.
   a. Thing
   b. Amount0
   c. Undefined
   d. Undefined

9. In elementary algebra, an _____ is a set that contains every real number between two indicated numbers and may contain the two numbers themselves.
   a. Interval0
   b. Thing
   c. Undefined
   d. Undefined

10. In mathematics, _____ geometry was the traditional name for the geometry of three-dimensional Euclidean space — for practical purposes the kind of space we live in.
   a. Solid0
   b. Thing
   c. Undefined
   d. Undefined

11. In the scientific method, an _____ (Latin: ex-+-periri, "of (or from) trying"), is a set of actions and observations, performed in the context of solving a particular problem or question, in order to support or falsify a hypothesis or research concerning phenomena.
   a. Thing
   b. Experiment0
   c. Undefined
   d. Undefined

12. In mathematics and the mathematical sciences, a _____ is a fixed, but possibly unspecified, value. This is in contrast to a variable, which is not fixed.
   a. Thing
   b. Constant0
   c. Undefined
   d. Undefined

13. _____ is defined as the rate of change or derivative with respect to time of velocity.
   a. Thing
   b. Acceleration0
   c. Undefined
   d. Undefined

14. A _____ of a number is the product of that number with any integer.
   a. Multiple0
   b. Thing
   c. Undefined
   d. Undefined

15. In plane geometry, a _____ is a polygon with four equal sides, four right angles, and parallel opposite sides. In algebra, the _____ of a number is that number multiplied by itself.
   a. Square0
   b. Thing
   c. Undefined
   d. Undefined

16. _____ of an object is its speed in a particular direction.
   a. Velocity0
   b. Thing
   c. Undefined
   d. Undefined

17. In navigation, a _____ is the clockwise angle between a reference direction and the direction to an object.
   a. Thing
   b. Bearing0
   c. Undefined
   d. Undefined

18. A bearing is a device to permit constrained relative motion between two parts, typically rotation or linear movement. _____ may be classified broadly according to the motions they allow and according to their principle of operation.
   a. Thing
   b. Bearings0
   c. Undefined
   d. Undefined

19. In physics, _____ is an influence that may cause an object to accelerate. It may be experienced as a lift, a push, or a pull. The actual acceleration of the body is determined by the vector sum of all forces acting on it, known as net _____ or resultant _____.

Chapter 2. Limits and Continuity

a. Force0
b. Thing
c. Undefined
d. Undefined

20. A _____ is a special kind of ratio, indicating a relationship between two measurements with different units, such as miles to gallons or cents to pounds.
   a. Thing
   b. Rate0
   c. Undefined
   d. Undefined

21. _____ is often used to describe the measurement of the steepness, incline, gradient, or grade of a straight line. The _____ is defined as the ratio of the "rise" divided by the "run" between two points on a line, or in other words, the ratio of the altitude change to the horizontal distance between any two points on the line.
   a. Slope0
   b. Thing
   c. Undefined
   d. Undefined

22. _____ is a trigonometric function that is the reciprocal of cosine.
   a. Secant0
   b. Thing
   c. Undefined
   d. Undefined

23. In mathematics, the concept of a _____ tries to capture the intuitive idea of a geometrical one-dimensional and continuous object. A simple example is the circle.
   a. Curve0
   b. Thing
   c. Undefined
   d. Undefined

24. In sociology and biology a _____ is the collection of people or organisms of a particular species living in a given geographic area or space, usually measured by a census.
   a. Thing
   b. Population0
   c. Undefined
   d. Undefined

25. _____, or Drosophila Melanoaster is a two-winged insect that belongs to the Diptera, the order of the flies. The species is commonly known as the fruit fly, and is one of the most commonly used model organisms in biology, including studies in genetics, physiology and life history evolution.
   a. Fruit flies0
   b. Thing
   c. Undefined
   d. Undefined

26. In mathematics, a _____ function in the sense of algebraic geometry is an everywhere-defined, polynomial function on an algebraic variety V with values in the field K over which V is defined.
   a. Thing
   b. Regular0
   c. Undefined
   d. Undefined

27. An _____ or member of a set is an object that when collected together make up the set.
   a. Thing
   b. Element0
   c. Undefined
   d. Undefined

28. In mathematics, the _____, or members of a set or more generally a class are all those objects which when collected together make up the set or class.

Chapter 2. Limits and Continuity

a. Elements0
b. Thing
c. Undefined
d. Undefined

29. In mathematics, a _____ is an ordered list of objects. Like a set, it contains members, also called elements or terms, and the number of terms is called the length of the _____. Unlike a set, order matters, and the exact same elements can appear multiple times at different positions in the _____.

a. Sequence0
b. Thing
c. Undefined
d. Undefined

30. In trigonometry, the _____ is a function defined as tan x = $^{\sin x}/_{\cos x}$. The function is so-named because it can be defined as the length of a certain segment of a _____ (in the geometric sense) to the unit circle. In plane geometry, a line is _____ to a curve, at some point, if both line and curve pass through the point with the same direction.

a. Thing
b. Tangent0
c. Undefined
d. Undefined

31. _____ has two distinct but etymologically-related meanings: one in geometry and one in trigonometry.

a. Tangent line0
b. Thing
c. Undefined
d. Undefined

32. _____ Any process by which a specified characteristic usually amplitude of the output of a device is prevented from exceeding a predetermined value.

a. Thing
b. Limiting0
c. Undefined
d. Undefined

33. _____ of a curve is a line that intersects two or more points on the curve.

a. Secant line0
b. Thing
c. Undefined
d. Undefined

34. _____ is the application of tools and a processing medium to the transformation of raw materials into finished goods for sale.

a. Thing
b. Manufacturing0
c. Undefined
d. Undefined

35. The _____, the average in everyday English, which is also called the arithmetic _____ (and is distinguished from the geometric _____ or harmonic _____). The average is also called the sample _____. The expected value of a random variable, which is also called the population _____.

a. Mean0
b. Thing
c. Undefined
d. Undefined

36. _____ is electromagnetic radiation with a wavelength that is visible to the eye (visible _____) or, in a technical or scientific context, electromagnetic radiation of any wavelength.

a. Thing
b. Light0
c. Undefined
d. Undefined

37. In mathematics, the _____ functions are functions of an angle; they are important when studying triangles and modeling periodic phenomena, among many other applications.

Chapter 2. Limits and Continuity

a. Trigonometric0
b. Thing
c. Undefined
d. Undefined

38. The _____ are functions of an angle; they are important when studying triangles and modeling periodic phenomena, among many other applications.
   a. Trigonometric functions0
   b. Thing
   c. Undefined
   d. Undefined

39. Two mathematical objects are equal if and only if they are precisely the same in every way. This defines a binary relation, _____, denoted by the sign of _____ "=" in such a way that the statement "x = y" means that x and y are equal.
   a. Equality0
   b. Thing
   c. Undefined
   d. Undefined

40. In combinatorial mathematics, a _____ is an un-ordered collection of unique elements.
   a. Concept
   b. Combination0
   c. Undefined
   d. Undefined

41. An _____ is an equality that remains true regardless of the values of any variables that appear within it, to distinguish it from an equality which is true under more particular conditions.
   a. Thing
   b. Identity0
   c. Undefined
   d. Undefined

42. An _____ is a function that does not have any effect: it always returns the same value that was used as its argument.
   a. Thing
   b. Identity function0
   c. Undefined
   d. Undefined

43. In mathematics, a _____ is an expression that is constructed from one or more variables and constants, using only the operations of addition, subtraction, multiplication, and constant positive whole number exponents. is a _____. Note in particular that division by an expression containing a variable is not in general allowed in polynomials. [1]
   a. Polynomial0
   b. Thing
   c. Undefined
   d. Undefined

44. _____ is a function whose values do not vary and thus are constant.
   a. Constant function0
   b. Thing
   c. Undefined
   d. Undefined

45. In mathematics, a _____ of a k-place relation $L \subseteq X_1 \times ... \times X_k$ is one of the sets X_j, $1 \leq j \leq k$. In the special case where k = 2 and $L \subseteq X_1 \times X_2$ is a function $L : X_1 \to X_2$, it is conventional to refer to X_1 as the _____ of the function and to refer to X_2 as the codomain of the function.
   a. Thing
   b. Domain0
   c. Undefined
   d. Undefined

46. In mathematics, a _____ may be described informally as a number that can be given by an infinite decimal representation.

a. Real number0
b. Thing
c. Undefined
d. Undefined

47. In mathematics, the _____ (or modulus) of a real number is its numerical value without regard to its sign.
   a. Thing
   b. Absolute value0
   c. Undefined
   d. Undefined

48. In linear algebra, the _____ of an n-by-n square matrix A is defined to be the sum of the elements on the main diagonal of A,
   a. Thing
   b. Trace0
   c. Undefined
   d. Undefined

49. In a mathematical proof or a syllogism, a _____ is a statement that is the logical consequence of preceding statements.
   a. Conclusion0
   b. Concept
   c. Undefined
   d. Undefined

50. _____ are procedures that allow people to exchange information by one of several methods.
   a. Thing
   b. Communications0
   c. Undefined
   d. Undefined

51. A _____ is the result of the addition of a set of numbers. The numbers may be natural numbers, complex numbers, matrices, or still more complicated objects. An infinite _____ is a subtle procedure known as a series.
   a. Thing
   b. Sum0
   c. Undefined
   d. Undefined

52. In mathematics, a _____ is a statement that can be proved on the basis of explicitly stated or previously agreed assumptions.
   a. Thing
   b. Theorem0
   c. Undefined
   d. Undefined

53. In mathematics, a _____ is the result of multiplying, or an expression that identifies factors to be multiplied.
   a. Thing
   b. Product0
   c. Undefined
   d. Undefined

54. In mathematics, a _____ is the end result of a division problem. It can also be expressed as the number of times the divisor divides into the dividend.
   a. Quotient0
   b. Thing
   c. Undefined
   d. Undefined

55. A _____ is the part of a fraction that tells how many equal parts make up a whole, and which is used in the name of the fraction: "halves", "thirds", "fourths" or "quarters", "fifths" and so on.
   a. Denominator0
   b. Concept
   c. Undefined
   d. Undefined

Chapter 2. Limits and Continuity

56. In mathematics, a _____ number is a number which can be expressed as a ratio of two integers. Non-integer _____ numbers (commonly called fractions) are usually written as the vulgar fraction a / b, where b is not zero.
   a. Thing
   b. Rational0
   c. Undefined
   d. Undefined

57. _____ has many meanings, most of which simply .
   a. Power0
   b. Thing
   c. Undefined
   d. Undefined

58. The _____ governs the differentiation of products of differentiable functions.
   a. Product rule0
   b. Thing
   c. Undefined
   d. Undefined

59. The _____ is a method of finding the derivative of a function that is the quotient of two other functions for which derivatives exist.
   a. Thing
   b. Quotient rule0
   c. Undefined
   d. Undefined

60. In mathematics, a _____ is any function which can be written as the ratio of two polynomial functions.
   a. Rational function0
   b. Thing
   c. Undefined
   d. Undefined

61. In calculus, the _____ in differentiation is a method of finding the derivative of a function that is the sum of two other functions for which derivatives exist.
   a. Sum Rule0
   b. Thing
   c. Undefined
   d. Undefined

62. _____ is a method for differentiating expressions involving exponentiation the power operation.
   a. Thing
   b. Power rule0
   c. Undefined
   d. Undefined

63. In mathematics, informally speaking, a _____ of a set S in a topological space X is a point x in X that can be "approximated" by points of S other than x as well as one pleases. This concept profitably generalizes the notion of a limit and is the underpinning of concepts such as closed set and topological closure.
   a. Thing
   b. Limit point0
   c. Undefined
   d. Undefined

64. A _____ is a numeral used to indicate a count. The most common use of the word today is to name the part of a fraction that tells the number or count of equal parts.
   a. Thing
   b. Numerator0
   c. Undefined
   d. Undefined

65. _____ is the largest positive integer that divides both numbers without remainder.
   a. Common Factor0
   b. Thing
   c. Undefined
   d. Undefined

Chapter 2. Limits and Continuity

66. In mathematics, factorization (British English: factorisation) or factoring is the decomposition of an object (for example, a number, a polynomial, or a matrix) into a product of other objects, or _____, which when multiplied together give the original.
   a. Factors0
   b. Thing
   c. Undefined
   d. Undefined

67. In mathematics, defined and _____ are used to explain whether or not expressions have meaningful, sensible, and unambiguous values.
   a. Undefined0
   b. Thing
   c. Undefined
   d. Undefined

68. In calculus, the _____ is a theorem regarding the limit of a function. The theorem asserts that if two functions approach the same limit at a point, and if a third function is "squeezed" between those functions, then the third function also approaches that limit at that point.
   a. Thing
   b. Squeeze Theorem0
   c. Undefined
   d. Undefined

69. _____ are the basic objects of study in graph theory. Informally speaking, a graph is a set of objects called points, nodes, or vertices connected by links called lines or edges.
   a. Graphs0
   b. Thing
   c. Undefined
   d. Undefined

70. In mathematics, an _____ is a statement about the relative size or order of two objects.
   a. Inequality0
   b. Thing
   c. Undefined
   d. Undefined

71. In mathematics, the _____ of a coordinate system is the point where the axes of the system intersect.
   a. Origin0
   b. Thing
   c. Undefined
   d. Undefined

72. The _____ of a solid object is the three-dimensional concept of how much space it occupies, often quantified numerically.
   a. Thing
   b. Volume0
   c. Undefined
   d. Undefined

73. In mathematics, a _____ is a quadric surface, with the following equation in Cartesian coordinates: $(x/_a)^2 + (y/_b)^2 = 1$.
   a. Cylinder0
   b. Thing
   c. Undefined
   d. Undefined

74. A _____ is a function that assigns a number to subsets of a given set.
   a. Measure0
   b. Thing
   c. Undefined
   d. Undefined

75. The _____ of measurement are a globally standardized and modernized form of the metric system.

a. Thing
b. Units0
c. Undefined
d. Undefined

76. The term _____ is defined dually as an element of P which is lesser than or equal to every element of S.
a. Thing
b. Lower bound0
c. Undefined
d. Undefined

77. In astronomy, geography, geometry and related sciences and contexts, a plane is said to be _____ at a given point if it is locally perpendicular to the gradient of the gravity field, i.e., with the direction of the gravitational force at that point.
a. Thing
b. Horizontal0
c. Undefined
d. Undefined

78. In mathematics, the _____ of a function is the set of all "output" values produced by that function. Given a function $f : A \to B$, the _____ of f, is defined to be the set $\{x \in B : x = f(a) \text{ for some } a \in A\}$.
a. Range0
b. Thing
c. Undefined
d. Undefined

79. In classical geometry, a _____ of a circle or sphere is any line segment from its center to its boundary. By extension, the _____ of a circle or sphere is the length of any such segment. The _____ is half the diameter. In science and engineering the term _____ of curvature is commonly used as a synonym for _____.
a. Thing
b. Radius0
c. Undefined
d. Undefined

80. A _____ is a symbolic representation denoting a quantity or expression. It often represents an "unknown" quantity that has the potential to change.
a. Thing
b. Variable0
c. Undefined
d. Undefined

81. _____ (Groups, Algorithms and Programming) is a computer algebra system for computational discrete algebra with particular emphasis on, but not restricted to, computational group theory.
a. Thing
b. Gap0
c. Undefined
d. Undefined

82. A _____ is a set of possible values that a variable can take on in order to satisfy a given set of conditions, which may include equations and inequalities.
a. Solution set0
b. Thing
c. Undefined
d. Undefined

83. In logic and mathematics, logical _____ is a logical relation that holds between a set T of formulas and a formula B when every model (or interpretation or valuation) of T is also a model of B.
a. Implication0
b. Concept
c. Undefined
d. Undefined

84. In geometry, an _____ is a point at which a line segment or ray terminates.

Chapter 2. Limits and Continuity

a. Endpoint0 b. Thing
c. Undefined d. Undefined

85. _____ means "constancy", i.e. if something retains a certain feature even after we change a way of looking at it, then it is symmetric.
a. Thing b. Symmetry0
c. Undefined d. Undefined

86. In Euclidean geometry, a uniform _____ is a linear transformation that enlargers or diminishes objects, and whose _____ factor is the same in all directions. This is also called homothethy.
a. Thing b. Scale0
c. Undefined d. Undefined

87. In mathematics, a _____ is a demonstration that, assuming certain axioms, some statement is necessarily true.
a. Proof0 b. Thing
c. Undefined d. Undefined

88. In financial mathematics, the _____ volatility of an option contract is the volatility _____ by the market price of the option based on an option pricing model.
a. Thing b. Implied0
c. Undefined d. Undefined

89. In common philosophical language, a proposition or _____, is the content of an assertion, that is, it is true-or-false and defined by the meaning of a particular piece of language.
a. Concept b. Statement0
c. Undefined d. Undefined

90. _____ is a measure of difference for interval and ratio variables between the observed value and the mean.
a. Deviation0 b. Thing
c. Undefined d. Undefined

91. In geometry, a _____ (Greek words diairo = divide and metro = measure) of a circle is any straight line segment that passes through the centre and whose endpoints are on the circular boundary, or, in more modern usage, the length of such a line segment. When using the word in the more modern sense, one speaks of the _____ rather than a _____, because all diameters of a circle have the same length. This length is twice the radius. The _____ of a circle is also the longest chord that the circle has.
a. Thing b. Diameter0
c. Undefined d. Undefined

92. _____ is the difference of electrical potential between two points of an electrical or electronic circuit, expressed in volts
a. Thing b. Voltage0
c. Undefined d. Undefined

93. The _____, in practice often shortened to amp, is a unit of electric current, or amount of electric charge per second.

Chapter 2. Limits and Continuity

    a. Amperes0   b. Thing
    c. Undefined   d. Undefined

94. Mathematical _____ is used to represent ideas.
    a. Thing
    b. Notation0
    c. Undefined
    d. Undefined

95. In mathematics, the multiplicative inverse of a number x, denoted 1/x or x^{-1}, is the number which, when multiplied by x, yields 1. The multiplicative inverse of x is also called the _____ of x.
    a. Thing
    b. Reciprocal0
    c. Undefined
    d. Undefined

96. _____ is the state of being greater than any finite real or natural number, however large.
    a. Thing
    b. Infinite0
    c. Undefined
    d. Undefined

97. _____ is the state of being greater than any finite number, however large.
    a. Thing
    b. Infinity0
    c. Undefined
    d. Undefined

98. In Euclidean geometry, an _____ is a closed segment of a differentiable curve in the two-dimensional plane; for example, a circular _____ is a segment of a circle.
    a. Arc0
    b. Concept
    c. Undefined
    d. Undefined

99. A _____ is a simplified and structured visual representation of concepts, ideas, constructions, relations, statistical data, anatomy etc used in all aspects of human activities to visualize and clarify the topic.
    a. Thing
    b. Diagram0
    c. Undefined
    d. Undefined

100. The plus and _____ signs are mathematical symbols used to represent the notions of positive and negative as well as the operations of addition and subtraction.
    a. Thing
    b. Minus0
    c. Undefined
    d. Undefined

101. A _____ function is a function for which, intuitively, small changes in the input result in small changes in the output.
    a. Event
    b. Continuous0
    c. Undefined
    d. Undefined

102. In statistics the _____ of an event i is the number n_i of times the event occurred in the experiment or the study. These frequencies are often graphically represented in histograms.
    a. Concept
    b. Frequency0
    c. Undefined
    d. Undefined

103. The word _____ comes from the 15th Century Latin word discretus which means separate.

a. Thing
b. Discrete0
c. Undefined
d. Undefined

104. In set theory and other branches of mathematics, the _____ of a collection of sets is the set that contains everything that belongs to any of the sets, but nothing else.
a. Thing
b. Union0
c. Undefined
d. Undefined

105. Continuous functions are of utmost importance in mathematics and applications. However, not all functions are continuous. If a function is not continuous at a point in its domain, one says that it has a _____ there. The set of all points of _____ of a function may be a discrete set, a dense set, or even the entire domain of the function.
a. Discontinuity0
b. Thing
c. Undefined
d. Undefined

106. A function on the real numbers is called a _____ if it can be written as a finite linear combination of indicator functions of half-open intervals.
a. Step function0
b. Thing
c. Undefined
d. Undefined

107. In mathematics, the additive inverse, or _____ of a number n is the number that, when added to n, yields zero. The additive inverse of n is denoted −n. For example, 7 is −7, because 7 + (−7) = 0, and the additive inverse of −0.3 is 0.3, because −0.3 + 0.3 = 0.
a. Thing
b. Opposite0
c. Undefined
d. Undefined

108. In mathematics, the _____ of a number n is the number that, when added to n, yields zero. The _____ of n is denoted −n. For example, 7 is −7, because 7 + (−7) = 0, and the _____ of −0.3 is 0.3, because −0.3 + 0.3 = 0.
a. Thing
b. Additive inverse0
c. Undefined
d. Undefined

109. In statistics, _____ means the most frequent value assumed by a random variable, or occurring in a sampling of a random variable.
a. Mode0
b. Concept
c. Undefined
d. Undefined

110. Acid _____ ratio measures the ability of a company to use its near cash or quick assets to immediately extinguish its current liabilities.
a. Test0
b. Thing
c. Undefined
d. Undefined

111. The _____ are the only integral domain whose positive elements are well-ordered, and in which order is preserved by addition. Like the natural numbers, the _____ form a countably infinite set. The set of all _____ is usually denoted in mathematics by a boldface Z .
a. Thing
b. Integers0
c. Undefined
d. Undefined

112. In mathematics, a _____ of a positive integer n is a way of writing n as a sum of positive integers.
  a. Composition0
  b. Thing
  c. Undefined
  d. Undefined

113. A _____ number is a positive integer which has a positive divisor other than one or itself.
  a. Thing
  b. Composite0
  c. Undefined
  d. Undefined

114. In mathematics, a set is called _____ if there is a bijection between the set and some set of the form {1, 2, ..., n} where n is a natural number.
  a. Finite0
  b. Thing
  c. Undefined
  d. Undefined

115. The _____ implies that on any great circle around the world, the temperature, pressure, elevation, carbon dioxide concentration, or anything else that varies continuously, there will always exist two antipodal points that share the same value for that variable.
  a. Intermediate Value Theorem0
  b. Thing
  c. Undefined
  d. Undefined

116. _____ is a set of numbers, in the broadest sense of the word, together with one or more operations, such as addition or multiplication.
  a. Thing
  b. Number system0
  c. Undefined
  d. Undefined

117. In mathematics, a _____ of a complex-valued function f is a member x of the domain of f such that f(x) vanishes at x, that is, x : f (x) = 0.
  a. Thing
  b. Root0
  c. Undefined
  d. Undefined

118. In mathematics, an _____ number is any real number that is not a rational number- that is, it is a number which cannot be expressed as a fraction m/n, where m and n are integers.
  a. Irrational0
  b. Thing
  c. Undefined
  d. Undefined

119. In mathematics, an _____ is any real number that is not a rational number ¡ª that is, it is a number which cannot be expressed as m/n, where m and n are integers.
  a. Thing
  b. Irrational number0
  c. Undefined
  d. Undefined

120. In mathematics, _____ are any real number that is not a rational number ¡ª that is, it is a number which cannot be expressed as m/n, where m and n are integers.
  a. Thing
  b. Irrational numbers0
  c. Undefined
  d. Undefined

121. The _____ is a unit of plane angle. It is represented by the symbol "rad" or, more rarely, by the superscript c (for "circular measure"). For example, an angle of 1.2 radians would be written "1.2 rad" or "1.2c" (second symbol can produce confusion with centigrads).
   a. Thing
   b. Radian0
   c. Undefined
   d. Undefined

122. In Euclidean geometry, a _____ is the set of all points in a plane at a fixed distance, called the radius, from a given point, the center.
   a. Circle0
   b. Thing
   c. Undefined
   d. Undefined

123. In geometry, two lines or planes if one falls on the other in such a way as to create congruent adjacent angles. The term may be used as a noun or adjective. Thus, referring to Figure 1, the line AB is the _____ to CD through the point B.
   a. Perpendicular0
   b. Thing
   c. Undefined
   d. Undefined

124. In geometry, the _____ of an object is a point in some sense in the middle of the object.
   a. Thing
   b. Center0
   c. Undefined
   d. Undefined

125. In mathematics, _____ are the intuitive idea of a geometrical one-dimensional and continuous object.
   a. Thing
   b. Curves0
   c. Undefined
   d. Undefined

126. In mathematics, the _____ is a conic section generated by the intersection of a right circular conical surface and a plane parallel to a generating straight line of that surface. It can also be defined as locus of points in a plane which are equidistant from a given point.
   a. Thing
   b. Parabola0
   c. Undefined
   d. Undefined

127. A _____ given two distinct points A and B on the _____, is the set of points C on the line containing points A and B such that A is not strictly between C and B.
   a. Thing
   b. Ray0
   c. Undefined
   d. Undefined

128. In mathematics, the _____ of two sets A and B is the set that contains all elements of A that also belong to B (or equivalently, all elements of B that also belong to A), but no other elements.
   a. Thing
   b. Intersection0
   c. Undefined
   d. Undefined

129. _____ was a highly influential French philosopher, mathematician, scientist, and writer. Dubbed the "Founder of Modern Philosophy", and the "Father of Modern Mathematics". His theories provided the basis for the calculus of Newton and Leibniz, by applying infinitesimal calculus to the tangent line problem, thus permitting the evolution of that branch of modern mathematics

Chapter 2. Limits and Continuity

a. Descartes0
b. Person
c. Undefined
d. Undefined

130. In mathematics, the _____ f is the collection of all ordered pairs. In particular, graph means the graphical representation of this collection, in the form of a curve or surface, together with axes, etc. Graphing on a Cartesian plane is sometimes referred to as curve sketching.
   a. Thing
   b. Graph of a function0
   c. Undefined
   d. Undefined

131. Equivalence is the condition of being _____ or essentially equal.
   a. Thing
   b. Equivalent0
   c. Undefined
   d. Undefined

132. An _____ is a combination of numbers, operators, grouping symbols and/or free variables and bound variables arranged in a meaningful way which can be evaluated..
   a. Thing
   b. Expression0
   c. Undefined
   d. Undefined

133. _____ was a French lawyer and a mathematician who is given credit for early developments that led to modern calculus. In particular, he is recognized for his discovery of an original method of finding the greatest and the smallest ordinates of curved lines, which is analogous to that of the then unknown differential calculus.
   a. Pierre de Fermat0
   b. Person
   c. Undefined
   d. Undefined

134. In mathematics, an inequality is a statement about the relative size or order of two objects. For example 14 > 10, or 14 is _____ 10.
   a. Greater than0
   b. Thing
   c. Undefined
   d. Undefined

135. In finance, a _____ is collateral that the holder of a position in securities, options, or futures contracts has to deposit to cover the credit risk of his counterparty.
   a. Margin0
   b. Thing
   c. Undefined
   d. Undefined

136. _____ are external two-dimensional outlines, with the appearance or configuration of some thing - in contrast to the matter or content or substance of which it is composed.
   a. Shapes0
   b. Thing
   c. Undefined
   d. Undefined

137. In geometry, the _____ or barycenter of an object X in n-dimensional space is the intersection of all hyperplanes that divide X into two parts of equal moment about the hyperplane
   a. Centroid0
   b. Thing
   c. Undefined
   d. Undefined

138. _____ is the branch of pure mathematics concerned with the properties of numbers in general, and integers in particular, as well as the wider classes of problems that arise from their study.

a. Number theory0 b. Thing
c. Undefined d. Undefined

139. In geometry, a _____ is defined as a quadrilateral where all four of its angles are right angles.
a. Thing b. Rectangle0
c. Undefined d. Undefined

140. _____, Greek for "knowledge of nature," is the branch of science concerned with the discovery and characterization of universal laws which govern matter, energy, space, and time.
a. Thing b. Physics0
c. Undefined d. Undefined

141. In mathematical analysis and related areas of mathematics, a set is called _____, if it is, in a certain sense, of finite size.
a. Bounded0 b. Thing
c. Undefined d. Undefined

142. In mathematics, a _____ is a two-dimensional manifold or surface that is perfectly flat.
a. Plane0 b. Thing
c. Undefined d. Undefined

143. The easiest _____ prime numbers resides in the use of the Sieve of Eratosthenes, an algorithm that discovers all prime numbers to a specified integer.
a. Thing b. Method for finding0
c. Undefined d. Undefined

144. _____ also called rectification of a curve—was historically difficult.
a. Thing b. Arc length0
c. Undefined d. Undefined

145. The term _____ refers to the largest and the smallest element of a set.
a. Extreme value0 b. Thing
c. Undefined d. Undefined

146. _____ determines whether a given stationary point of a function is a maximum or a minimum.
a. Thing b. Second derivative test0
c. Undefined d. Undefined

147. The _____ is a measurement of how a function changes when the values of its inputs change.
a. Thing b. Derivative0
c. Undefined d. Undefined

148. The function difference divided by the point difference is known as the _____
a. Difference quotient0 b. Thing
c. Undefined d. Undefined

Chapter 2. Limits and Continuity 37

149. A _____ is a vehicle, missile or aircraft which obtains thrust by the reaction to the ejection of fast moving fluid from within a _____ engine.
 a. Thing
 b. Rocket0
 c. Undefined
 d. Undefined

150. _____ is a mathematical operation, written a^n, involving two numbers, the base a and the exponent n.
 a. Exponentiating0
 b. Thing
 c. Undefined
 d. Undefined

151. _____ is a mathematical operation, written a^n, involving two numbers, the base a and the exponent n.
 a. Thing
 b. Exponentiation0
 c. Undefined
 d. Undefined

152. In mathematics, a _____ is a polynomial equation of the second degree. The general form is $ax^2 + bx + c = 0$.
 a. Quadratic equation0
 b. Thing
 c. Undefined
 d. Undefined

153. In logic, and especially in its applications to mathematics and philosophy, a _____ is an exception to a proposed general rule, i.e., a specific instance of the falsity of a universal quantification (a "for all" statement).
 a. Thing
 b. Counterexample0
 c. Undefined
 d. Undefined

154. In mathematics, a _____ of a number x is a number r such that $r^2 = x$, or in words, a number r whose square (the result of multiplying the number by itself) is x.
 a. Square root0
 b. Thing
 c. Undefined
 d. Undefined

155. _____ is a physical property of a system that underlies the common notions of hot and cold; something that is hotter has the greater _____.
 a. Thing
 b. Temperature0
 c. Undefined
 d. Undefined

156. The _____ (symbol _____) and the millibar (symbol mbar, also mb) are units of pressure.
 a. Bar0
 b. Thing
 c. Undefined
 d. Undefined

157. In mathematics, especially in order theory, an _____ of a subset S of some partially ordered set is an element of P which is greater than or equal to every element of S.
 a. Thing
 b. Upper bound0
 c. Undefined
 d. Undefined

158. In mathematics, a _____ is a number which can be expressed as a ratio of two integers. Non-integer rational numbers (commonly called fractions) are usually written as the vulgar fraction a / b, where b is not zero.
 a. Concept
 b. Rational Number0
 c. Undefined
 d. Undefined

159. A _____ is an instrument used in geometry technical drawing and engineering/building to measure distances and/or to rule straight lines.
   a. Ruler0
   b. Thing
   c. Undefined
   d. Undefined

Chapter 3. Derivatives

1. _____ is often used to describe the measurement of the steepness, incline, gradient, or grade of a straight line. The _____ is defined as the ratio of the "rise" divided by the "run" between two points on a line, or in other words, the ratio of the altitude change to the horizontal distance between any two points on the line.
   a. Slope0
   b. Thing
   c. Undefined
   d. Undefined

2. In mathematics, the concept of a _____ tries to capture the intuitive idea of a geometrical one-dimensional and continuous object. A simple example is the circle.
   a. Thing
   b. Curve0
   c. Undefined
   d. Undefined

3. An _____ in policy debate is part of a speech which is flagged as not responding to the line-by-line arguments on the flow.
   a. Thing
   b. Overview0
   c. Undefined
   d. Undefined

4. _____ is a trigonometric function that is the reciprocal of cosine.
   a. Thing
   b. Secant0
   c. Undefined
   d. Undefined

5. _____ of an object is its speed in a particular direction.
   a. Thing
   b. Velocity0
   c. Undefined
   d. Undefined

6. _____ is the estimation of a physical quantity such as distance, energy, temperature, or time.
   a. Measurement0
   b. Thing
   c. Undefined
   d. Undefined

7. The _____ is a measurement of how a function changes when the values of its inputs change.
   a. Derivative0
   b. Thing
   c. Undefined
   d. Undefined

8. _____ is defined as the rate of change or derivative with respect to time of velocity.
   a. Thing
   b. Acceleration0
   c. Undefined
   d. Undefined

9. A _____ is a symbolic representation denoting a quantity or expression. It often represents an "unknown" quantity that has the potential to change.
   a. Thing
   b. Variable0
   c. Undefined
   d. Undefined

10. The mathematical concept of a _____ expresses the intuitive idea of deterministic dependence between two quantities, one of which is viewed as primary and the other as secondary. A _____ then is a way to associate a unique output for each input of a specified type, for example, a real number or an element of a given set.
    a. Thing
    b. Function0
    c. Undefined
    d. Undefined

Chapter 3. Derivatives

11. In mathematics, a _____ of a k-place relation $L \subseteq X_1 \times \ldots \times X_k$ is one of the sets X_j, $1 \leq j \leq k$. In the special case where k = 2 and $L \subseteq X_1 \times X_2$ is a function $L : X_1 \to X_2$, it is conventional to refer to X_1 as the _____ of the function and to refer to X_2 as the codomain of the function.
   - a. Thing
   - b. Domain0
   - c. Undefined
   - d. Undefined

12. Mathematical _____ is used to represent ideas.
    - a. Thing
    - b. Notation0
    - c. Undefined
    - d. Undefined

13. In mathematics, a _____ number (or a _____) is a natural number that has exactly two (distinct) natural number divisors, which are 1 and the _____ number itself.
    - a. Prime0
    - b. Thing
    - c. Undefined
    - d. Undefined

14. In mathematics, an _____ is any of the arguments, i.e. "inputs", to a function. Thus if we have a function f(x), then x is a _____.
    - a. Thing
    - b. Independent variable0
    - c. Undefined
    - d. Undefined

15. _____, a field in mathematics, is the study of how functions change when their inputs change. The primary object of study in _____ is the derivative.
    - a. Thing
    - b. Differential calculus0
    - c. Undefined
    - d. Undefined

16. Sir Isaac _____, was an English physicist, mathematician, astronomer, natural philosopher, and alchemist, regarded by many as the greatest figure in the history of science
    - a. Newton0
    - b. Person
    - c. Undefined
    - d. Undefined

17. A _____ is a simplified and structured visual representation of concepts, ideas, constructions, relations, statistical data, anatomy etc used in all aspects of human activities to visualize and clarify the topic.
    - a. Thing
    - b. Diagram0
    - c. Undefined
    - d. Undefined

18. In finance, a _____ is collateral that the holder of a position in securities, options, or futures contracts has to deposit to cover the credit risk of his counterparty.
    - a. Thing
    - b. Margin0
    - c. Undefined
    - d. Undefined

19. _____ was a German mathematician and philosopher. He invented calculus independently of Newton, and his notation is the one in general use since.
    - a. Leibniz0
    - b. Person
    - c. Undefined
    - d. Undefined

Chapter 3. Derivatives

20. In mathematics, a _____ is the end result of a division problem. It can also be expressed as the number of times the divisor divides into the dividend.
    a. Quotient0
    b. Thing
    c. Undefined
    d. Undefined

21. An _____ is a combination of numbers, operators, grouping symbols and/or free variables and bound variables arranged in a meaningful way which can be evaluated..
    a. Thing
    b. Expression0
    c. Undefined
    d. Undefined

22. The function difference divided by the point difference is known as the _____
    a. Difference quotient0
    b. Thing
    c. Undefined
    d. Undefined

23. Equivalence is the condition of being _____ or essentially equal.
    a. Thing
    b. Equivalent0
    c. Undefined
    d. Undefined

24. In trigonometry, the _____ is a function defined as $\tan x = \sin x / \cos x$. The function is so-named because it can be defined as the length of a certain segment of a _____ (in the geometric sense) to the unit circle. In plane geometry, a line is _____ to a curve, at some point, if both line and curve pass through the point with the same direction.
    a. Tangent0
    b. Thing
    c. Undefined
    d. Undefined

25. _____ has two distinct but etymologically-related meanings: one in geometry and one in trigonometry.
    a. Thing
    b. Tangent line0
    c. Undefined
    d. Undefined

26. _____ are the basic objects of study in graph theory. Informally speaking, a graph is a set of objects called points, nodes, or vertices connected by links called lines or edges.
    a. Thing
    b. Graphs0
    c. Undefined
    d. Undefined

27. _____ is the path a moving object follows through space.
    a. Thing
    b. Projectile motion0
    c. Undefined
    d. Undefined

28. A _____ is a function that assigns a number to subsets of a given set.
    a. Thing
    b. Measure0
    c. Undefined
    d. Undefined

29. In mathematics, _____ are the intuitive idea of a geometrical one-dimensional and continuous object.
    a. Curves0
    b. Thing
    c. Undefined
    d. Undefined

30. _____ is a synonym for information.

a. Thing
c. Undefined
b. Data0
d. Undefined

31. Acid _____ ratio measures the ability of a company to use its near cash or quick assets to immediately extinguish its current liabilities.
   a. Test0
   c. Undefined
   b. Thing
   d. Undefined

32. In geometry, a line _____ is a part of a line that is bounded by two end points, and contains every point on the line between its end points.
   a. Segment0
   c. Undefined
   b. Concept
   d. Undefined

33. A _____ is a part of a line that is bounded by two end points, and contains every point on the line between its end points.
   a. Thing
   c. Undefined
   b. Line segment0
   d. Undefined

34. In mathematics and the mathematical sciences, a _____ is a fixed, but possibly unspecified, value. This is in contrast to a variable, which is not fixed.
   a. Constant0
   c. Undefined
   b. Thing
   d. Undefined

35. In topology and related areas of mathematics a _____ or Moore-Smith sequence is a generalization of a sequence, intended to unify the various notions of limit and generalize them to arbitrary topological spaces.
   a. Net0
   c. Undefined
   b. Thing
   d. Undefined

36. A _____ is a special kind of ratio, indicating a relationship between two measurements with different units, such as miles to gallons or cents to pounds.
   a. Rate0
   c. Undefined
   b. Thing
   d. Undefined

37. In mathematics, a _____ or rhodonea curve is a sinusoid plotted in polar coordinates.
   a. Rose0
   c. Undefined
   b. Thing
   d. Undefined

38. A _____ is a set of numbers that designate location in a given reference system, such as x,y in a planar _____ system or an x,y,z in a three-dimensional _____ system.
   a. Thing
   c. Undefined
   b. Coordinate0
   d. Undefined

39. A function on the real numbers is called a _____ if it can be written as a finite linear combination of indicator functions of half-open intervals.

Chapter 3. Derivatives

a. Step function0
c. Undefined
b. Thing
d. Undefined

40. An _____ is when two lines intersect somewhere on a plane creating a right angle at intersection
   a. Thing
   b. Axes0
   c. Undefined
   d. Undefined

41. An _____ is a straight line around which a geometric figure can be rotated.
   a. Thing
   b. Axis0
   c. Undefined
   d. Undefined

42. In astronomy, geography, geometry and related sciences and contexts, a plane is said to be _____ at a given point if it is locally perpendicular to the gradient of the gravity field, i.e., with the direction of the gravitational force at that point.
   a. Thing
   b. Horizontal0
   c. Undefined
   d. Undefined

43. In elementary algebra, an _____ is a set that contains every real number between two indicated numbers and may contain the two numbers themselves.
   a. Interval0
   b. Thing
   c. Undefined
   d. Undefined

44. The _____ of measurement are a globally standardized and modernized form of the metric system.
   a. Units0
   b. Thing
   c. Undefined
   d. Undefined

45. _____ is the state of being greater than any finite real or natural number, however large.
   a. Thing
   b. Infinite0
   c. Undefined
   d. Undefined

46. In mathematics, a set is called _____ if there is a bijection between the set and some set of the form {1, 2, ..., n} where n is a natural number.
   a. Finite0
   b. Thing
   c. Undefined
   d. Undefined

47. In geometry, an _____ is a point at which a line segment or ray terminates.
   a. Endpoint0
   b. Thing
   c. Undefined
   d. Undefined

48. In mathematics, a _____ is a statement that can be proved on the basis of explicitly stated or previously agreed assumptions.
   a. Theorem0
   b. Thing
   c. Undefined
   d. Undefined

49. In mathematics, the _____ of a coordinate system is the point where the axes of the system intersect.

44   *Chapter 3. Derivatives*

    a. Origin0   b. Thing
    c. Undefined   d. Undefined

50. _____ Any process by which a specified characteristic usually amplitude of the output of a device is prevented from exceeding a predetermined value.
    a. Thing   b. Limiting0
    c. Undefined   d. Undefined

51. _____ of a curve is a line that intersects two or more points on the curve.
    a. Thing   b. Secant line0
    c. Undefined   d. Undefined

52. Continuous functions are of utmost importance in mathematics and applications. However, not all functions are continuous. If a function is not continuous at a point in its domain, one says that it has a _____ there. The set of all points of _____ of a function may be a discrete set, a dense set, or even the entire domain of the function.
    a. Thing   b. Discontinuity0
    c. Undefined   d. Undefined

53. In mathematics, the _____ (or modulus) of a real number is its numerical value without regard to its sign.
    a. Absolute value0   b. Thing
    c. Undefined   d. Undefined

54. A _____ function is a function for which, intuitively, small changes in the input result in small changes in the output.
    a. Event   b. Continuous0
    c. Undefined   d. Undefined

55. The _____ of an angle is the ratio of the length of the adjacent side to the length of the hypotenuse.
    a. Concept   b. Cosine0
    c. Undefined   d. Undefined

56. A _____ is the result of the addition of a set of numbers. The numbers may be natural numbers, complex numbers, matrices, or still more complicated objects. An infinite _____ is a subtle procedure known as a series.
    a. Sum0   b. Thing
    c. Undefined   d. Undefined

57. In statistics the _____ of an event i is the number n_i of times the event occurred in the experiment or the study. These frequencies are often graphically represented in histograms.
    a. Concept   b. Frequency0
    c. Undefined   d. Undefined

58. _____ is an adjective usually refering to being in the centre.
    a. Thing   b. Central0
    c. Undefined   d. Undefined

Chapter 3. Derivatives

59. _____ is a mathematical subject that includes the study of limits, derivatives, integrals, and power series and constitutes a major part of modern university curriculum.
    a. Thing
    b. Calculus0
    c. Undefined
    d. Undefined

60. A _____ is a deliberate process for transforming one or more inputs into one or more results.
    a. Thing
    b. Calculation0
    c. Undefined
    d. Undefined

61. In mathematics, a _____ is the result of multiplying, or an expression that identifies factors to be multiplied.
    a. Thing
    b. Product0
    c. Undefined
    d. Undefined

62. In economics _____ means before deductions brutto, e.g. _____ domestic or national product, or _____ profit or income
    a. Gross0
    b. Thing
    c. Undefined
    d. Undefined

63. In sociology and biology a _____ is the collection of people or organisms of a particular species living in a given geographic area or space, usually measured by a census.
    a. Thing
    b. Population0
    c. Undefined
    d. Undefined

64. _____ is the ability to hold, receive or absorb, or a measure thereof, similar to the concept of volume.
    a. Capacity0
    b. Concept
    c. Undefined
    d. Undefined

65. _____ usually refers to the biological _____ of a population level that can be supported for an organism, given the quantity of food, habitat, water and other life infrastructure present.
    a. Carrying capacity0
    b. Thing
    c. Undefined
    d. Undefined

66. A _____ of a number is the product of that number with any integer.
    a. Multiple0
    b. Thing
    c. Undefined
    d. Undefined

67. _____ has many meanings, most of which simply .
    a. Thing
    b. Power0
    c. Undefined
    d. Undefined

68. _____ is a function whose values do not vary and thus are constant.
    a. Thing
    b. Constant function0
    c. Undefined
    d. Undefined

69. In mathematics, a _____ is a demonstration that, assuming certain axioms, some statement is necessarily true.

Chapter 3. Derivatives

    a. Thing
    c. Undefined
    b. Proof0
    d. Undefined

70. The _____ are the only integral domain whose positive elements are well-ordered, and in which order is preserved by addition. Like the natural numbers, the _____ form a countably infinite set. The set of all _____ is usually denoted in mathematics by a boldface Z .
    a. Thing
    c. Undefined
    b. Integers0
    d. Undefined

71. _____ is a method for differentiating expressions involving exponentiation the power operation.
    a. Thing
    c. Undefined
    b. Power rule0
    d. Undefined

72. In mathematics, a _____ is an n-tuple with n being 3.
    a. Triple0
    c. Undefined
    b. Thing
    d. Undefined

73. In calculus, the _____ in differentiation is a method of finding the derivative of a function that is the sum of two other functions for which derivatives exist.
    a. Sum Rule0
    c. Undefined
    b. Thing
    d. Undefined

74. A _____ signifies a point or points of probability on a subject e.g., the _____ of creativity, which allows for the formation of rule or norm or law by interpretation of the phenomena events that can be created.
    a. Thing
    c. Undefined
    b. Principle0
    d. Undefined

75. In mathematics, an inequality is a statement about the relative size or order of two objects. For example 14 > 10, or 14 is _____ 10.
    a. Greater than0
    c. Undefined
    b. Thing
    d. Undefined

76. An _____ is any starting assumption from which other statements are logically derived
    a. Axiom0
    c. Undefined
    b. Thing
    d. Undefined

77. _____ is a method of mathematical proof typically used to establish that a given statement is true of all natural numbers
    a. Thing
    c. Undefined
    b. Mathematical induction0
    d. Undefined

78. In mathematics, a _____ is an expression that is constructed from one or more variables and constants, using only the operations of addition, subtraction, multiplication, and constant positive whole number exponents. is a _____. Note in particular that division by an expression containing a variable is not in general allowed in polynomials. [1]

Chapter 3. Derivatives 47

    a. Polynomial0   b. Thing
    c. Undefined   d. Undefined

79. A _____ is a negotiable instrument instructing a financial institution to pay a specific amount of a specific currency from a specific demand account held in the maker/depositor's name with that institution. Both the maker and payee may be natural persons or legal entities.
    a. Check0   b. Thing
    c. Undefined   d. Undefined

80. In common philosophical language, a proposition or _____, is the content of an assertion, that is, it is true-or-false and defined by the meaning of a particular piece of language.
    a. Statement0   b. Concept
    c. Undefined   d. Undefined

81. The _____ governs the differentiation of products of differentiable functions.
    a. Thing   b. Product rule0
    c. Undefined   d. Undefined

82. A _____ is a numeral used to indicate a count. The most common use of the word today is to name the part of a fraction that tells the number or count of equal parts.
    a. Thing   b. Numerator0
    c. Undefined   d. Undefined

83. The _____ is a method of finding the derivative of a function that is the quotient of two other functions for which derivatives exist.
    a. Quotient rule0   b. Thing
    c. Undefined   d. Undefined

84. In mathematics, _____ is an elementary arithmetic operation. When one of the numbers is a whole number, _____ is the repeated sum of the other number.
    a. Thing   b. Multiplication0
    c. Undefined   d. Undefined

85. The _____, the average in everyday English, which is also called the arithmetic _____ (and is distinguished from the geometric _____ or harmonic _____). The average is also called the sample _____. The expected value of a random variable, which is also called the population _____.
    a. Thing   b. Mean0
    c. Undefined   d. Undefined

86. _____ are objects, characters, or other concrete representations of ideas, concepts, or other abstractions.
    a. Thing   b. Symbols0
    c. Undefined   d. Undefined

87. In mathematics, factorization (British English: factorisation) or factoring is the decomposition of an object (for example, a number, a polynomial, or a matrix) into a product of other objects, or _____, which when multiplied together give the original.

48   *Chapter 3. Derivatives*

    a. Thing   b. Factors0
    c. Undefined   d. Undefined

88. In mathematics, the _____, sometimes called the witch of Maria Agnesi is the curve defined as follows.Starting with a fixed circle, a point O on the circle is chosen. For any other point A on the circle, the secant line OA is drawn. The point M is diametrically opposite O. The line OA intersects the tangent at M at the point N. The line parallel to OM through N, and the line perpedicular to OM through A intersect at P. As the point A is varied, the path of P is the witch.
    a. Thing   b. Witch of Agnesi0
    c. Undefined   d. Undefined

89. In linear algebra, the _____ of an n-by-n square matrix A is defined to be the sum of the elements on the main diagonal of A,
    a. Trace0   b. Thing
    c. Undefined   d. Undefined

90. In mathematics, the _____ of two sets A and B is the set that contains all elements of A that also belong to B (or equivalently, all elements of B that also belong to A), but no other elements.
    a. Thing   b. Intersection0
    c. Undefined   d. Undefined

91. The _____ of a solid object is the three-dimensional concept of how much space it occupies, often quantified numerically.
    a. Volume0   b. Thing
    c. Undefined   d. Undefined

92. _____ is a physical property of a system that underlies the common notions of hot and cold; something that is hotter has the greater _____.
    a. Thing   b. Temperature0
    c. Undefined   d. Undefined

93. _____ is a kind of property which exists as magnitude or multitude. It is among the basic classes of things along with quality, substance, change, and relation.
    a. Thing   b. Amount0
    c. Undefined   d. Undefined

94. In mathematics, there are several meanings of _____ depending on the subject.
    a. Degree0   b. Thing
    c. Undefined   d. Undefined

95. In mathematics, the multiplicative inverse of a number x, denoted 1/x or x^{-1}, is the number which, when multiplied by x, yields 1. The multiplicative inverse of x is also called the _____ of x.
    a. Reciprocal0   b. Thing
    c. Undefined   d. Undefined

96. _____ is a branch of mathematics concerning the study of structure, relation and quantity.

Chapter 3. Derivatives

a. Algebra0
b. Concept
c. Undefined
d. Undefined

97. In mathematics, a _____ number is a number which can be expressed as a ratio of two integers. Non-integer _____ numbers (commonly called fractions) are usually written as the vulgar fraction a / b, where b is not zero.
a. Rational0
b. Thing
c. Undefined
d. Undefined

98. _____ is the fee paid on borrowed money.
a. Thing
b. Interest0
c. Undefined
d. Undefined

99. An _____ is the fee paid on borrow money.
a. Concept
b. Interest rate0
c. Undefined
d. Undefined

100. _____ or investing is a term with several closely-related meanings in business management, finance and economics, related to saving or deferring consumption.
a. Investment0
b. Thing
c. Undefined
d. Undefined

101. In mathematics, an _____, mean, or central tendency of a data set refers to a measure of the "middle" or "expected" value of the data set.
a. Concept
b. Average0
c. Undefined
d. Undefined

102. In geometry, a _____ (Greek words diairo = divide and metro = measure) of a circle is any straight line segment that passes through the centre and whose endpoints are on the circular boundary, or, in more modern usage, the length of such a line segment. When using the word in the more modern sense, one speaks of the _____ rather than a _____, because all diameters of a circle have the same length. This length is twice the radius. The _____ of a circle is also the longest chord that the circle has.
a. Diameter0
b. Thing
c. Undefined
d. Undefined

103. _____ is the transport of people on a trip/journey or the process or time involved in a person or object moving from one location to another.
a. Thing
b. Travel0
c. Undefined
d. Undefined

104. _____ statistics are statistics that estimate population parameters.
a. Thing
b. Parametric0
c. Undefined
d. Undefined

105. In statistics, _____ means the most frequent value assumed by a random variable, or occurring in a sampling of a random variable.

Chapter 3. Derivatives

a. Concept
b. Mode0
c. Undefined
d. Undefined

106. In mathematics, the _____ is a conic section generated by the intersection of a right circular conical surface and a plane parallel to a generating straight line of that surface. It can also be defined as locus of points in a plane which are equidistant from a given point.
   a. Parabola0
   b. Thing
   c. Undefined
   d. Undefined

107. In physics, _____ is an influence that may cause an object to accelerate. It may be experienced as a lift, a push, or a pull. The actual acceleration of the body is determined by the vector sum of all forces acting on it, known as net _____ or resultant _____.
   a. Thing
   b. Force0
   c. Undefined
   d. Undefined

108. _____ was a Greek philosopher, a student of Plato and teacher of Alexander the Great. He wrote on diverse subjects, including physics, metaphysics, poetry, biology and zoology, logic, rhetoric, politics, government, and ethics.
   a. Aristotle0
   b. Person
   c. Undefined
   d. Undefined

109. _____ was an Italian physicist, mathematician, astronomer, and philosopher who is closely associated with the scientific revolution.
   a. Person
   b. Galileo Galilei0
   c. Undefined
   d. Undefined

110. In mathematics, two quantities are called _____ if they vary in such a way that one of the quantities is a constant multiple of the other, or equivalently if they have a constant ratio.
   a. Proportional0
   b. Thing
   c. Undefined
   d. Undefined

111. In plane geometry, a _____ is a polygon with four equal sides, four right angles, and parallel opposite sides. In algebra, the _____ of a number is that number multiplied by itself.
   a. Thing
   b. Square0
   c. Undefined
   d. Undefined

112. In mathematics, the word _____ is used informally to refer to certain distinct bodies of knowledge about mathematics.
   a. Thing
   b. Theoretical0
   c. Undefined
   d. Undefined

113. In mathematics a _____ is a function which defines a distance between elements of a set.
   a. Metric0
   b. Thing
   c. Undefined
   d. Undefined

114. In navigation, a _____ is the clockwise angle between a reference direction and the direction to an object.

Chapter 3. Derivatives

a. Bearing0
b. Thing
c. Undefined
d. Undefined

115. In mathematics and its applications, a _____ is a system for assigning an n-tuple of numbers or scalars to each point in an n-dimensional space.
   a. Concept
   b. Coordinate system0
   c. Undefined
   d. Undefined

116. _____ is a concept in traditional logic referring to a "type of immediate inference in which from a given proposition another proposition is inferred which has as its subject the predicate of the original proposition and as its predicate the subject of the original proposition (the quality of the proposition being retained)."
   a. Conversion0
   b. Concept
   c. Undefined
   d. Undefined

117. In botany, _____ are above-ground plant organs specialized for photosynthesis. Their characteristics are typically analyzed by using Fiobonacci's sequences.
   a. Thing
   b. Leaves0
   c. Undefined
   d. Undefined

118. In mathematics, _____ bear slight similarity to functions: they allow one to use arbitrary values, called parameters, in place of independent variables in equations, which in turn provide values for dependent variables. A simple kinematical example is when one uses a time parameter to determine the position, velocity, and other information about a body in motion.
   a. Thing
   b. Parametric equations0
   c. Undefined
   d. Undefined

119. The deductive-nomological model is a formalized view of scientific _____ in natural language.
   a. Explanation0
   b. Thing
   c. Undefined
   d. Undefined

120. _____ is the application of tools and a processing medium to the transformation of raw materials into finished goods for sale.
   a. Manufacturing0
   b. Thing
   c. Undefined
   d. Undefined

121. _____ is the change in total cost that arises when the quantity produced changes by one unit.
   a. Marginal cost0
   b. Thing
   c. Undefined
   d. Undefined

122. A _____ is a quantity that denotes the proportional amount or magnitude of one quantity relative to another.
   a. Thing
   b. Ratio0
   c. Undefined
   d. Undefined

123. _____ is a special mathematical relationship between two quantities. Two quantities are called proportional if they vary in such a way that one of the quantities is a constant multiple of the other, or equivalently if they have a constant ratio.

a. Proportionality0
b. Thing
c. Undefined
d. Undefined

124. In banking and accountancy, the outstanding _____ is the amount of money owned, or due, that remains in a deposit account or a loan account at a given date, after all past remittances, payments and withdrawal have been accounted for.
  a. Thing
  b. Balance0
  c. Undefined
  d. Undefined

125. _____ is the extra revenue that an additional unit of product will bring a firm. It can also be described as the change in total revenue/change in number of units sold.
  a. Thing
  b. Marginal revenue0
  c. Undefined
  d. Undefined

126. _____ is a business term for the amount of money that a company receives from its activities in a given period, mostly from sales of products and/or services to customers
  a. Revenue0
  b. Thing
  c. Undefined
  d. Undefined

127. The _____ (symbol _____) and the millibar (symbol mbar, also mb) are units of pressure.
  a. Bar0
  b. Thing
  c. Undefined
  d. Undefined

128. The metre (or _____, see spelling differences) is a measure of length. It is the basic unit of length in the metric system and in the International System of Units (SI), used around the world for general and scientific purposes.
  a. Meter0
  b. Concept
  c. Undefined
  d. Undefined

129. A _____, as defined by the International Astronomical Union, is a celestial body orbiting a star or stellar remnant that is massive enough to be rounded by its own gravity, not massive enough to cause thermonuclear fusion in its core, and has cleared its neighboring region of planetesimals.
  a. Thing
  b. Planet0
  c. Undefined
  d. Undefined

130. In the scientific method, an _____ (Latin: ex-+-periri, "of (or from) trying"), is a set of actions and observations, performed in the context of solving a particular problem or question, in order to support or falsify a hypothesis or research concerning phenomena.
  a. Experiment0
  b. Thing
  c. Undefined
  d. Undefined

131. In a mathematical proof or a syllogism, a _____ is a statement that is the logical consequence of preceding statements.
  a. Conclusion0
  b. Concept
  c. Undefined
  d. Undefined

Chapter 3. Derivatives

132. A _____ is a one-dimensional picture in which the integers are shown as specially-marked points evenly spaced on a line.
   a. Number line0
   b. Thing
   c. Undefined
   d. Undefined

133. A _____ is a vehicle, missile or aircraft which obtains thrust by the reaction to the ejection of fast moving fluid from within a _____ engine.
   a. Thing
   b. Rocket0
   c. Undefined
   d. Undefined

134. A _____ is an instrument used in geometry technical drawing and engineering/building to measure distances and/or to rule straight lines.
   a. Ruler0
   b. Thing
   c. Undefined
   d. Undefined

135. In mathematics, the _____ functions are functions of an angle; they are important when studying triangles and modeling periodic phenomena, among many other applications.
   a. Trigonometric0
   b. Thing
   c. Undefined
   d. Undefined

136. In classical geometry, a _____ of a circle or sphere is any line segment from its center to its boundary. By extension, the _____ of a circle or sphere is the length of any such segment. The _____ is half the diameter. In science and engineering the term _____ of curvature is commonly used as a synonym for _____.
   a. Thing
   b. Radius0
   c. Undefined
   d. Undefined

137. The _____ are functions of an angle; they are important when studying triangles and modeling periodic phenomena, among many other applications.
   a. Thing
   b. Trigonometric functions0
   c. Undefined
   d. Undefined

138. _____ is a trigonemtric function that is important when studying triangles and modeling periodic phenomena, among other applications.
   a. Sine0
   b. Thing
   c. Undefined
   d. Undefined

139. In combinatorial mathematics, a _____ is an un-ordered collection of unique elements.
   a. Concept
   b. Combination0
   c. Undefined
   d. Undefined

140. A _____ is a function that repeats its values after some definite period has been added to its independent variable.
   a. Thing
   b. Periodic function0
   c. Undefined
   d. Undefined

Chapter 3. Derivatives

141. _____ are the cyclic rizing and falling of Earth's ocean surface caused by the tidal forces of the Moon and the sun acting on the oceans.
   a. Thing
   b. Tides0
   c. Undefined
   d. Undefined

142. In mathematics, an _____ is a statement about the relative size or order of two objects.
   a. Inequality0
   b. Thing
   c. Undefined
   d. Undefined

143. The _____ is a unit of plane angle. It is represented by the symbol "rad" or, more rarely, by the superscript c (for "circular measure"). For example, an angle of 1.2 radians would be written "1.2 rad" or "1.2c" (second symbol can produce confusion with centigrads).
   a. Thing
   b. Radian0
   c. Undefined
   d. Undefined

144. In geometry, _____, or general position for a set of points, or other configuration, means the general case situation, as opposed to some more special or coincidental cases that are possible.
   a. Standard position0
   b. Thing
   c. Undefined
   d. Undefined

145. In Euclidean geometry, an _____ is a closed segment of a differentiable curve in the two-dimensional plane; for example, a circular _____ is a segment of a circle.
   a. Concept
   b. Arc0
   c. Undefined
   d. Undefined

146. A _____ is one of the basic shapes of geometry: a polygon with three vertices and three sides which are straight line segments.
   a. Triangle0
   b. Thing
   c. Undefined
   d. Undefined

147. _____ is a relation in Euclidean geometry among the three sides of a right triangle.
   a. Thing
   b. Pythagorean Theorem0
   c. Undefined
   d. Undefined

148. _____ is a circle with a unit radius, i.e., a circle whose radius is 1.
   a. Unit circle0
   b. Thing
   c. Undefined
   d. Undefined

149. In Euclidean geometry, a _____ is the set of all points in a plane at a fixed distance, called the radius, from a given point, the center.
   a. Circle0
   b. Thing
   c. Undefined
   d. Undefined

150. _____ has one 90° internal angle a right angle.

Chapter 3. Derivatives

a. Right triangle0
b. Thing
c. Undefined
d. Undefined

151. In mathematics, a _____ of a number x is a number r such that $r^2 = x$, or in words, a number r whose square (the result of multiplying the number by itself) is x.
   a. Square root0
   b. Thing
   c. Undefined
   d. Undefined

152. In calculus, the _____ is a theorem regarding the limit of a function. The theorem asserts that if two functions approach the same limit at a point, and if a third function is "squeezed" between those functions, then the third function also approaches that limit at that point.
   a. Thing
   b. Squeeze Theorem0
   c. Undefined
   d. Undefined

153. In mathematics, a _____ of a complex-valued function f is a member x of the domain of f such that f(x) vanishes at x, that is, $x : f(x) = 0$.
   a. Root0
   b. Thing
   c. Undefined
   d. Undefined

154. In Euclidean geometry, a uniform _____ is a linear transformation that enlargers or diminishes objects, and whose _____ factor is the same in all directions. This is also called homothethy.
   a. Scale0
   b. Thing
   c. Undefined
   d. Undefined

155. _____ means "constancy", i.e. if something retains a certain feature even after we change a way of looking at it, then it is symmetric.
   a. Symmetry0
   b. Thing
   c. Undefined
   d. Undefined

156. An _____ is an equality that remains true regardless of the values of any variables that appear within it, to distinguish it from an equality which is true under more particular conditions.
   a. Thing
   b. Identity0
   c. Undefined
   d. Undefined

157. A circular _____ or circle _____ also known as a pie piece is the portion of a circle enclosed by two radii and an arc.
   a. Sector0
   b. Thing
   c. Undefined
   d. Undefined

158. _____ is a unit of plane angle, equal to 180/δ degrees, or about 57.2958 degrees
   a. Thing
   b. Radian measure0
   c. Undefined
   d. Undefined

159. In mathematics, a _____ is a mathematical statement which appears likely to be true, but has not been formally proven to be true under the rules of mathematical logic.

Chapter 3. Derivatives

    a. Conjecture0
    b. Concept
    c. Undefined
    d. Undefined

160. In mathematics, science including computer science, linguistics and engineering, an _____ is, generally speaking, an independent variable or input to a function.
    a. Thing
    b. Argument0
    c. Undefined
    d. Undefined

161. An _____ is an increase, either of some fixed amount, for example added regularly, or of a variable amount.
    a. Increment0
    b. Thing
    c. Undefined
    d. Undefined

162. In business, particularly accounting, a _____ is the time intervals that the accounts, statement, payments, or other calculations cover.
    a. Thing
    b. Period0
    c. Undefined
    d. Undefined

163. The _____ is a nonnegative scalar measure of a wave's magnitude of oscillation, that is, the magnitude of the maximum disturbance in the medium during one wave cycle.
    a. Thing
    b. Amplitude0
    c. Undefined
    d. Undefined

164. The _____ of a mathematical object is its size: a property by which it can be larger or smaller than other objects of the same kind; in technical terms, an ordering of the class of objects to which it belongs.
    a. Magnitude0
    b. Thing
    c. Undefined
    d. Undefined

165. In physics, _____ is the rate of change of acceleration; more precisely, the derivative of acceleration with respect to time, the second derivative of velocity, or the third derivative of displacement. _____ is described by the following equation:
    a. Thing
    b. Jerk0
    c. Undefined
    d. Undefined

166. In mathematics, a function f is _____ of a function g if f whenever A and B are complementary angles. This definition typically applies to trigonometric functions.
    a. Cofunction0
    b. Thing
    c. Undefined
    d. Undefined

167. The plus and _____ signs are mathematical symbols used to represent the notions of positive and negative as well as the operations of addition and subtraction.
    a. Minus0
    b. Thing
    c. Undefined
    d. Undefined

168. _____ is the chance that something is likely to happen or be the case.

Chapter 3. Derivatives

a. Thing
b. Probability0
c. Undefined
d. Undefined

169. _____ is the design, analysis, and/or construction of works for practical purposes.
   a. Engineering0
   b. Thing
   c. Undefined
   d. Undefined

170. _____, Greek for "knowledge of nature," is the branch of science concerned with the discovery and characterization of universal laws which govern matter, energy, space, and time.
   a. Physics0
   b. Thing
   c. Undefined
   d. Undefined

171. A _____ is traditionally an infinitesimally small change in a variable.
   a. Thing
   b. Differential0
   c. Undefined
   d. Undefined

172. A _____ is a mathematical equation for an unknown function of one or several variables which relates the values of the function itself and of its derivatives of various orders.
   a. Thing
   b. Differential equation0
   c. Undefined
   d. Undefined

173. In acoustics and telecommunication, the _____ of a wave is a component frequency of the signal that is an integer multiple of the fundamental frequency.
   a. Harmonic0
   b. Thing
   c. Undefined
   d. Undefined

174. Simple _____ is the motion of a simple harmonic oscillator, a motion that is neither driven nor damped. Complex _____ is the superposition — linear combination — of several simultaneous simple harmonic motions.
   a. Harmonic motion0
   b. Thing
   c. Undefined
   d. Undefined

175. In calculus, the _____ is a formula for the derivative of the composite of two functions.
   a. Chain rule0
   b. Concept
   c. Undefined
   d. Undefined

176. A _____ number is a positive integer which has a positive divisor other than one or itself.
   a. Thing
   b. Composite0
   c. Undefined
   d. Undefined

177. A _____ is 360° or 2∂ radians.
   a. Thing
   b. Turn0
   c. Undefined
   d. Undefined

178. _____ is the mathematical action of repeatedly adding or subtracting one, usually to find out how many objects there are or to set aside a desired number of objects.

Chapter 3. Derivatives

a. Thing
b. Counting0
c. Undefined
d. Undefined

179. The _____ is the distance around a closed curve. _____ is a kind of perimeter.
a. Thing
b. Circumference0
c. Undefined
d. Undefined

180. A _____, formed by the composition of one function on another, represents the application of the former to the result of the application of the latter to the argument of the composite.
a. Composite function0
b. Thing
c. Undefined
d. Undefined

181. _____ named in honor of the 17th century German philosopher and mathematician Gottfried Wilhelm Leibniz, was originally the use of expressions such as dx and dy and to represent "infinitely small" or infinitesimal increments of quantities x and y, just as Äx and Äy represent finite increments of x and y respectively.
a. Thing
b. Leibniz notation0
c. Undefined
d. Undefined

182. _____ interest refers to the fact that whenever interest is calculated, it is based not only on the original principal, but also on any unpaid interest that has been added to the principal.
a. Thing
b. Compound0
c. Undefined
d. Undefined

183. A _____ is a three-dimensional solid object bounded by six square faces, facets, or sides, with three meeting at each vertex.
a. Thing
b. Cube0
c. Undefined
d. Undefined

184. _____ are of a number n in its third power-the result of multiplying it by itself three times.
a. Cubes0
b. Thing
c. Undefined
d. Undefined

185. A _____ is an abstract model that uses mathematical language to describe the behavior of a system. Eykhoff defined a _____ as 'a representation of the essential aspects of an existing system which presents knowledge of that system in usable form'.
a. Thing
b. Mathematical model0
c. Undefined
d. Undefined

186. A _____ is a statement or claimt that a particular event will occur in the future in more certain terms than a forecast.
a. Thing
b. Prediction0
c. Undefined
d. Undefined

187. In functional analysis and related areas of mathematics the _____ set of a given subset of a vector space is a certain set in the dual space.

Chapter 3. Derivatives

a. Polar0
b. Thing
c. Undefined
d. Undefined

188. An n-sided _____ is a polyhedron formed by connecting an n-sided polygonal base and a point, called the apex, by n triangular faces. In other words, it is a conic solid with polygonal base.
   a. Pyramid0
   b. Thing
   c. Undefined
   d. Undefined

189. In mathematics, _____ geometry was the traditional name for the geometry of three-dimensional Euclidean space — for practical purposes the kind of space we live in.
   a. Thing
   b. Solid0
   c. Undefined
   d. Undefined

190. _____ is a temperature scale named after the German physicist Daniel Gabriel _____ , who proposed it in 1724.
   a. Thing
   b. Fahrenheit0
   c. Undefined
   d. Undefined

191. In geometry, the _____ of an object is a point in some sense in the middle of the object.
   a. Center0
   b. Thing
   c. Undefined
   d. Undefined

192. A _____ is a unit of length in the metric system, equal to one thousand metres, the current SI base unit of length
   a. Kilometer0
   b. Thing
   c. Undefined
   d. Undefined

193. A _____ is an object that is attached to a pivot point so that it can swing freely.
   a. Thing
   b. Pendulum0
   c. Undefined
   d. Undefined

194. _____ is a finite linear combination of sin and cos nx with n a natural number.
   a. Thing
   b. Trigonometric polynomial0
   c. Undefined
   d. Undefined

195. _____ is a mathematical operation, written a^n, involving two numbers, the base a and the exponent n.
   a. Thing
   b. Exponentiating0
   c. Undefined
   d. Undefined

196. _____ is a mathematical operation, written a^n, involving two numbers, the base a and the exponent n.
   a. Thing
   b. Exponentiation0
   c. Undefined
   d. Undefined

197. _____ is to give an equation R(x,y) = S(x,y) that at least in part has the same graph as y = f(x).
   a. Implicit differentiation0
   b. Thing
   c. Undefined
   d. Undefined

Chapter 3. Derivatives

198. In mathematics, the _____ (e) for L-functions are a class of summation formulae, expressing sums taken over the complex number zeroes of a given L-function, typically in terms of quantities studied by number theory by use of the theory of special functions.
   a. Thing
   b. Explicit formula0
   c. Undefined
   d. Undefined

199. A quadratic equation with real solutions, called roots, which may be real or complex, is given by the _____ : $x = \frac{-b \pm \sqrt{b^2 - 4ac}}{2a}$.
   a. Quadratic formula0
   b. Thing
   c. Undefined
   d. Undefined

200. _____ is the study of geometry using the principles of algebra. _____ can be explained more simply: it is concerned with defining geometrical shapes in a numerical way and extracting numerical information from that representation.
   a. Thing
   b. Analytic geometry0
   c. Undefined
   d. Undefined

201. In geometry, two lines or planes if one falls on the other in such a way as to create congruent adjacent angles. The term may be used as a noun or adjective. Thus, referring to Figure 1, the line AB is the _____ to CD through the point B.
   a. Perpendicular0
   b. Thing
   c. Undefined
   d. Undefined

202. _____ is electromagnetic radiation with a wavelength that is visible to the eye (visible _____) or, in a technical or scientific context, electromagnetic radiation of any wavelength.
   a. Light0
   b. Thing
   c. Undefined
   d. Undefined

203. A _____ given two distinct points A and B on the _____, is the set of points C on the line containing points A and B such that A is not strictly between C and B.
   a. Ray0
   b. Thing
   c. Undefined
   d. Undefined

204. In mathematics, an _____ .
   a. Ellipse0
   b. Thing
   c. Undefined
   d. Undefined

205. In geometry, an _____ polygon is a polygon which has all sides of the same length.
   a. Equilateral0
   b. Thing
   c. Undefined
   d. Undefined

206. An _____ is a triangle in which all sides are of equal length.
   a. Equilateral triangle0
   b. Thing
   c. Undefined
   d. Undefined

Chapter 3. Derivatives

207. In mathematics, a _____ is an ordered list of objects. Like a set, it contains members, also called elements or terms, and the number of terms is called the length of the _____. Unlike a set, order matters, and the exact same elements can appear multiple times at different positions in the _____.
   a. Sequence0
   b. Thing
   c. Undefined
   d. Undefined

208. A _____ is a curve derived from a fixed point O and two other curves á and â. Every line through O cutting á at A and â at B cuts the _____ at the midpoint of AB.
   a. Thing
   b. Cissoid0
   c. Undefined
   d. Undefined

209. _____ (July 31, 1704 - January 4, 1752) was a Swiss mathematician, born in Geneva.
   a. Person
   b. Gabriel Cramer0
   c. Undefined
   d. Undefined

210. In differential calculus, _____ problems involve finding the rate at which a quantity is changing by relating that quantity to other quantities whose rates of change are known.
   a. Thing
   b. Related rates0
   c. Undefined
   d. Undefined

211. In mathematics, a _____ is a quadric surface, with the following equation in Cartesian coordinates: $(x/_a)^2 + (y/_b)^2 = 1$.
   a. Cylinder0
   b. Thing
   c. Undefined
   d. Undefined

212. In mathematics, the _____ of a function is the set of all "output" values produced by that function. Given a function $f : A \to B$, the _____ of f, is defined to be the set $\{x \in B : x = f(a)$ for some $a \in A\}$.
   a. Thing
   b. Range0
   c. Undefined
   d. Undefined

213. The _____ of a geographic location is its height above a fixed reference point, often the mean sea level.
   a. Thing
   b. Elevation0
   c. Undefined
   d. Undefined

214. _____ is a three-dimensional geometric shape formed by straight lines through a fixed point vertex to the points of a fixed curve directrix.
   a. Right circular cone0
   b. Thing
   c. Undefined
   d. Undefined

215. A _____ is a three-dimensional geometric shape formed by straight lines through a fixed point (vertex) to the points of a fixed curve (directrix)
   a. Cone0
   b. Concept
   c. Undefined
   d. Undefined

216. The _____, in practice often shortened to amp, is a unit of electric current, or amount of electric charge per second.

Chapter 3. Derivatives

    a. Amperes0
    c. Undefined
    b. Thing
    d. Undefined

217. In geometry, a _____ is defined as a quadrilateral where all four of its angles are right angles.
    a. Rectangle0
    c. Undefined
    b. Thing
    d. Undefined

218. _____ is the distance around a given two-dimensional object. As a general rule, the _____ of a polygon can always be calculated by adding all the length of the sides together. So, the formula for triangles is P = a + b + c, where a, b and c stand for each side of it. For quadrilaterals the equation is P = a + b + c + d. For equilateral polygons, P = na, where n is the number of sides and a is the side length.
    a. Thing
    c. Undefined
    b. Perimeter0
    d. Undefined

219. A _____ can refer to a line joining two nonadjacent vertices of a polygon or polyhedron, or in some contexts any upward or downward sloping line. .
    a. Thing
    c. Undefined
    b. Diagonal0
    d. Undefined

220. The _____ rule, also known as a slipstick, is a mechanical analog computer, consisting of at least two finely divided scales , most often a fixed outer pair and a movable inner one, with a sliding window called the cursor.
    a. Thing
    c. Undefined
    b. Slide0
    d. Undefined

221. In geometry and trigonometry, a _____ is defined as an angle between two straight intersecting lines of ninety degrees, or one-quarter of a circle.
    a. Thing
    c. Undefined
    b. Right angle0
    d. Undefined

222. A _____, sea mile or nautimile is a unit of length. It is accepted for use with the International System of Units (SI), but it is not an SI unit.[1] The _____ is used around the world for maritime and aviation purposes. It is commonly used in international law and treaties, especially regarding the limits of territorial waters. It developed from the geographical mile.
    a. Nautical mile0
    c. Undefined
    b. Thing
    d. Undefined

223. A _____ is a method for fastening or securing linear material such as rope by tying or interweaving. It may consist of a length of one or more segments of rope, string, webbing, twine, strap or even chain interwoven so as to create in the line the ability to bind to itself or to some other object - the "load". Knots have been the subject of interest both for their ancient origins, common use, and the mathematical implications of _____ theory.
    a. Knot0
    c. Undefined
    b. Thing
    d. Undefined

224. In mathematics, a _____ is a two-dimensional manifold or surface that is perfectly flat.

Chapter 3. Derivatives

a. Plane0
b. Thing
c. Undefined
d. Undefined

225. A _____ is a unit of length, usually used to measure distance, in a number of different systems, including Imperial units, United States customary units and Norwegian/Swedish mil. Its size can vary from system to system, but in each is between 1 and 10 kilometers. In contemporary English contexts _____ refers to either:
a. Thing
b. Mile0
c. Undefined
d. Undefined

226. _____ is a unit of speed, expressing the number of international miles covered per hour.
a. Thing
b. Miles per hour0
c. Undefined
d. Undefined

227. In geometry a _____, or deltoid, is a quadrilateral with two pairs of congruent adjacent sides.
a. Kite0
b. Thing
c. Undefined
d. Undefined

228. In geometry, a _____ is a special kind of point, usually a corner of a polygon, polyhedron, or higher dimensional polytope. In the geometry of curves a _____ is a point of where the first derivative of curvature is zero. In graph theory, a _____ is the fundamental unit out of which graphs are formed
a. Thing
b. Vertex0
c. Undefined
d. Undefined

229. In mathematics, a _____ is an algebraic structure in which addition and multiplication are defined and have properties listed below.
a. Thing
b. Ring0
c. Undefined
d. Undefined

230. _____ is the volume of blood being pumped by the heart, in particular a ventricle in a minute.
a. Thing
b. Cardiac output0
c. Undefined
d. Undefined

231. A _____ consists of one quarter of the coordinate plane.
a. Thing
b. Quadrant0
c. Undefined
d. Undefined

232. A _____, lamp post, street lamp, light standard or lamp standard, is a raised source of light on the edge of a road, turned on or lit at a certain time every night.
a. Streetlight0
b. Thing
c. Undefined
d. Undefined

233. In business, _____, _____ cost or _____ expense refers to an ongoing expense of operating a business.
a. Overhead0
b. Thing
c. Undefined
d. Undefined

Chapter 3. Derivatives

234. Initial objects are also called _____, and terminal objects are also called final.
   a. Coterminal0
   b. Thing
   c. Undefined
   d. Undefined

235. _____ is the property of a physical object that quantifies the amount of matter and energy it is equivalent to.
   a. Thing
   b. Mass0
   c. Undefined
   d. Undefined

236. In mathematics, a _____ is a countable collection of open covers of a topological space that satisfies certain separation axioms.
   a. Thing
   b. Development0
   c. Undefined
   d. Undefined

237. A _____ is a polynomial function of the form $f(x) = ax^2 + bx + c$, where a, b, c are real numbers and a , 0.
   a. Quadratic function0
   b. Event
   c. Undefined
   d. Undefined

238. _____ is the middle point of a line segment.
   a. Midpoint0
   b. Thing
   c. Undefined
   d. Undefined

Chapter 4. Applications of Derivatives 65

1. A _____ function is a function for which, intuitively, small changes in the input result in small changes in the output.
   a. Event
   b. Continuous0
   c. Undefined
   d. Undefined

2. In mathematics, a _____ is a statement that can be proved on the basis of explicitly stated or previously agreed assumptions.
   a. Theorem0
   b. Thing
   c. Undefined
   d. Undefined

3. The mathematical concept of a _____ expresses the intuitive idea of deterministic dependence between two quantities, one of which is viewed as primary and the other as secondary. A _____ then is a way to associate a unique output for each input of a specified type, for example, a real number or an element of a given set.
   a. Function0
   b. Thing
   c. Undefined
   d. Undefined

4. In elementary algebra, an _____ is a set that contains every real number between two indicated numbers and may contain the two numbers themselves.
   a. Thing
   b. Interval0
   c. Undefined
   d. Undefined

5. A _____ is a function for which, intuitively, small changes in the input result in small changes in the output.
   a. Event
   b. Continuous function0
   c. Undefined
   d. Undefined

6. _____ is a free computer algebra system based on a 1982 version of Macsyma
   a. Maxima0
   b. Thing
   c. Undefined
   d. Undefined

7. _____ are points in the domain of a function at which the function takes a largest value or smallest value, either within a given neighborhood or on the function domain in its entirety.
   a. Maxima and minima0
   b. Thing
   c. Undefined
   d. Undefined

8. The _____ is a measurement of how a function changes when the values of its inputs change.
   a. Thing
   b. Derivative0
   c. Undefined
   d. Undefined

9. In mathematics, maxima and _____, known collectively as extrema, are points in the domain of a function at which the function takes a largest value .
   a. Thing
   b. Minima0
   c. Undefined
   d. Undefined

10. In a mathematical proof or a syllogism, a _____ is a statement that is the logical consequence of preceding statements.
    a. Concept
    b. Conclusion0
    c. Undefined
    d. Undefined

Chapter 4. Applications of Derivatives

11. _____ are the basic objects of study in graph theory. Informally speaking, a graph is a set of objects called points, nodes, or vertices connected by links called lines or edges.
    a. Thing
    b. Graphs0
    c. Undefined
    d. Undefined

12. The term _____ refers to the largest and the smallest element of a set.
    a. Thing
    b. Extreme value0
    c. Undefined
    d. Undefined

13. in mathematics, maxima and minima, known collectively as _____, are the largest value maximum or smallest value minimum, that a function takes in a point either within a given neighborhood or on the function domain in its entirety global extremum.
    a. Thing
    b. Extrema0
    c. Undefined
    d. Undefined

14. An _____ or an extremal point is a point that belongs to the extremity of something.
    a. Extreme point0
    b. Thing
    c. Undefined
    d. Undefined

15. In mathematics, the concept of a _____ tries to capture the intuitive idea of a geometrical one-dimensional and continuous object. A simple example is the circle.
    a. Thing
    b. Curve0
    c. Undefined
    d. Undefined

16. In mathematics, maxima and minima, known collectively as extrema, are the largest value maximum or smallest value minimum, that a function takes in a point either within a given neighborhood local _____ or on the function domain in its entirety global _____.
    a. Extremum0
    b. Thing
    c. Undefined
    d. Undefined

17. In mathematics, a _____ of a k-place relation $L \subseteq X_1 \times ... \times X_k$ is one of the sets X_j, $1 \leq j \leq k$. In the special case where k = 2 and $L \subseteq X_1 \times X_2$ is a function $L : X_1 \to X_2$, it is conventional to refer to X_1 as the _____ of the function and to refer to X_2 as the codomain of the function.
    a. Thing
    b. Domain0
    c. Undefined
    d. Undefined

18. A real-valued function f defined on the real line is said to have a _____ point at the point $x*$, if there exists some $\varepsilon > 0$, such that f when $x - x* < \varepsilon$.
    a. Local maximum0
    b. Thing
    c. Undefined
    d. Undefined

19. In mathematics, a _____ is a demonstration that, assuming certain axioms, some statement is necessarily true.
    a. Proof0
    b. Thing
    c. Undefined
    d. Undefined

20. The _____ integers are all the integers from zero on upwards.

Chapter 4. Applications of Derivatives

    a. Nonnegative0
    b. Thing
    c. Undefined
    d. Undefined

21. _____ is often used to describe the measurement of the steepness, incline, gradient, or grade of a straight line. The _____ is defined as the ratio of the "rise" divided by the "run" between two points on a line, or in other words, the ratio of the altitude change to the horizontal distance between any two points on the line.
    a. Slope0
    b. Thing
    c. Undefined
    d. Undefined

22. In mathematics, an _____ is a statement about the relative size or order of two objects.
    a. Inequality0
    b. Thing
    c. Undefined
    d. Undefined

23. In mathematics, defined and _____ are used to explain whether or not expressions have meaningful, sensible, and unambiguous values.
    a. Thing
    b. Undefined0
    c. Undefined
    d. Undefined

24. _____ is a point on the domain of a function
    a. Critical point0
    b. Thing
    c. Undefined
    d. Undefined

25. In geometry, an _____ is a point at which a line segment or ray terminates.
    a. Endpoint0
    b. Thing
    c. Undefined
    d. Undefined

26. A _____ is a negotiable instrument instructing a financial institution to pay a specific amount of a specific currency from a specific demand account held in the maker/depositor's name with that institution. Both the maker and payee may be natural persons or legal entities.
    a. Check0
    b. Thing
    c. Undefined
    d. Undefined

27. When _____ symmetry one can determine whether or not an object is symmetric with respect to a given mathematical operation, if, when applied to the object, this operation does not change the object or its appearance.
    a. Thing
    b. Investigating0
    c. Undefined
    d. Undefined

28. In trigonometry, the _____ is a function defined as $\tan x = \sin x / \cos x$. The function is so-named because it can be defined as the length of a certain segment of a _____ (in the geometric sense) to the unit circle. In plane geometry, a line is _____ to a curve, at some point, if both line and curve pass through the point with the same direction.
    a. Thing
    b. Tangent0
    c. Undefined
    d. Undefined

29. In astronomy, geography, geometry and related sciences and contexts, a plane is said to be _____ at a given point if it is locally perpendicular to the gradient of the gravity field, i.e., with the direction of the gravitational force at that point.

68   *Chapter 4. Applications of Derivatives*

    a. Thing   b. Horizontal0
    c. Undefined   d. Undefined

30. In mathematics, a _____ is an expression that is constructed from one or more variables and constants, using only the operations of addition, subtraction, multiplication, and constant positive whole number exponents. is a _____. Note in particular that division by an expression containing a variable is not in general allowed in polynomials. [1]
    a. Thing   b. Polynomial0
    c. Undefined   d. Undefined

31. _____ is a mathematical subject that includes the study of limits, derivatives, integrals, and power series and constitutes a major part of modern university curriculum.
    a. Calculus0   b. Thing
    c. Undefined   d. Undefined

32. A _____ consists either of a suggested explanation for a phenomenon or of a reasoned proposal suggesting a possible correlation between multiple phenomena.
    a. Hypothesis0   b. Thing
    c. Undefined   d. Undefined

33. In mathematics and the mathematical sciences, a _____ is a fixed, but possibly unspecified, value. This is in contrast to a variable, which is not fixed.
    a. Constant0   b. Thing
    c. Undefined   d. Undefined

34. _____ consists either of a suggested explanation for a phenomenon or of a reasoned proposal suggesting a possible correlation between multiple phenomena.
    a. Event   b. Hypotheses0
    c. Undefined   d. Undefined

35. The _____, the average in everyday English, which is also called the arithmetic _____ (and is distinguished from the geometric _____ or harmonic _____). The average is also called the sample _____. The expected value of a random variable, which is also called the population _____.
    a. Mean0   b. Thing
    c. Undefined   d. Undefined

36. In mathematics, an _____, mean, or central tendency of a data set refers to a measure of the "middle" or "expected" value of the data set.
    a. Average0   b. Concept
    c. Undefined   d. Undefined

37. _____ is defined as the rate of change or derivative with respect to time of velocity.
    a. Acceleration0   b. Thing
    c. Undefined   d. Undefined

38. A _____ is a mathematical statement which follows easily from a previously proven statement, typically a mathematical theorem.

Chapter 4. Applications of Derivatives

    a. Thing
    c. Undefined
    b. Corollary0
    d. Undefined

39. A _____ is a special kind of ratio, indicating a relationship between two measurements with different units, such as miles to gallons or cents to pounds.
    a. Thing
    c. Undefined
    b. Rate0
    d. Undefined

40. _____ has many meanings, most of which simply .
    a. Power0
    c. Undefined
    b. Thing
    d. Undefined

41. In mathematics, a _____ of a complex-valued function f is a member x of the domain of f such that f(x) vanishes at x, that is, x : f (x) = 0.
    a. Root0
    c. Undefined
    b. Thing
    d. Undefined

42. A _____ is a polynomial function of the form f(x) = ax^2 + bx +c , where a, b, c are real numbers and a , 0.
    a. Event
    c. Undefined
    b. Quadratic function0
    d. Undefined

43. _____ is the mathematical action of repeatedly adding or subtracting one, usually to find out how many objects there are or to set aside a desired number of objects.
    a. Counting0
    c. Undefined
    b. Thing
    d. Undefined

44. _____ is a trigonemtric function that is important when studying triangles and modeling periodic phenomena, among other applications.
    a. Thing
    c. Undefined
    b. Sine0
    d. Undefined

45. Acid _____ ratio measures the ability of a company to use its near cash or quick assets to immediately extinguish its current liabilities.
    a. Test0
    c. Undefined
    b. Thing
    d. Undefined

46. _____ determines whether a given critical point of a function is a maximum, a minimum, or neither.
    a. Thing
    c. Undefined
    b. First Derivative Test0
    d. Undefined

47. In mathematics, a _____ may be described informally as a number that can be given by an infinite decimal representation.
    a. Thing
    c. Undefined
    b. Real number0
    d. Undefined

Chapter 4. Applications of Derivatives

48. In mathematics, factorization (British English: factorisation) or factoring is the decomposition of an object (for example, a number, a polynomial, or a matrix) into a product of other objects, or _____, which when multiplied together give the original.
    a. Factors0
    b. Thing
    c. Undefined
    d. Undefined

49. In mathematics, the _____ of a coordinate system is the point where the axes of the system intersect.
    a. Thing
    b. Origin0
    c. Undefined
    d. Undefined

50. A _____ is 360° or 2δ radians.
    a. Thing
    b. Turn0
    c. Undefined
    d. Undefined

51. A _____ consists of one quarter of the coordinate plane.
    a. Quadrant0
    b. Thing
    c. Undefined
    d. Undefined

52. _____ determines whether a given stationary point of a function is a maximum or a minimum.
    a. Thing
    b. Second derivative test0
    c. Undefined
    d. Undefined

53. The word _____ means curving in or hollowed inward.
    a. Thing
    b. Concavity0
    c. Undefined
    d. Undefined

54. In mathematics, the _____ is a conic section generated by the intersection of a right circular conical surface and a plane parallel to a generating straight line of that surface. It can also be defined as locus of points in a plane which are equidistant from a given point.
    a. Thing
    b. Parabola0
    c. Undefined
    d. Undefined

55. In mathematics, the _____ f is the collection of all ordered pairs . In particular, graph means the graphical representation of this collection, in the form of a curve or surface, together with axes, etc. Graphing on a Cartesian plane is sometimes referred to as curve sketching.
    a. Thing
    b. Graph of a function0
    c. Undefined
    d. Undefined

56. _____ has two distinct but etymologically-related meanings: one in geometry and one in trigonometry.
    a. Tangent line0
    b. Thing
    c. Undefined
    d. Undefined

57. In acoustics and telecommunication, the _____ of a wave is a component frequency of the signal that is an integer multiple of the fundamental frequency.

Chapter 4. Applications of Derivatives

a. Harmonic0
b. Thing
c. Undefined
d. Undefined

58. Simple _____ is the motion of a simple harmonic oscillator, a motion that is neither driven nor damped. Complex _____ is the superposition — linear combination — of several simultaneous simple harmonic motions.
    a. Harmonic motion0
    b. Thing
    c. Undefined
    d. Undefined

59. _____ is the change in total cost that arises when the quantity produced changes by one unit.
    a. Thing
    b. Marginal cost0
    c. Undefined
    d. Undefined

60. _____ is a a point on a curve at which the tangent crosses the curve itself.
    a. Inflection point0
    b. Thing
    c. Undefined
    d. Undefined

61. Any point where a graph makes contact with an coordinate axis is called an _____ of the graph
    a. Intercept0
    b. Thing
    c. Undefined
    d. Undefined

62. A _____ is a set of numbers that designate location in a given reference system, such as x,y in a planar _____ system or an x,y,z in a three-dimensional _____ system.
    a. Thing
    b. Coordinate0
    c. Undefined
    d. Undefined

63. _____ is the application of tools and a processing medium to the transformation of raw materials into finished goods for sale.
    a. Thing
    b. Manufacturing0
    c. Undefined
    d. Undefined

64. In mathematics, there are several meanings of _____ depending on the subject.
    a. Degree0
    b. Thing
    c. Undefined
    d. Undefined

65. An _____ is a straight line or curve A to which another curve B approaches closer and closer as one moves along it. As one moves along B, the space between it and the _____ A becomes smaller and smaller, and can in fact be made as small as one could wish by going far enough along. A curve may or may not touch or cross its _____. In fact, the curve may intersect the _____ an infinite number of times.
    a. Thing
    b. Asymptote0
    c. Undefined
    d. Undefined

66. The _____ of a mathematical object is its size: a property by which it can be larger or smaller than other objects of the same kind; in technical terms, an ordering of the class of objects to which it belongs.
    a. Magnitude0
    b. Thing
    c. Undefined
    d. Undefined

Chapter 4. Applications of Derivatives

67. _____ is the state of being greater than any finite number, however large.
 a. Infinity0
 b. Thing
 c. Undefined
 d. Undefined

68. In logic and mathematics, logical _____ is a logical relation that holds between a set T of formulas and a formula B when every model (or interpretation or valuation) of T is also a model of B.
 a. Concept
 b. Implication0
 c. Undefined
 d. Undefined

69. A _____ is a numeral used to indicate a count. The most common use of the word today is to name the part of a fraction that tells the number or count of equal parts.
 a. Thing
 b. Numerator0
 c. Undefined
 d. Undefined

70. In mathematics, a _____ number is a number which can be expressed as a ratio of two integers. Non-integer _____ numbers (commonly called fractions) are usually written as the vulgar fraction a / b, where b is not zero.
 a. Thing
 b. Rational0
 c. Undefined
 d. Undefined

71. In mathematics, a _____ is any function which can be written as the ratio of two polynomial functions.
 a. Thing
 b. Rational function0
 c. Undefined
 d. Undefined

72. In Euclidean geometry, a uniform _____ is a linear transformation that enlargers or diminishes objects, and whose _____ factor is the same in all directions. This is also called homothethy.
 a. Thing
 b. Scale0
 c. Undefined
 d. Undefined

73. A _____ is the part of a fraction that tells how many equal parts make up a whole, and which is used in the name of the fraction: "halves", "thirds", "fourths" or "quarters", "fifths" and so on.
 a. Denominator0
 b. Concept
 c. Undefined
 d. Undefined

74. In mathematics, an inequality is a statement about the relative size or order of two objects. For example 14 > 10, or 14 is _____ 10.
 a. Thing
 b. Greater than0
 c. Undefined
 d. Undefined

75. A _____ is a quantity that denotes the proportional amount or magnitude of one quantity relative to another.
 a. Ratio0
 b. Thing
 c. Undefined
 d. Undefined

76. _____ is a straight line or curve A to which another curve B the one being studied approaches closer and closer as one moves along it.

Chapter 4. Applications of Derivatives

a. Thing
b. Vertical asymptote0
c. Undefined
d. Undefined

77. An _____ is when two lines intersect somewhere on a plane creating a right angle at intersection
a. Thing
b. Axes0
c. Undefined
d. Undefined

78. A _____ of a number is the product of that number with any integer.
a. Multiple0
b. Thing
c. Undefined
d. Undefined

79. In mathematics, _____ are the intuitive idea of a geometrical one-dimensional and continuous object.
a. Curves0
b. Thing
c. Undefined
d. Undefined

80. The _____ of measurement are a globally standardized and modernized form of the metric system.
a. Units0
b. Thing
c. Undefined
d. Undefined

81. A _____ is the part of the dividend that is left over when the dividend is not evenly divisible by the divisor.
a. Thing
b. Remainder0
c. Undefined
d. Undefined

82. _____ are functions which satisfy particular symmetry relations, with respect to taking additive inverses.
a. Even function0
b. Thing
c. Undefined
d. Undefined

83. _____ means "constancy", i.e. if something retains a certain feature even after we change a way of looking at it, then it is symmetric.
a. Thing
b. Symmetry0
c. Undefined
d. Undefined

84. In mathematics, a set is called _____ if there is a bijection between the set and some set of the form {1, 2, ..., n} where n is a natural number.
a. Thing
b. Finite0
c. Undefined
d. Undefined

85. Continuous functions are of utmost importance in mathematics and applications. However, not all functions are continuous. If a function is not continuous at a point in its domain, one says that it has a _____ there. The set of all points of _____ of a function may be a discrete set, a dense set, or even the entire domain of the function.
a. Discontinuity0
b. Thing
c. Undefined
d. Undefined

86. In calculus, the _____ is a theorem regarding the limit of a function. The theorem asserts that if two functions approach the same limit at a point, and if a third function is "squeezed" between those functions, then the third function also approaches that limit at that point.

74   Chapter 4. Applications of Derivatives

     a. Thing   b. Squeeze Theorem0
     c. Undefined   d. Undefined

87. In geometry, an _____ angle is an angle that is not a 90 degree angle, or an angle that is divisible by 90: 180, 270, 360/0
     a. Thing   b. Oblique0
     c. Undefined   d. Undefined

88. The word _____ comes from the Latin word linearis, which means created by lines.
     a. Linear0   b. Thing
     c. Undefined   d. Undefined

89. Sir Isaac _____, was an English physicist, mathematician, astronomer, natural philosopher, and alchemist, regarded by many as the greatest figure in the history of science
     a. Person   b. Newton0
     c. Undefined   d. Undefined

90. A _____ is the result of the addition of a set of numbers. The numbers may be natural numbers, complex numbers, matrices, or still more complicated objects. An infinite _____ is a subtle procedure known as a series.
     a. Sum0   b. Thing
     c. Undefined   d. Undefined

91. A _____ is a symbolic representation denoting a quantity or expression. It often represents an "unknown" quantity that has the potential to change.
     a. Thing   b. Variable0
     c. Undefined   d. Undefined

92. An _____ is a combination of numbers, operators, grouping symbols and/or free variables and bound variables arranged in a meaningful way which can be evaluated..
     a. Thing   b. Expression0
     c. Undefined   d. Undefined

93. A _____ is an abstract model that uses mathematical language to describe the behavior of a system. Eykhoff defined a _____ as 'a representation of the essential aspects of an existing system which presents knowledge of that system in usable form'.
     a. Mathematical model0   b. Thing
     c. Undefined   d. Undefined

94. _____ is the fee paid on borrowed money.
     a. Thing   b. Interest0
     c. Undefined   d. Undefined

95. In plane geometry, a _____ is a polygon with four equal sides, four right angles, and parallel opposite sides. In algebra, the _____ of a number is that number multiplied by itself.

Chapter 4. Applications of Derivatives

a. Thing
b. Square0
c. Undefined
d. Undefined

96. The _____ of a solid object is the three-dimensional concept of how much space it occupies, often quantified numerically.
a. Volume0
b. Thing
c. Undefined
d. Undefined

97. In mathematics, a _____ is a quadric surface, with the following equation in Cartesian coordinates: $(x/a)^2 + (y/b)^2 = 1$.
a. Thing
b. Cylinder0
c. Undefined
d. Undefined

98. In geometry, a _____ (Greek words diairo = divide and metro = measure) of a circle is any straight line segment that passes through the centre and whose endpoints are on the circular boundary, or, in more modern usage, the length of such a line segment. When using the word in the more modern sense, one speaks of the _____ rather than a _____, because all diameters of a circle have the same length. This length is twice the radius. The _____ of a circle is also the longest chord that the circle has.
a. Diameter0
b. Thing
c. Undefined
d. Undefined

99. _____ or arithmetics is the oldest and most elementary branch of mathematics, used by almost everyone, for tasks ranging from simple daily counting to advanced science and business calculations.
a. Thing
b. Arithmetic0
c. Undefined
d. Undefined

100. _____, Greek for "knowledge of nature," is the branch of science concerned with the discovery and characterization of universal laws which govern matter, energy, space, and time.
a. Thing
b. Physics0
c. Undefined
d. Undefined

101. In mathematics, a _____ is the result of multiplying, or an expression that identifies factors to be multiplied.
a. Product0
b. Thing
c. Undefined
d. Undefined

102. In geometry, a _____ is defined as a quadrilateral where all four of its angles are right angles.
a. Rectangle0
b. Thing
c. Undefined
d. Undefined

103. _____ is the transport of people on a trip/journey or the process or time involved in a person or object moving from one location to another.
a. Thing
b. Travel0
c. Undefined
d. Undefined

104. A _____ signifies a point or points of probability on a subject e.g., the _____ of creativity, which allows for the formation of rule or norm or law by interpretation of the phenomena events that can be created.

76   Chapter 4. Applications of Derivatives

    a. Thing
    b. Principle0
    c. Undefined
    d. Undefined

105. The _____ in a vacuum is an important physical constant denoted by the letter c for constant or the Latin word celeritas meaning "swiftness
    a. Thing
    b. Speed of light0
    c. Undefined
    d. Undefined

106. _____ is electromagnetic radiation with a wavelength that is visible to the eye (visible _____) or, in a technical or scientific context, electromagnetic radiation of any wavelength.
    a. Light0
    b. Thing
    c. Undefined
    d. Undefined

107. A _____ given two distinct points A and B on the _____, is the set of points C on the line containing points A and B such that A is not strictly between C and B.
    a. Thing
    b. Ray0
    c. Undefined
    d. Undefined

108. In geometry, the relations of _____ are those such as 'lies on' between points and lines (as in 'point P lies on line L'), and 'intersects' (as in 'line L_1 intersects line L_2', in three-dimensional space). That is, they are the binary relations describing how subsets meet.
    a. Incidence0
    b. Thing
    c. Undefined
    d. Undefined

109. _____ of an object is its speed in a particular direction.
    a. Velocity0
    b. Thing
    c. Undefined
    d. Undefined

110. _____ is a physical property of a system that underlies the common notions of hot and cold; something that is hotter has the greater _____.
    a. Thing
    b. Temperature0
    c. Undefined
    d. Undefined

111. Claudius Ptolemaeus, known in English as _____, was a Hellenistic mathematician, geographer, astronomer, and astrologer. The Almagest is widely held to be the first systematic treatise on astronomy in antiquity. Babylonian astronomers had developed arithmetical techniques for calculating astronomical phenomena; Greek astronomers such as Hipparchus had produced geometric models for calculating celestial motions; _____, however, clearly derived his geometrical models from selected astronomical observations by his predecessors spanning more than 800 years.
    a. Ptolemy0
    b. Person
    c. Undefined
    d. Undefined

112. _____, from Latin meaning "to make progress", is defined in two different ways. Pure economic _____ is the increase in wealth that an investor has from making an investment, taking into consideration all costs associated with that investment including the opportunity cost of capital.

Chapter 4. Applications of Derivatives

a. Profit0
b. Thing
c. Undefined
d. Undefined

113. _____ is the extra revenue that an additional unit of product will bring a firm. It can also be described as the change in total revenue/change in number of units sold.
  a. Thing
  b. Marginal revenue0
  c. Undefined
  d. Undefined

114. _____ is a business term for the amount of money that a company receives from its activities in a given period, mostly from sales of products and/or services to customers
  a. Revenue0
  b. Thing
  c. Undefined
  d. Undefined

115. In combinatorial mathematics, a _____ is an un-ordered collection of unique elements.
  a. Concept
  b. Combination0
  c. Undefined
  d. Undefined

116. _____ is a synonym for information.
  a. Data0
  b. Thing
  c. Undefined
  d. Undefined

117. A circular _____ or circle _____ also known as a pie piece is the portion of a circle enclosed by two radii and an arc.
  a. Sector0
  b. Thing
  c. Undefined
  d. Undefined

118. In Euclidean geometry, a _____ is the set of all points in a plane at a fixed distance, called the radius, from a given point, the center.
  a. Circle0
  b. Thing
  c. Undefined
  d. Undefined

119. In classical geometry, a _____ of a circle or sphere is any line segment from its center to its boundary. By extension, the _____ of a circle or sphere is the length of any such segment. The _____ is half the diameter. In science and engineering the term _____ of curvature is commonly used as a synonym for _____.
  a. Radius0
  b. Thing
  c. Undefined
  d. Undefined

120. In Euclidean geometry, an _____ is a closed segment of a differentiable curve in the two-dimensional plane; for example, a circular _____ is a segment of a circle.
  a. Concept
  b. Arc0
  c. Undefined
  d. Undefined

121. _____ is the distance around a given two-dimensional object. As a general rule, the _____ of a polygon can always be calculated by adding all the length of the sides together. So, the formula for triangles is P = a + b + c, where a, b and c stand for each side of it. For quadrilaterals the equation is P = a + b + c + d. For equilateral polygons, P = na, where n is the number of sides and a is the side length.

a. Thing
b. Perimeter0
c. Undefined
d. Undefined

122. A _____ is one of the basic shapes of geometry: a polygon with three vertices and three sides which are straight line segments.
a. Triangle0
b. Thing
c. Undefined
d. Undefined

123. The _____ of a right triangle is the triangle's longest side; the side opposite the right angle.
a. Thing
b. Hypotenuse0
c. Undefined
d. Undefined

124. _____ has one 90° internal angle a right angle.
a. Right triangle0
b. Thing
c. Undefined
d. Undefined

125. An _____ triange is a triangle with at least two sides of equal length.
a. Isosceles0
b. Thing
c. Undefined
d. Undefined

126. In mathematics, two quantities are called _____ if they vary in such a way that one of the quantities is a constant multiple of the other, or equivalently if they have a constant ratio.
a. Proportional0
b. Thing
c. Undefined
d. Undefined

127. In finance, a _____ is collateral that the holder of a position in securities, options, or futures contracts has to deposit to cover the credit risk of his counterparty.
a. Thing
b. Margin0
c. Undefined
d. Undefined

128. A _____ is a function that assigns a number to subsets of a given set.
a. Thing
b. Measure0
c. Undefined
d. Undefined

129. In mathematical analysis and related areas of mathematics, a set is called _____, if it is, in a certain sense, of finite size.
a. Bounded0
b. Thing
c. Undefined
d. Undefined

130. Compass and straightedge or ruler-and-compass _____ is the _____ of lengths or angles using only an idealized ruler and compass.
a. Construction0
b. Thing
c. Undefined
d. Undefined

131. In a right triangle, the _____ of the triangle are the two sides that are perpendicular to each other, as opposed to the hypotenuse.

Chapter 4. Applications of Derivatives

   a. Legs0   b. Thing
   c. Undefined   d. Undefined

132. _____ is a three-dimensional geometric shape formed by straight lines through a fixed point vertex to the points of a fixed curve directrix.
   a. Right circular cone0   b. Thing
   c. Undefined   d. Undefined

133. A _____ is a three-dimensional geometric shape formed by straight lines through a fixed point (vertex) to the points of a fixed curve (directrix)
   a. Cone0   b. Concept
   c. Undefined   d. Undefined

134. The metre (or _____, see spelling differences) is a measure of length. It is the basic unit of length in the metric system and in the International System of Units (SI), used around the world for general and scientific purposes.
   a. Concept   b. Meter0
   c. Undefined   d. Undefined

135. A _____ is a three-dimensional solid object bounded by six square faces, facets, or sides, with three meeting at each vertex.
   a. Thing   b. Cube0
   c. Undefined   d. Undefined

136. A _____, sea mile or nautimile is a unit of length. It is accepted for use with the International System of Units (SI), but it is not an SI unit.[1] The _____ is used around the world for maritime and aviation purposes. It is commonly used in international law and treaties, especially regarding the limits of territorial waters. It developed from the geographical mile.
   a. Nautical mile0   b. Thing
   c. Undefined   d. Undefined

137. A _____ is a method for fastening or securing linear material such as rope by tying or interweaving. It may consist of a length of one or more segments of rope, string, webbing, twine, strap or even chain interwoven so as to create in the line the ability to bind to itself or to some other object - the "load". Knots have been the subject of interest both for their ancient origins, common use, and the mathematical implications of _____ theory.
   a. Knot0   b. Thing
   c. Undefined   d. Undefined

138. A _____ is a unit of length, usually used to measure distance, in a number of different systems, including Imperial units, United States customary units and Norwegian/Swedish mil. Its size can vary from system to system, but in each is between 1 and 10 kilometers. In contemporary English contexts _____ refers to either:
   a. Mile0   b. Thing
   c. Undefined   d. Undefined

139. _____ is a unit of speed, expressing the number of international miles covered per hour.

Chapter 4. Applications of Derivatives

    a. Thing
    b. Miles per hour0
    c. Undefined
    d. Undefined

140. In mathematics, a class _____ is a structure used to organize the various Galois groups and modules that appear in class field theory. They were invented by Emil Artin and John Tate.
    a. Formation0
    b. Thing
    c. Undefined
    d. Undefined

141. _____ is a kind of property which exists as magnitude or multitude. It is among the basic classes of things along with quality, substance, change, and relation.
    a. Thing
    b. Amount0
    c. Undefined
    d. Undefined

142. In mathematics, a _____ (also spelled reflexion) is a map that transforms an object into its mirror image.
    a. Reflection0
    b. Concept
    c. Undefined
    d. Undefined

143. In mathematics, a _____ is a two-dimensional manifold or surface that is perfectly flat.
    a. Thing
    b. Plane0
    c. Undefined
    d. Undefined

144. _____ is the force that opposes the relative motion or tendency toward such motion of two surfaces in contact.
    a. Thing
    b. Friction0
    c. Undefined
    d. Undefined

145. In mathematics and its applications, _____ refers to finding the linear approximation to a function at a given point.
    a. Linearization0
    b. Thing
    c. Undefined
    d. Undefined

146. A _____ is traditionally an infinitesimally small change in a variable.
    a. Differential0
    b. Thing
    c. Undefined
    d. Undefined

147. _____ is an approximation of a general function using a linear function more precisely, an affine function.
    a. Thing
    b. Linear approximation0
    c. Undefined
    d. Undefined

148. In geometry, the _____ of an object is a point in some sense in the middle of the object.
    a. Center0
    b. Thing
    c. Undefined
    d. Undefined

149. A _____ is a deliberate process for transforming one or more inputs into one or more results.
    a. Thing
    b. Calculation0
    c. Undefined
    d. Undefined

Chapter 4. Applications of Derivatives   81

150. In mathematics, a _____ of a number x is a number r such that $r^2 = x$, or in words, a number r whose square (the result of multiplying the number by itself) is x.
   a. Thing
   b. Square root0
   c. Undefined
   d. Undefined

151. In mathematics, an _____ is any of the arguments, i.e. "inputs", to a function. Thus if we have a function f(x), then x is a _____.
   a. Thing
   b. Independent variable0
   c. Undefined
   d. Undefined

152. In a function the _____, is the variable which is the value, i.e. the "output", of the function.
   a. Thing
   b. Dependent variable0
   c. Undefined
   d. Undefined

153. In mathematics, a _____ is the end result of a division problem. It can also be expressed as the number of times the divisor divides into the dividend.
   a. Thing
   b. Quotient0
   c. Undefined
   d. Undefined

154. In mathematics, a _____ is the set of all points in three-dimensional space (R^3) which are at distance r from a fixed point of that space, where r is a positive real number called the radius of the _____. The fixed point is called the center or centre, and is not part of the _____ itself.
   a. Sphere0
   b. Thing
   c. Undefined
   d. Undefined

155. An _____ is an increase, either of some fixed amount, for example added regularly, or of a variable amount.
   a. Increment0
   b. Thing
   c. Undefined
   d. Undefined

156. _____ is the estimation of a physical quantity such as distance, energy, temperature, or time.
   a. Thing
   b. Measurement0
   c. Undefined
   d. Undefined

157. _____, either of the curved-bracket punctuation marks that together make a set of _____
   a. Parentheses0
   b. Thing
   c. Undefined
   d. Undefined

158. In the mathematical field of numerical analysis, the _____ in some data is the discrepancy between an exact value and some approximation to it.
   a. Approximation Error0
   b. Thing
   c. Undefined
   d. Undefined

159. The function difference divided by the point difference is known as the _____
   a. Difference quotient0
   b. Thing
   c. Undefined
   d. Undefined

Chapter 4. Applications of Derivatives

160. In calculus, the _____ is a formula for the derivative of the composite of two functions.
 a. Concept
 b. Chain rule0
 c. Undefined
 d. Undefined

161. A _____ number is a positive integer which has a positive divisor other than one or itself.
 a. Thing
 b. Composite0
 c. Undefined
 d. Undefined

162. _____ is the property of a physical object that quantifies the amount of matter and energy it is equivalent to.
 a. Mass0
 b. Thing
 c. Undefined
 d. Undefined

163. The _____ of an object is the extra energy which it possesses due to its motion.
 a. Thing
 b. Kinetic energy0
 c. Undefined
 d. Undefined

164. In mathematics, the _____ functions are functions of an angle; they are important when studying triangles and modeling periodic phenomena, among many other applications.
 a. Thing
 b. Trigonometric0
 c. Undefined
 d. Undefined

165. The _____ are functions of an angle; they are important when studying triangles and modeling periodic phenomena, among many other applications.
 a. Trigonometric functions0
 b. Thing
 c. Undefined
 d. Undefined

166. In mathematics, a _____ is a number which can be expressed as a ratio of two integers. Non-integer rational numbers (commonly called fractions) are usually written as the vulgar fraction a / b, where b is not zero.
 a. Concept
 b. Rational Number0
 c. Undefined
 d. Undefined

167. _____ is a method for differentiating expressions involving exponentiation the power operation.
 a. Power rule0
 b. Thing
 c. Undefined
 d. Undefined

168. In mathematics, an _____ number is any real number that is not a rational number- that is, it is a number which cannot be expressed as a fraction m/n, where m and n are integers.
 a. Thing
 b. Irrational0
 c. Undefined
 d. Undefined

169. In mathematics, an _____ is any real number that is not a rational number ¡ª that is, it is a number which cannot be expressed as m/n, where m and n are integers.
 a. Thing
 b. Irrational number0
 c. Undefined
 d. Undefined

Chapter 4. Applications of Derivatives

170. A _____ surface is the surface or face of a solid on its sides. It can also be defined as any face or surface that is not a base.
   a. Lateral0
   b. Thing
   c. Undefined
   d. Undefined

171. _____ is mass m per unit volume V.
   a. Density0
   b. Thing
   c. Undefined
   d. Undefined

172. Initial objects are also called _____, and terminal objects are also called final.
   a. Thing
   b. Coterminal0
   c. Undefined
   d. Undefined

173. The _____ (symbol _____) and the millibar (symbol mbar, also mb) are units of pressure.
   a. Thing
   b. Bar0
   c. Undefined
   d. Undefined

174. A _____ is an object that is attached to a pivot point so that it can swing freely.
   a. Pendulum0
   b. Thing
   c. Undefined
   d. Undefined

175. In business, particularly accounting, a _____ is the time intervals that the accounts, statement, payments, or other calculations cover.
   a. Period0
   b. Thing
   c. Undefined
   d. Undefined

176. In mathematics, a _____ is a polynomial equation of the second degree. The general form is $ax^2 + bx + c = 0$.
   a. Quadratic equation0
   b. Thing
   c. Undefined
   d. Undefined

177. In mathematics and elsewhere, the adjective _____ means fourth order, such as the function x4. A _____ number is a number which equals the fourth power of an integer.
   a. Thing
   b. Quartic0
   c. Undefined
   d. Undefined

178. In mathematics, a _____ is an ordered list of objects. Like a set, it contains members, also called elements or terms, and the number of terms is called the length of the _____. Unlike a set, order matters, and the exact same elements can appear multiple times at different positions in the _____.
   a. Thing
   b. Sequence0
   c. Undefined
   d. Undefined

179. The act of _____ is the calculated approximation of a result which is usable even if input data may be incomplete, uncertain, or noisy.
   a. Thing
   b. Estimating0
   c. Undefined
   d. Undefined

Chapter 4. Applications of Derivatives

180. The traditional _____ are addition, subtraction, multiplication and division, although more advanced operations (such as manipulations of percentages, square root, exponentiation, and logarithmic functions) are also sometimes included in this subject.
   a. Concept
   b. Arithmetic operations0
   c. Undefined
   d. Undefined

181. In mathematics, computing, linguistics, and related disciplines, an _____ is a finite list of well-defined instructions for accomplishing some task which, given an initial state, will terminate in a defined end-state.
   a. Concept
   b. Algorithm0
   c. Undefined
   d. Undefined

182. A _____ decimal is a number whose decimal representation eventually becomes periodic (i.e. the same number sequence _____ indefinitely).
   a. Thing
   b. Repeating0
   c. Undefined
   d. Undefined

183. _____ denotes the approach toward a definite value, as time goes on; or to a definite point, a common view or opinion, or toward a fixed or equilibrium state.
   a. Thing
   b. Convergence0
   c. Undefined
   d. Undefined

184. A _____ function curves downwards. The graph of a _____ function of one variable remains above its tangents and below its cords.
   a. Convex0
   b. Thing
   c. Undefined
   d. Undefined

185. _____ means in succession or back-to-back
   a. Consecutive0
   b. Thing
   c. Undefined
   d. Undefined

186. an _____ is a set to which the system evolves after a long enough time.
   a. Attractor0
   b. Thing
   c. Undefined
   d. Undefined

187. The _____ implies that on any great circle around the world, the temperature, pressure, elevation, carbon dioxide concentration, or anything else that varies continuously, there will always exist two antipodal points that share the same value for that variable.
   a. Thing
   b. Intermediate Value Theorem0
   c. Undefined
   d. Undefined

188. In linear algebra, the _____ of an n-by-n square matrix A is defined to be the sum of the elements on the main diagonal of A,
   a. Trace0
   b. Thing
   c. Undefined
   d. Undefined

Chapter 4. Applications of Derivatives

189. _____ is a set, with some particular properties and usually some additional structure, such as the operations of addition or multiplication, for instance.
- a. Space0
- b. Thing
- c. Undefined
- d. Undefined

190. A _____, as defined by the International Astronomical Union, is a celestial body orbiting a star or stellar remnant that is massive enough to be rounded by its own gravity, not massive enough to cause thermonuclear fusion in its core, and has cleared its neighboring region of planetesimals.
- a. Planet0
- b. Thing
- c. Undefined
- d. Undefined

191. In mathematics, _____ is the decomposition of an object into a product of other objects, or factors, which when multiplied together give the original.
- a. Thing
- b. Factoring0
- c. Undefined
- d. Undefined

192. _____ is a method of defining functions in which the function being defined is applied within its own definition. The term is also used more generally to describe a process of repeating objects in a self-similar way.
- a. Recursion0
- b. Thing
- c. Undefined
- d. Undefined

193. In the scientific method, an _____ (Latin: ex-+-periri, "of (or from) trying"), is a set of actions and observations, performed in the context of solving a particular problem or question, in order to support or falsify a hypothesis or research concerning phenomena.
- a. Experiment0
- b. Thing
- c. Undefined
- d. Undefined

194. In geographic information systems, a _____ comprises an entity with a geographic location, typically determined by points, arcs, or polygons. Carriageways and cadastres exemplify _____ data.
- a. Thing
- b. Feature0
- c. Undefined
- d. Undefined

195. In geometry, a _____ is a special kind of point, usually a corner of a polygon, polyhedron, or higher dimensional polytope. In the geometry of curves a _____ is a point of where the first derivative of curvature is zero. In graph theory, a _____ is the fundamental unit out of which graphs are formed
- a. Vertex0
- b. Thing
- c. Undefined
- d. Undefined

196. An _____ is a straight line around which a geometric figure can be rotated.
- a. Axis0
- b. Thing
- c. Undefined
- d. Undefined

197. _____ is a circle on the surface of a sphere that has the same circumference as the sphere, dividing the sphere into two equal hemispheres.

a. Thing
b. Great circle0
c. Undefined
d. Undefined

198. The _____ is the distance around a closed curve. _____ is a kind of perimeter.
a. Circumference0
b. Thing
c. Undefined
d. Undefined

199. _____ is a function whose values do not vary and thus are constant.
a. Thing
b. Constant function0
c. Undefined
d. Undefined

200. _____ is a circle with a unit radius, i.e., a circle whose radius is 1.
a. Unit circle0
b. Thing
c. Undefined
d. Undefined

201. _____ (or proportionality) are two quantities that vary in such a way that one of the quatities is a constant multiple of the other, or equivalently if they have a constant ratio.
a. Thing
b. Proportions0
c. Undefined
d. Undefined

202. _____ are external two-dimensional outlines, with the appearance or configuration of some thing - in contrast to the matter or content or substance of which it is composed.
a. Shapes0
b. Thing
c. Undefined
d. Undefined

Chapter 5. Integration

1. The _____ is a measurement of how a function changes when the values of its inputs change.
   a. Derivative0
   b. Thing
   c. Undefined
   d. Undefined

2. The mathematical concept of a _____ expresses the intuitive idea of deterministic dependence between two quantities, one of which is viewed as primary and the other as secondary. A _____ then is a way to associate a unique output for each input of a specified type, for example, a real number or an element of a given set.
   a. Function0
   b. Thing
   c. Undefined
   d. Undefined

3. The _____ of a solid object is the three-dimensional concept of how much space it occupies, often quantified numerically.
   a. Thing
   b. Volume0
   c. Undefined
   d. Undefined

4. _____ is a process of combining or accumulating. It may also refer to:
   a. Thing
   b. Integration0
   c. Undefined
   d. Undefined

5. _____, a field in mathematics, is the study of how functions change when their inputs change. The primary object of study in _____ is the derivative.
   a. Thing
   b. Differential calculus0
   c. Undefined
   d. Undefined

6. Sir Isaac _____, was an English physicist, mathematician, astronomer, natural philosopher, and alchemist, regarded by many as the greatest figure in the history of science
   a. Person
   b. Newton0
   c. Undefined
   d. Undefined

7. _____ was a German mathematician and philosopher. He invented calculus independently of Newton, and his notation is the one in general use since.
   a. Person
   b. Leibniz0
   c. Undefined
   d. Undefined

8. _____ of an object is its speed in a particular direction.
   a. Thing
   b. Velocity0
   c. Undefined
   d. Undefined

9. The _____ of a function is an extension of the concept of a sum, and are identified or found through the use of integration.
   a. Thing
   b. Integral0
   c. Undefined
   d. Undefined

10. _____ is a mathematical subject that includes the study of limits, derivatives, integrals, and power series and constitutes a major part of modern university curriculum.

Chapter 5. Integration

a. Calculus0
b. Thing
c. Undefined
d. Undefined

11. A _____ is a special kind of ratio, indicating a relationship between two measurements with different units, such as miles to gallons or cents to pounds.
    a. Rate0
    b. Thing
    c. Undefined
    d. Undefined

12. _____ is a set, with some particular properties and usually some additional structure, such as the operations of addition or multiplication, for instance.
    a. Thing
    b. Space0
    c. Undefined
    d. Undefined

13. _____ is a subset of a population.
    a. Thing
    b. Sample0
    c. Undefined
    d. Undefined

14. _____ the expected value of a random variable displays the average or central value of the variable. It is a summary value of the distribution of the variable.
    a. Thing
    b. Determining0
    c. Undefined
    d. Undefined

15. An _____ of a function f is a function F whose derivative is equal to f, i.e., $F' = f$.
    a. Antiderivative0
    b. Thing
    c. Undefined
    d. Undefined

16. A _____ is a mathematical statement which follows easily from a previously proven statement, typically a mathematical theorem.
    a. Thing
    b. Corollary0
    c. Undefined
    d. Undefined

17. The _____, the average in everyday English, which is also called the arithmetic _____ (and is distinguished from the geometric _____ or harmonic _____). The average is also called the sample _____. The expected value of a random variable, which is also called the population _____.
    a. Thing
    b. Mean0
    c. Undefined
    d. Undefined

18. In mathematics, a _____ is a statement that can be proved on the basis of explicitly stated or previously agreed assumptions.
    a. Thing
    b. Theorem0
    c. Undefined
    d. Undefined

19. In mathematics, a _____ of a k-place relation $L \subseteq X_1 \times \ldots \times X_k$ is one of the sets X_j, $1 \leq j \leq k$. In the special case where k = 2 and $L \subseteq X_1 \times X_2$ is a function $L : X_1 \to X_2$, it is conventional to refer to X_1 as the _____ of the function and to refer to X_2 as the codomain of the function.

Chapter 5. Integration

a. Domain0
b. Thing
c. Undefined
d. Undefined

20. A _____ is a symbolic representation denoting a quantity or expression. It often represents an "unknown" quantity that has the potential to change.
    a. Variable0
    b. Thing
    c. Undefined
    d. Undefined

21. _____ is a function that extends the concept of an ordinary sum
    a. Thing
    b. Integrand0
    c. Undefined
    d. Undefined

22. In mathematics and the mathematical sciences, a _____ is a fixed, but possibly unspecified, value. This is in contrast to a variable, which is not fixed.
    a. Constant0
    b. Thing
    c. Undefined
    d. Undefined

23. A _____ is a negotiable instrument instructing a financial institution to pay a specific amount of a specific currency from a specific demand account held in the maker/depositor's name with that institution. Both the maker and payee may be natural persons or legal entities.
    a. Thing
    b. Check0
    c. Undefined
    d. Undefined

24. A _____ of a number is the product of that number with any integer.
    a. Multiple0
    b. Thing
    c. Undefined
    d. Undefined

25. _____ is a branch of mathematics concerning the study of structure, relation and quantity.
    a. Algebra0
    b. Concept
    c. Undefined
    d. Undefined

26. A _____ is the result of the addition of a set of numbers. The numbers may be natural numbers, complex numbers, matrices, or still more complicated objects. An infinite _____ is a subtle procedure known as a series.
    a. Thing
    b. Sum0
    c. Undefined
    d. Undefined

27. In mathematics, a _____ number (or a _____) is a natural number that has exactly two (distinct) natural number divisors, which are 1 and the _____ number itself.
    a. Thing
    b. Prime0
    c. Undefined
    d. Undefined

28. In calculus, the indefinite integral of a given function i.e. the set of all antiderivatives of the function is always written with a constant, the _____.
    a. Thing
    b. Constant of integration0
    c. Undefined
    d. Undefined

Chapter 5. Integration

29. In mathematics, the _____ functions are functions of an angle; they are important when studying triangles and modeling periodic phenomena, among many other applications.
    a. Thing
    b. Trigonometric0
    c. Undefined
    d. Undefined

30. _____ is a trigonemtric function that is important when studying triangles and modeling periodic phenomena, among other applications.
    a. Sine0
    b. Thing
    c. Undefined
    d. Undefined

31. An _____ is an equality that remains true regardless of the values of any variables that appear within it, to distinguish it from an equality which is true under more particular conditions.
    a. Thing
    b. Identity0
    c. Undefined
    d. Undefined

32. Initial objects are also called _____, and terminal objects are also called final.
    a. Coterminal0
    b. Thing
    c. Undefined
    d. Undefined

33. _____ is a differential equation together with specified value, called the initial condition, of the unknown function at a given point in the domain of the solution.
    a. Initial value problem0
    b. Thing
    c. Undefined
    d. Undefined

34. A _____ is traditionally an infinitesimally small change in a variable.
    a. Thing
    b. Differential0
    c. Undefined
    d. Undefined

35. A _____ is a mathematical equation for an unknown function of one or several variables which relates the values of the function itself and of its derivatives of various orders.
    a. Differential equation0
    b. Thing
    c. Undefined
    d. Undefined

36. In mathematics, in the field of differential equations, an initial value problem is a differential equation together with specified value, called the _____, of the unknown function at a given point in the domain of the solution.
    a. Initial condition0
    b. Thing
    c. Undefined
    d. Undefined

37. A _____ is any object propelled through space by the applicationp of a force.
    a. Thing
    b. Projectile0
    c. Undefined
    d. Undefined

38. _____ is the path a moving object follows through space.
    a. Thing
    b. Projectile motion0
    c. Undefined
    d. Undefined

Chapter 5. Integration

39. _____ is defined as the rate of change or derivative with respect to time of velocity.
   a. Acceleration0
   b. Thing
   c. Undefined
   d. Undefined

40. In physics, _____ is an influence that may cause an object to accelerate. It may be experienced as a lift, a push, or a pull. The actual acceleration of the body is determined by the vector sum of all forces acting on it, known as net _____ or resultant _____.
   a. Force0
   b. Thing
   c. Undefined
   d. Undefined

41. In mathematics, the concept of a _____ tries to capture the intuitive idea of a geometrical one-dimensional and continuous object. A simple example is the circle.
   a. Thing
   b. Curve0
   c. Undefined
   d. Undefined

42. In mathematics, _____ are the intuitive idea of a geometrical one-dimensional and continuous object.
   a. Curves0
   b. Thing
   c. Undefined
   d. Undefined

43. In mathematics, the _____(e) for L-functions are a class of summation formulae, expressing sums taken over the complex number zeroes of a given L-function, typically in terms of quantities studied by number theory by use of the theory of special functions.
   a. Explicit formula0
   b. Thing
   c. Undefined
   d. Undefined

44. _____ is a point on the domain of a function
   a. Thing
   b. Critical point0
   c. Undefined
   d. Undefined

45. in mathematics, maxima and minima, known collectively as _____, are the largest value maximum or smallest value minimum, that a function takes in a point either within a given neighborhood or on the function domain in its entirety global extremum.
   a. Thing
   b. Extrema0
   c. Undefined
   d. Undefined

46. _____ is often used to describe the measurement of the steepness, incline, gradient, or grade of a straight line. The _____ is defined as the ratio of the "rise" divided by the "run" between two points on a line, or in other words, the ratio of the altitude change to the horizontal distance between any two points on the line.
   a. Thing
   b. Slope0
   c. Undefined
   d. Undefined

47. The word _____ means curving in or hollowed inward.
   a. Concavity0
   b. Thing
   c. Undefined
   d. Undefined

48. _____ is a a point on a curve at which the tangent crosses the curve itself.

a. Inflection point0   b. Thing
c. Undefined   d. Undefined

49. A _____ is a three-dimensional geometric shape formed by straight lines through a fixed point (vertex) to the points of a fixed curve (directrix)
    a. Cone0   b. Concept
    c. Undefined   d. Undefined

50. In geographic information systems, a _____ comprises an entity with a geographic location, typically determined by points, arcs, or polygons. Carriageways and cadastres exemplify _____ data.
    a. Feature0   b. Thing
    c. Undefined   d. Undefined

51. A _____ is an abstract model that uses mathematical language to describe the behavior of a system. Eykhoff defined a _____ as 'a representation of the essential aspects of an existing system which presents knowledge of that system in usable form'.
    a. Thing   b. Mathematical model0
    c. Undefined   d. Undefined

52. In navigation, a _____ is the clockwise angle between a reference direction and the direction to an object.
    a. Thing   b. Bearing0
    c. Undefined   d. Undefined

53. In mathematics, a _____ is a countable collection of open covers of a topological space that satisfies certain separation axioms.
    a. Thing   b. Development0
    c. Undefined   d. Undefined

54. In a mathematical proof or a syllogism, a _____ is a statement that is the logical consequence of preceding statements.
    a. Conclusion0   b. Concept
    c. Undefined   d. Undefined

55. _____ is electromagnetic radiation with a wavelength that is visible to the eye (visible _____) or, in a technical or scientific context, electromagnetic radiation of any wavelength.
    a. Thing   b. Light0
    c. Undefined   d. Undefined

56. In the scientific method, an _____ (Latin: ex-+-periri, "of (or from) trying"), is a set of actions and observations, performed in the context of solving a particular problem or question, in order to support or falsify a hypothesis or research concerning phenomena.
    a. Experiment0   b. Thing
    c. Undefined   d. Undefined

57. In _____ algebra, a *-ring is an associative ring with an antilinear, antiautomorphism * : A ¨ A which is an involution.

Chapter 5. Integration

a. Thing
b. Star0
c. Undefined
d. Undefined

58. _____ are an imitation of some real thing, state of affairs, or process.
a. Thing
b. Simulations0
c. Undefined
d. Undefined

59. _____ are external two-dimensional outlines, with the appearance or configuration of some thing - in contrast to the matter or content or substance of which it is composed.
a. Thing
b. Shapes0
c. Undefined
d. Undefined

60. In mathematics, _____ is a part of the set theoretic notion of function.
a. Thing
b. Image0
c. Undefined
d. Undefined

61. A _____ is a set of numbers that designate location in a given reference system, such as x,y in a planar _____ system or an x,y,z in a three-dimensional _____ system.
a. Coordinate0
b. Thing
c. Undefined
d. Undefined

62. A _____ is a vehicle, missile or aircraft which obtains thrust by the reaction to the ejection of fast moving fluid from within a _____ engine.
a. Thing
b. Rocket0
c. Undefined
d. Undefined

63. A _____, as defined by the International Astronomical Union, is a celestial body orbiting a star or stellar remnant that is massive enough to be rounded by its own gravity, not massive enough to cause thermonuclear fusion in its core, and has cleared its neighboring region of planetesimals.
a. Planet0
b. Thing
c. Undefined
d. Undefined

64. The plus and _____ signs are mathematical symbols used to represent the notions of positive and negative as well as the operations of addition and subtraction.
a. Thing
b. Minus0
c. Undefined
d. Undefined

65. A _____ is 360° or 2δ radians.
a. Thing
b. Turn0
c. Undefined
d. Undefined

66. In calculus, the _____ is a formula for the derivative of the composite of two functions.
a. Concept
b. Chain rule0
c. Undefined
d. Undefined

Chapter 5. Integration

67. _____ is a tool for finding antiderivatives and integrals. Using the fundamental theorem of calculus often requires finding an antiderivative. For this and other reasons, this rule is a relatively important tool for mathematicians. It is the counterpart to the chain rule of differentiation.
   a. Thing
   b. Integration by substitution0
   c. Undefined
   d. Undefined

68. The _____ is used to discard one of the variables in an equation, only to replace it with the actual value when solving multiple equations.
   a. Thing
   b. Substitution method0
   c. Undefined
   d. Undefined

69. In mathematics, a _____ number is a number which can be expressed as a ratio of two integers. Non-integer _____ numbers (commonly called fractions) are usually written as the vulgar fraction a / b, where b is not zero.
   a. Rational0
   b. Thing
   c. Undefined
   d. Undefined

70. _____ has many meanings, most of which simply .
   a. Thing
   b. Power0
   c. Undefined
   d. Undefined

71. _____ is a method for differentiating expressions involving exponentiation the power operation.
   a. Thing
   b. Power rule0
   c. Undefined
   d. Undefined

72. The _____ are functions of an angle; they are important when studying triangles and modeling periodic phenomena, among many other applications.
   a. Trigonometric functions0
   b. Thing
   c. Undefined
   d. Undefined

73. _____ is a notation for writing numbers that is often used by scientists and mathematicians to make it easier to write large and small numbers.
   a. Scientific notation0
   b. Thing
   c. Undefined
   d. Undefined

74. A _____ function is a function for which, intuitively, small changes in the input result in small changes in the output.
   a. Event
   b. Continuous0
   c. Undefined
   d. Undefined

75. In mathematics, _____ expressions is used to reduce the expression into the lowest possible term.
   a. Simplifying0
   b. Thing
   c. Undefined
   d. Undefined

76. In mathematics, a set is called _____ if there is a bijection between the set and some set of the form {1, 2, ..., n} where n is a natural number.

Chapter 5. Integration

    a. Finite0
    b. Thing
    c. Undefined
    d. Undefined

77. _____ is the volume of blood being pumped by the heart, in particular a ventricle in a minute.
    a. Cardiac output0
    b. Thing
    c. Undefined
    d. Undefined

78. _____ is the flow of blood in the cardiovascular system.
    a. Blood flow0
    b. Thing
    c. Undefined
    d. Undefined

79. The _____ of measurement are a globally standardized and modernized form of the metric system.
    a. Thing
    b. Units0
    c. Undefined
    d. Undefined

80. _____ is a kind of property which exists as magnitude or multitude. It is among the basic classes of things along with quality, substance, change, and relation.
    a. Amount0
    b. Thing
    c. Undefined
    d. Undefined

81. The act of _____ is the calculated approximation of a result which is usable even if input data may be incomplete, uncertain, or noisy.
    a. Estimating0
    b. Thing
    c. Undefined
    d. Undefined

82. In geometry, a _____ is defined as a quadrilateral where all four of its angles are right angles.
    a. Thing
    b. Rectangle0
    c. Undefined
    d. Undefined

83. _____ is the middle point of a line segment.
    a. Midpoint0
    b. Thing
    c. Undefined
    d. Undefined

84. In mathematics, an _____, mean, or central tendency of a data set refers to a measure of the "middle" or "expected" value of the data set.
    a. Concept
    b. Average0
    c. Undefined
    d. Undefined

85. In elementary algebra, an _____ is a set that contains every real number between two indicated numbers and may contain the two numbers themselves.
    a. Thing
    b. Interval0
    c. Undefined
    d. Undefined

86. In mathematics, a _____ is the result of multiplying, or an expression that identifies factors to be multiplied.

a. Thing
b. Product0
c. Undefined
d. Undefined

87. In mathematics, a _____ or rhodonea curve is a sinusoid plotted in polar coordinates.
   a. Thing
   b. Rose0
   c. Undefined
   d. Undefined

88. _____ is the addition of a set of numbers; the result is their sum. The "numbers" to be summed may be natural numbers, complex numbers, matrices, or still more complicated objects. An infinite sum is a subtle procedure known as a series.
   a. Thing
   b. Summation0
   c. Undefined
   d. Undefined

89. In geometry, an _____ is a point at which a line segment or ray terminates.
   a. Thing
   b. Endpoint0
   c. Undefined
   d. Undefined

90. The _____ of a mathematical object is its size: a property by which it can be larger or smaller than other objects of the same kind; in technical terms, an ordering of the class of objects to which it belongs.
   a. Magnitude0
   b. Thing
   c. Undefined
   d. Undefined

91. In geometry, a _____ is the intersection of a body in 2-dimensional space with a line, or of a body in 3-dimensional space with a plane
   a. Thing
   b. Cross section0
   c. Undefined
   d. Undefined

92. In mathematics, _____ geometry was the traditional name for the geometry of three-dimensional Euclidean space — for practical purposes the kind of space we live in.
   a. Thing
   b. Solid0
   c. Undefined
   d. Undefined

93. In plane geometry, a _____ is a polygon with four equal sides, four right angles, and parallel opposite sides. In algebra, the _____ of a number is that number multiplied by itself.
   a. Thing
   b. Square0
   c. Undefined
   d. Undefined

94. An _____ is a straight line around which a geometric figure can be rotated.
   a. Thing
   b. Axis0
   c. Undefined
   d. Undefined

95. In geometry, two lines or planes if one falls on the other in such a way as to create congruent adjacent angles. The term may be used as a noun or adjective. Thus, referring to Figure 1, the line AB is the _____ to CD through the point B.
   a. Thing
   b. Perpendicular0
   c. Undefined
   d. Undefined

Chapter 5. Integration

96. In mathematics, a _____ is a two-dimensional manifold or surface that is perfectly flat.
   a. Plane0
   b. Thing
   c. Undefined
   d. Undefined

97. In mathematics, _____ are two-dimensional manifolds or surfaces that are perfectly flat.
   a. Planes0
   b. Thing
   c. Undefined
   d. Undefined

98. Generally, a _____ is a splitting of something into parts.
   a. Thing
   b. Partition0
   c. Undefined
   d. Undefined

99. In mathematics, a _____ is a quadric surface, with the following equation in Cartesian coordinates: $(x/_a)^2 + (y/_b)^2 = 1$.
   a. Thing
   b. Cylinder0
   c. Undefined
   d. Undefined

100. In classical geometry, a _____ of a circle or sphere is any line segment from its center to its boundary. By extension, the _____ of a circle or sphere is the length of any such segment. The _____ is half the diameter. In science and engineering the term _____ of curvature is commonly used as a synonym for _____.
   a. Radius0
   b. Thing
   c. Undefined
   d. Undefined

101. In mathematics, a _____ is the set of all points in three-dimensional space (R^3) which are at distance r from a fixed point of that space, where r is a positive real number called the radius of the _____. The fixed point is called the center or centre, and is not part of the _____ itself.
   a. Sphere0
   b. Thing
   c. Undefined
   d. Undefined

102. _____ is the part of statistical practice concerned with the selection of individual observations intended to yield some knowledge about a population of concern, especially for the purposes of statistical inference.
   a. Thing
   b. Sampling0
   c. Undefined
   d. Undefined

103. _____ are activities that are governed by a set of rules or customs and often engaged in competitively.
   a. Thing
   b. Sports0
   c. Undefined
   d. Undefined

104. _____ is a synonym for information.
   a. Thing
   b. Data0
   c. Undefined
   d. Undefined

105. In geometry, a _____ (Greek words diairo = divide and metro = measure) of a circle is any straight line segment that passes through the centre and whose endpoints are on the circular boundary, or, in more modern usage, the length of such a line segment. When using the word in the more modern sense, one speaks of the _____ rather than a _____, because all diameters of a circle have the same length. This length is twice the radius. The _____ of a circle is also the longest chord that the circle has.
  a. Thing
  b. Diameter0
  c. Undefined
  d. Undefined

106. _____ means "constancy", i.e. if something retains a certain feature even after we change a way of looking at it, then it is symmetric.
  a. Symmetry0
  b. Thing
  c. Undefined
  d. Undefined

107. _____ of a two-dimensional figure is a line such that, if a perpendicular is constructed, any two points lying on the perpendicular at equal distances from the _____ are identical.
  a. Axis of symmetry0
  b. Thing
  c. Undefined
  d. Undefined

108. In mathematics, the _____ is a conic section generated by the intersection of a right circular conical surface and a plane parallel to a generating straight line of that surface. It can also be defined as locus of points in a plane which are equidistant from a given point.
  a. Thing
  b. Parabola0
  c. Undefined
  d. Undefined

109. A _____ is one of the basic shapes of geometry: a polygon with three vertices and three sides which are straight line segments.
  a. Thing
  b. Triangle0
  c. Undefined
  d. Undefined

110. In geometry, an _____ polygon is a polygon which has all sides of the same length.
  a. Equilateral0
  b. Thing
  c. Undefined
  d. Undefined

111. An _____ is a triangle in which all sides are of equal length.
  a. Equilateral triangle0
  b. Thing
  c. Undefined
  d. Undefined

112. In geometry, a _____ planar shape or solid is one that encloses and "fits snugly" around another geometric shape or solid.
  a. Circumscribed0
  b. Thing
  c. Undefined
  d. Undefined

113. _____ is a way of expressing a number as a fraction of 100 per cent meaning "per hundred".
  a. Percent0
  b. Thing
  c. Undefined
  d. Undefined

Chapter 5. Integration

114. _____ is a quadric
   a. Thing
   b. Paraboloid0
   c. Undefined
   d. Undefined

115. _____ is the estimation of a physical quantity such as distance, energy, temperature, or time.
   a. Measurement0
   b. Thing
   c. Undefined
   d. Undefined

116. _____ is an extension of the concept of a sum.
   a. Definite integral0
   b. Thing
   c. Undefined
   d. Undefined

117. _____ is a method for approximating the values of integrals.
   a. Riemann sum0
   b. Thing
   c. Undefined
   d. Undefined

118. _____ is the eighteenth letter of the Greek alphabet.
   a. Thing
   b. Sigma0
   c. Undefined
   d. Undefined

119. _____ is used as the symbol for summation. Summation is the addition of a set of numbers; the result is their sum. The "numbers" to be summed may be natural numbers, complex numbers, matrices, or still more complicated objects. An infinite sum is a subtle procedure known as a series.
   a. Thing
   b. Sigma notation0
   c. Undefined
   d. Undefined

120. Mathematical _____ is used to represent ideas.
   a. Thing
   b. Notation0
   c. Undefined
   d. Undefined

121. The _____ are the only integral domain whose positive elements are well-ordered, and in which order is preserved by addition. Like the natural numbers, the _____ form a countably infinite set. The set of all _____ is usually denoted in mathematics by a boldface Z .
   a. Integers0
   b. Thing
   c. Undefined
   d. Undefined

122. In calculus, the _____ in differentiation is a method of finding the derivative of a function that is the sum of two other functions for which derivatives exist.
   a. Thing
   b. Sum Rule0
   c. Undefined
   d. Undefined

123. A _____ is a three-dimensional solid object bounded by six square faces, facets, or sides, with three meeting at each vertex.
   a. Thing
   b. Cube0
   c. Undefined
   d. Undefined

Chapter 5. Integration

124. _____ are of a number n in its third power-the result of multiplying it by itself three times.
   a. Cubes0
   b. Thing
   c. Undefined
   d. Undefined

125. _____ Any process by which a specified characteristic usually amplitude of the output of a device is prevented from exceeding a predetermined value.
   a. Thing
   b. Limiting0
   c. Undefined
   d. Undefined

126. Acid _____ ratio measures the ability of a company to use its near cash or quick assets to immediately extinguish its current liabilities.
   a. Thing
   b. Test0
   c. Undefined
   d. Undefined

127. The _____ integers are all the integers from zero on upwards.
   a. Thing
   b. Nonnegative0
   c. Undefined
   d. Undefined

128. In mathematics, science including computer science, linguistics and engineering, an _____ is, generally speaking, an independent variable or input to a function.
   a. Thing
   b. Argument0
   c. Undefined
   d. Undefined

129. In mathematics, a _____ is a demonstration that, assuming certain axioms, some statement is necessarily true.
   a. Proof0
   b. Thing
   c. Undefined
   d. Undefined

130. In mathematics, an _____ is a theorem with a statement beginning 'there exist ...'. That is, in more formal terms of symbolic logic, it is a theorem with a statement involving the existential quantifier.
   a. Existence theorem0
   b. Thing
   c. Undefined
   d. Undefined

131. In mathematics, an _____ number is any real number that is not a rational number- that is, it is a number which cannot be expressed as a fraction m/n, where m and n are integers.
   a. Thing
   b. Irrational0
   c. Undefined
   d. Undefined

132. _____ is the study of terms and their use — of words and compound words that are used in specific contexts.
   a. Terminology0
   b. Thing
   c. Undefined
   d. Undefined

133. In mathematics, an _____ is any of the arguments, i.e. "inputs", to a function. Thus if we have a function f(x), then x is a _____.

Chapter 5. Integration

a. Independent variable0
b. Thing
c. Undefined
d. Undefined

134. _____ is a function whose values do not vary and thus are constant.
  a. Thing
  b. Constant function0
  c. Undefined
  d. Undefined

135. A _____ is a quadrilateral, which is defined as a shape with four sides, which has a pair of parallel sides.
  a. Trapezoid0
  b. Thing
  c. Undefined
  d. Undefined

136. Equivalence is the condition of being _____ or essentially equal.
  a. Thing
  b. Equivalent0
  c. Undefined
  d. Undefined

137. A _____ can refer to a line joining two nonadjacent vertices of a polygon or polyhedron, or in some contexts any upward or downward sloping line. .
  a. Diagonal0
  b. Thing
  c. Undefined
  d. Undefined

138. In mathematics, an _____ is a statement about the relative size or order of two objects.
  a. Inequality0
  b. Thing
  c. Undefined
  d. Undefined

139. Mathematical _____ are demonstrations that,assuming certain axioms, some statement is necessarily true.
  a. Proofs0
  b. Thing
  c. Undefined
  d. Undefined

140. _____ is a method of mathematical proof typically used to establish that a given statement is true of all natural numbers
  a. Thing
  b. Mathematical induction0
  c. Undefined
  d. Undefined

141. In mathematics and logic, a _____ proof is a way of showing the truth or falsehood of a given statement by a straightforward combination of established facts, usually existing lemmas and theorems, without making any further assumptions.
  a. Direct0
  b. Thing
  c. Undefined
  d. Undefined

142. In mathematics, especially in order theory, an _____ of a subset S of some partially ordered set is an element of P which is greater than or equal to every element of S.
  a. Upper bound0
  b. Thing
  c. Undefined
  d. Undefined

143. The term _____ is defined dually as an element of P which is lesser than or equal to every element of S.

Chapter 5. Integration

    a. Thing
    b. Lower bound0
    c. Undefined
    d. Undefined

144. In mathematics, the notion of _____ is a generalization of the notion of invertible.
    a. Thing
    b. Cancellation0
    c. Undefined
    d. Undefined

145. In mathematics, the _____ (or modulus) of a real number is its numerical value without regard to its sign.
    a. Thing
    b. Absolute value0
    c. Undefined
    d. Undefined

146. In common philosophical language, a proposition or _____, is the content of an assertion, that is, it is true-or-false and defined by the meaning of a particular piece of language.
    a. Concept
    b. Statement0
    c. Undefined
    d. Undefined

147. The population _____ is the total number of human beings alive on the planet Earth at a given time.
    a. Of the world0
    b. Thing
    c. Undefined
    d. Undefined

148. In number theory, the _____ of arithmetic (or unique factorization theorem) states that every natural number greater than 1 can be written as a unique product of prime numbers.
    a. Concept
    b. Fundamental theorem0
    c. Undefined
    d. Undefined

149. _____ of calculus is the statement that the two central operations of calculus, differentiation and integration, are inverse operations: if a continuous function is first integrated and then differentiated, the original function is retrieved.
    a. Thing
    b. Fundamental Theorem of Calculus0
    c. Undefined
    d. Undefined

150. A _____ is a numeral used to indicate a count. The most common use of the word today is to name the part of a fraction that tells the number or count of equal parts.
    a. Numerator0
    b. Thing
    c. Undefined
    d. Undefined

151. In mathematics, a _____ is the end result of a division problem. It can also be expressed as the number of times the divisor divides into the dividend.
    a. Thing
    b. Quotient0
    c. Undefined
    d. Undefined

152. The function difference divided by the point difference is known as the _____
    a. Difference quotient0
    b. Thing
    c. Undefined
    d. Undefined

153. A _____ number is a positive integer which has a positive divisor other than one or itself.

Chapter 5. Integration

a. Thing
b. Composite0
c. Undefined
d. Undefined

154. _____ is the difference of electrical potential between two points of an electrical or electronic circuit, expressed in volts
   a. Thing
   b. Voltage0
   c. Undefined
   d. Undefined

155. In statistics the _____ of an event i is the number n_i of times the event occurred in the experiment or the study. These frequencies are often graphically represented in histograms.
   a. Concept
   b. Frequency0
   c. Undefined
   d. Undefined

156. The metre (or _____, see spelling differences) is a measure of length. It is the basic unit of length in the metric system and in the International System of Units (SI), used around the world for general and scientific purposes.
   a. Meter0
   b. Concept
   c. Undefined
   d. Undefined

157. In mathematics, a _____ of a number x is a number r such that $r^2 = x$, or in words, a number r whose square (the result of multiplying the number by itself) is x.
   a. Square root0
   b. Thing
   c. Undefined
   d. Undefined

158. A _____ is a number, figure, or indicator that appears below the normal line of type, typically used in a formula, mathematical expression, or description of a chemical compound.
   a. Subscript0
   b. Thing
   c. Undefined
   d. Undefined

159. A _____ is a function that assigns a number to subsets of a given set.
   a. Measure0
   b. Thing
   c. Undefined
   d. Undefined

160. In mathematics, a _____ of a complex-valued function f is a member x of the domain of f such that f(x) vanishes at x, that is, x : f (x) = 0.
   a. Thing
   b. Root0
   c. Undefined
   d. Undefined

161. _____ of Syracuse was an ancient Greek mathematician, physicist and engineer. In addition to making important discoveries in the field of mathematics and geometry, he is credited with producing machines that were well ahead of their time.
   a. Archimedes0
   b. Person
   c. Undefined
   d. Undefined

162. An _____ is a combination of numbers, operators, grouping symbols and/or free variables and bound variables arranged in a meaningful way which can be evaluated..

a. Expression0
b. Thing
c. Undefined
d. Undefined

163. _____ is the change in total cost that arises when the quantity produced changes by one unit.
  a. Thing
  b. Marginal cost0
  c. Undefined
  d. Undefined

164. _____ was an English divine, scholar and mathematician who is generally given minor credit for his role in the development of modern calculus; in particular, for his work regarding the tangent; for example, Barrow is given credit for being the first to calculate the tangents of the kappa curve. Isaac Newton was a student of Barrow's. Lunar crater Barrow is named after him.
  a. Isaac Barrow0
  b. Thing
  c. Undefined
  d. Undefined

165. _____ is the chance that something is likely to happen or be the case.
  a. Thing
  b. Probability0
  c. Undefined
  d. Undefined

166. In Euclidean geometry, a _____ is moving every point a constant distance in a specified direction.
  a. Translation0
  b. Concept
  c. Undefined
  d. Undefined

167. In geometry, two sets are called _____ if one can be transformed into the other by an isometry, i.e., a combination of translations, rotations and reflections.
  a. Congruent0
  b. Thing
  c. Undefined
  d. Undefined

168. _____ constitutes a broad family of algorithms for calculating the numerical value of a definite integral, and by extension, the term is also sometimes used to describe the numerical solution of differential equations.
  a. Thing
  b. Numerical integration0
  c. Undefined
  d. Undefined

169. _____ the American term is a way to approximately calculate the definite integral
  a. Thing
  b. Trapezoidal Rule0
  c. Undefined
  d. Undefined

170. In mathematics, a _____ is an expression that is constructed from one or more variables and constants, using only the operations of addition, subtraction, multiplication, and constant positive whole number exponents. is a _____. Note in particular that division by an expression containing a variable is not in general allowed in polynomials. [1]
  a. Polynomial0
  b. Thing
  c. Undefined
  d. Undefined

171. In mathematics, there are several meanings of _____ depending on the subject.
  a. Degree0
  b. Thing
  c. Undefined
  d. Undefined

Chapter 5. Integration

172. In geometry, a line _____ is a part of a line that is bounded by two end points, and contains every point on the line between its end points.
   a. Segment0
   b. Concept
   c. Undefined
   d. Undefined

173. _____ are the basic objects of study in graph theory. Informally speaking, a graph is a set of objects called points, nodes, or vertices connected by links called lines or edges.
   a. Graphs0
   b. Thing
   c. Undefined
   d. Undefined

174. A _____ is a part of a line that is bounded by two end points, and contains every point on the line between its end points.
   a. Thing
   b. Line segment0
   c. Undefined
   d. Undefined

175. A _____ is a deliberate process for transforming one or more inputs into one or more results.
   a. Thing
   b. Calculation0
   c. Undefined
   d. Undefined

176. In Euclidean geometry, an _____ is a closed segment of a differentiable curve in the two-dimensional plane; for example, a circular _____ is a segment of a circle.
   a. Arc0
   b. Concept
   c. Undefined
   d. Undefined

177. The word _____ comes from the Latin word linearis, which means created by lines.
   a. Thing
   b. Linear0
   c. Undefined
   d. Undefined

178. In mathematics, the conjugate _____ or adjoint matrix of an m-by-n matrix A with complex entries is the n-by-m matrix A* obtained from A by taking the transpose and then taking the complex conjugate of each entry.
   a. Pairs0
   b. Thing
   c. Undefined
   d. Undefined

179. _____ or arithmetics is the oldest and most elementary branch of mathematics, used by almost everyone, for tasks ranging from simple daily counting to advanced science and business calculations.
   a. Thing
   b. Arithmetic0
   c. Undefined
   d. Undefined

180. _____ is the study of algorithms for the problems of continuous mathematics as distinguished from discrete mathematics.
   a. Numerical analysis0
   b. Thing
   c. Undefined
   d. Undefined

181. In astronomy, geography, geometry and related sciences and contexts, a plane is said to be _____ at a given point if it is locally perpendicular to the gradient of the gravity field, i.e., with the direction of the gravitational force at that point.

a. Horizontal0 b. Thing
c. Undefined d. Undefined

182. In Euclidean geometry, a uniform _____ is a linear transformation that enlargers or diminishes objects, and whose _____ factor is the same in all directions. This is also called homothethy.
a. Scale0 b. Thing
c. Undefined d. Undefined

183. _____ is mass m per unit volume V.
a. Density0 b. Thing
c. Undefined d. Undefined

184. A _____ is a first degree polynomial mathematical function of the form: f(x) = mx + b where m and b are real constants and x is a real variable.
a. Linear function0 b. Thing
c. Undefined d. Undefined

185. _____ is the design, analysis, and/or construction of works for practical purposes.
a. Thing b. Engineering0
c. Undefined d. Undefined

186. In linear algebra, the _____ of an n-by-n square matrix A is defined to be the sum of the elements on the main diagonal of A,
a. Trace0 b. Thing
c. Undefined d. Undefined

187. _____ is a physical property of a system that underlies the common notions of hot and cold; something that is hotter has the greater _____.
a. Thing b. Temperature0
c. Undefined d. Undefined

188. _____ is the property of a physical object that quantifies the amount of matter and energy it is equivalent to.
a. Thing b. Mass0
c. Undefined d. Undefined

189. In economics, supply and _____ describe market relations between prospective sellers and buyers of a good.
a. Thing b. Demand0
c. Undefined d. Undefined

190. In botany, _____ are above-ground plant organs specialized for photosynthesis. Their characteristics are typically analyzed by using Fiobonacci's sequences.
a. Leaves0 b. Thing
c. Undefined d. Undefined

191. _____ is a list of goods and materials, or those goods and materials themselves, held available in stock by a business

Chapter 5. Integration

a. Inventory0
b. Thing
c. Undefined
d. Undefined

192. In business, particularly accounting, a _____ is the time intervals that the accounts, statement, payments, or other calculations cover.
a. Thing
b. Period0
c. Undefined
d. Undefined

193. The _____ (symbol _____) and the millibar (symbol mbar, also mb) are units of pressure.
a. Thing
b. Bar0
c. Undefined
d. Undefined

194. According to the United Nations Statistics Division, _____ is the resale sale without transformation of new and used goods to retailers, to industrial, commercial, institutional or professional users, or to other wholesalers, or involves acting as an agent or broker in buying merchandise for, or selling merchandise, to such persons or companies.
a. Wholesale0
b. Thing
c. Undefined
d. Undefined

195. A _____ defined function $f(x)$ of a real variable x is a function whose definition is given differently on disjoint subsets of its domain.
a. Piecewise0
b. Thing
c. Undefined
d. Undefined

196. In mathematical analysis and related areas of mathematics, a set is called _____, if it is, in a certain sense, of finite size.
a. Thing
b. Bounded0
c. Undefined
d. Undefined

197. In topology and related areas of mathematics a _____ or Moore-Smith sequence is a generalization of a sequence, intended to unify the various notions of limit and generalize them to arbitrary topological spaces.
a. Net0
b. Thing
c. Undefined
d. Undefined

198. In economics, economic _____ is simply a state of the world where economic forces are balanced and in the absence of external influences the values of economic variables will not change.
a. Thing
b. Equilibrium0
c. Undefined
d. Undefined

Chapter 6. Applications of Integrals

1. The _____ of a solid object is the three-dimensional concept of how much space it occupies, often quantified numerically.
   a. Thing
   b. Volume0
   c. Undefined
   d. Undefined

2. A _____ is a set of numbers that designate location in a given reference system, such as x,y in a planar _____ system or an x,y,z in a three-dimensional _____ system.
   a. Thing
   b. Coordinate0
   c. Undefined
   d. Undefined

3. In mathematics, _____ geometry was the traditional name for the geometry of three-dimensional Euclidean space — for practical purposes the kind of space we live in.
   a. Thing
   b. Solid0
   c. Undefined
   d. Undefined

4. In mathematics, the concept of a _____ tries to capture the intuitive idea of a geometrical one-dimensional and continuous object. A simple example is the circle.
   a. Curve0
   b. Thing
   c. Undefined
   d. Undefined

5. In mathematics, _____ are the intuitive idea of a geometrical one-dimensional and continuous object.
   a. Curves0
   b. Thing
   c. Undefined
   d. Undefined

6. An _____ in policy debate is part of a speech which is flagged as not responding to the line-by-line arguments on the flow.
   a. Thing
   b. Overview0
   c. Undefined
   d. Undefined

7. The _____ of a function is an extension of the concept of a sum, and are identified or found through the use of integration.
   a. Integral0
   b. Thing
   c. Undefined
   d. Undefined

8. _____ is a kind of property which exists as magnitude or multitude. It is among the basic classes of things along with quality, substance, change, and relation.
   a. Amount0
   b. Thing
   c. Undefined
   d. Undefined

9. In banking and accountancy, the outstanding _____ is the amount of money owned, or due, that remains in a deposit account or a loan account at a given date, after all past remittances, payments and withdrawal have been accounted for.
   a. Thing
   b. Balance0
   c. Undefined
   d. Undefined

Chapter 6. Applications of Integrals

10. In physics, _____ is an influence that may cause an object to accelerate. It may be experienced as a lift, a push, or a pull. The actual acceleration of the body is determined by the vector sum of all forces acting on it, known as net _____ or resultant _____.
    a. Thing
    b. Force0
    c. Undefined
    d. Undefined

11. A _____ function is a function for which, intuitively, small changes in the input result in small changes in the output.
    a. Event
    b. Continuous0
    c. Undefined
    d. Undefined

12. The mathematical concept of a _____ expresses the intuitive idea of deterministic dependence between two quantities, one of which is viewed as primary and the other as secondary. A _____ then is a way to associate a unique output for each input of a specified type, for example, a real number or an element of a given set.
    a. Thing
    b. Function0
    c. Undefined
    d. Undefined

13. In geometry, a _____ is defined as a quadrilateral where all four of its angles are right angles.
    a. Rectangle0
    b. Thing
    c. Undefined
    d. Undefined

14. Generally, a _____ is a splitting of something into parts.
    a. Partition0
    b. Thing
    c. Undefined
    d. Undefined

15. _____ is a process of combining or accumulating. It may also refer to:
    a. Thing
    b. Integration0
    c. Undefined
    d. Undefined

16. In mathematics, the _____ of two sets A and B is the set that contains all elements of A that also belong to B (or equivalently, all elements of B that also belong to A), but no other elements.
    a. Intersection0
    b. Thing
    c. Undefined
    d. Undefined

17. In mathematics, the _____ is a conic section generated by the intersection of a right circular conical surface and a plane parallel to a generating straight line of that surface. It can also be defined as locus of points in a plane which are equidistant from a given point.
    a. Parabola0
    b. Thing
    c. Undefined
    d. Undefined

18. _____ are the basic objects of study in graph theory. Informally speaking, a graph is a set of objects called points, nodes, or vertices connected by links called lines or edges.
    a. Graphs0
    b. Thing
    c. Undefined
    d. Undefined

19. In mathematics, a _____ of a complex-valued function f is a member x of the domain of f such that f(x) vanishes at x, that is, x : f (x) = 0.
- a. Thing
- b. Root0
- c. Undefined
- d. Undefined

20. _____ is a mathematical subject that includes the study of limits, derivatives, integrals, and power series and constitutes a major part of modern university curriculum.
- a. Thing
- b. Calculus0
- c. Undefined
- d. Undefined

21. In topology, the _____ are subsets S of a topological space X is the set of points which can be approached both from S and from the outside of S.
- a. Thing
- b. Boundaries0
- c. Undefined
- d. Undefined

22. In geometry, _____ lines are two lines that share one or more common points.
- a. Intersecting0
- b. Thing
- c. Undefined
- d. Undefined

23. A _____ consists of one quarter of the coordinate plane.
- a. Thing
- b. Quadrant0
- c. Undefined
- d. Undefined

24. In mathematical analysis and related areas of mathematics, a set is called _____, if it is, in a certain sense, of finite size.
- a. Bounded0
- b. Thing
- c. Undefined
- d. Undefined

25. _____ variables are variables other than the independent variable that may bear any effect on the behavior of the subject being studied.
- a. Extraneous0
- b. Thing
- c. Undefined
- d. Undefined

26. In astronomy, geography, geometry and related sciences and contexts, a plane is said to be _____ at a given point if it is locally perpendicular to the gradient of the gravity field, i.e., with the direction of the gravitational force at that point.
- a. Horizontal0
- b. Thing
- c. Undefined
- d. Undefined

27. The _____ integers are all the integers from zero on upwards.
- a. Nonnegative0
- b. Thing
- c. Undefined
- d. Undefined

28. A _____ is one of the basic shapes of geometry: a polygon with three vertices and three sides which are straight line segments.

Chapter 6. Applications of Integrals

a. Triangle0
b. Thing
c. Undefined
d. Undefined

29. The plus and _____ signs are mathematical symbols used to represent the notions of positive and negative as well as the operations of addition and subtraction.
    a. Thing
    b. Minus0
    c. Undefined
    d. Undefined

30. In elementary algebra, an _____ is a set that contains every real number between two indicated numbers and may contain the two numbers themselves.
    a. Thing
    b. Interval0
    c. Undefined
    d. Undefined

31. In Euclidean geometry, a uniform _____ is a linear transformation that enlargers or diminishes objects, and whose _____ factor is the same in all directions. This is also called homothethy.
    a. Scale0
    b. Thing
    c. Undefined
    d. Undefined

32. In mathematics, a _____ is a quadric surface, with the following equation in Cartesian coordinates: $(x/_a)^2 + (y/_b)^2 = 1$.
    a. Cylinder0
    b. Thing
    c. Undefined
    d. Undefined

33. In geometry, a _____ is the intersection of a body in 2-dimensional space with a line, or of a body in 3-dimensional space with a plane
    a. Cross section0
    b. Thing
    c. Undefined
    d. Undefined

34. In mathematics, a _____ is a two-dimensional manifold or surface that is perfectly flat.
    a. Plane0
    b. Thing
    c. Undefined
    d. Undefined

35. In mathematics, _____ are two-dimensional manifolds or surfaces that are perfectly flat.
    a. Thing
    b. Planes0
    c. Undefined
    d. Undefined

36. A _____ is the result of the addition of a set of numbers. The numbers may be natural numbers, complex numbers, matrices, or still more complicated objects. An infinite _____ is a subtle procedure known as a series.
    a. Thing
    b. Sum0
    c. Undefined
    d. Undefined

37. _____ is a method for approximating the values of integrals.
    a. Thing
    b. Riemann sum0
    c. Undefined
    d. Undefined

38. An n-sided _____ is a polyhedron formed by connecting an n-sided polygonal base and a point, called the apex, by n triangular faces. In other words, it is a conic solid with polygonal base.
   a. Pyramid0
   b. Thing
   c. Undefined
   d. Undefined

39. In plane geometry, a _____ is a polygon with four equal sides, four right angles, and parallel opposite sides. In algebra, the _____ of a number is that number multiplied by itself.
   a. Thing
   b. Square0
   c. Undefined
   d. Undefined

40. In geometry, a _____ is a special kind of point, usually a corner of a polygon, polyhedron, or higher dimensional polytope. In the geometry of curves a _____ is a point of where the first derivative of curvature is zero. In graph theory, a _____ is the fundamental unit out of which graphs are formed
   a. Thing
   b. Vertex0
   c. Undefined
   d. Undefined

41. In geometry, two lines or planes if one falls on the other in such a way as to create congruent adjacent angles. The term may be used as a noun or adjective. Thus, referring to Figure 1, the line AB is the _____ to CD through the point B.
   a. Perpendicular0
   b. Thing
   c. Undefined
   d. Undefined

42. In geometry, an _____ of a triangle is a straight line through a vertex and perpendicular to (i.e. forming a right angle with) the opposite side or an extension of the opposite side.
   a. Altitude0
   b. Concept
   c. Undefined
   d. Undefined

43. The metre (or _____, see spelling differences) is a measure of length. It is the basic unit of length in the metric system and in the International System of Units (SI), used around the world for general and scientific purposes.
   a. Meter0
   b. Concept
   c. Undefined
   d. Undefined

44. Bonaventura Francesco _____ was an Italian mathematician known for _____'s principle,
   a. Person
   b. Cavalieri0
   c. Undefined
   d. Undefined

45. _____ was an Italian physicist, mathematician, astronomer, and philosopher who is closely associated with the scientific revolution.
   a. Galileo Galilei0
   b. Person
   c. Undefined
   d. Undefined

46. In mathematics, a _____ is a statement that can be proved on the basis of explicitly stated or previously agreed assumptions.
   a. Theorem0
   b. Thing
   c. Undefined
   d. Undefined

Chapter 6. Applications of Integrals

47. In classical geometry, a _____ of a circle or sphere is any line segment from its center to its boundary. By extension, the _____ of a circle or sphere is the length of any such segment. The _____ is half the diameter. In science and engineering the term _____ of curvature is commonly used as a synonym for _____.
- a. Radius0
- b. Thing
- c. Undefined
- d. Undefined

48. An _____ is a straight line around which a geometric figure can be rotated.
- a. Thing
- b. Axis0
- c. Undefined
- d. Undefined

49. In geometry, a _____ (Greek words diairo = divide and metro = measure) of a circle is any straight line segment that passes through the centre and whose endpoints are on the circular boundary, or, in more modern usage, the length of such a line segment. When using the word in the more modern sense, one speaks of the _____ rather than a _____, because all diameters of a circle have the same length. This length is twice the radius. The _____ of a circle is also the longest chord that the circle has.
- a. Diameter0
- b. Thing
- c. Undefined
- d. Undefined

50. In geometry, an _____ polygon is a polygon which has all sides of the same length.
- a. Thing
- b. Equilateral0
- c. Undefined
- d. Undefined

51. An _____ is a triangle in which all sides are of equal length.
- a. Equilateral triangle0
- b. Thing
- c. Undefined
- d. Undefined

52. A _____ can refer to a line joining two nonadjacent vertices of a polygon or polyhedron, or in some contexts any upward or downward sloping line. .
- a. Diagonal0
- b. Thing
- c. Undefined
- d. Undefined

53. A _____ is 360° or 2ð radians.
- a. Thing
- b. Turn0
- c. Undefined
- d. Undefined

54. In mathematics, a matrix can be thought of as each row or _____ being a vector. Hence, a space formed by row vectors or _____ vectors are said to be a row space or a _____ space.
- a. Concept
- b. Column0
- c. Undefined
- d. Undefined

55. _____ has one 90° internal angle a right angle.
- a. Right triangle0
- b. Thing
- c. Undefined
- d. Undefined

56. An _____ triange is a triangle with at least two sides of equal length.

a. Isosceles0
b. Thing
c. Undefined
d. Undefined

57. _____ is a three-dimensional geometric shape formed by straight lines through a fixed point vertex to the points of a fixed curve directrix.
   a. Thing
   b. Right circular cone0
   c. Undefined
   d. Undefined

58. A _____ is a three-dimensional geometric shape formed by straight lines through a fixed point (vertex) to the points of a fixed curve (directrix)
   a. Cone0
   b. Concept
   c. Undefined
   d. Undefined

59. _____ are external two-dimensional outlines, with the appearance or configuration of some thing - in contrast to the matter or content or substance of which it is composed.
   a. Thing
   b. Shapes0
   c. Undefined
   d. Undefined

60. An _____ is when two lines intersect somewhere on a plane creating a right angle at intersection
   a. Axes0
   b. Thing
   c. Undefined
   d. Undefined

61. A _____ is a movement of an object in a circular motion. A two-dimensional object rotates around a center (or point) of _____. A three-dimensional object rotates around a line called an axis. If the axis of _____ is within the body, the body is said to rotate upon itself, or spin—which implies relative speed and perhaps free-movement with angular momentum. A circular motion about an external point, e.g. the Earth about the Sun, is called an orbit or more properly an orbital revolution.
   a. Rotation0
   b. Thing
   c. Undefined
   d. Undefined

62. _____ is a means of calculating the volume of a solid of revolution, when integrating along the axis of revolution. This method models the generated 3 dimensional shape as a "stack" of an infinite number of disks of infinitesimal thickness.
   a. Disk method0
   b. Thing
   c. Undefined
   d. Undefined

63. In geometry, a line _____ is a part of a line that is bounded by two end points, and contains every point on the line between its end points.
   a. Segment0
   b. Concept
   c. Undefined
   d. Undefined

64. A _____ is a part of a line that is bounded by two end points, and contains every point on the line between its end points.
   a. Thing
   b. Line segment0
   c. Undefined
   d. Undefined

Chapter 6. Applications of Integrals 115

65. In Euclidean geometry, a _____ is the set of all points in a plane at a fixed distance, called the radius, from a given point, the center.
- a. Circle0
- b. Thing
- c. Undefined
- d. Undefined

66. In mathematics, a _____ is the set of all points in three-dimensional space (R^3) which are at distance r from a fixed point of that space, where r is a positive real number called the radius of the _____. The fixed point is called the center or centre, and is not part of the _____ itself.
- a. Sphere0
- b. Thing
- c. Undefined
- d. Undefined

67. In mathematics, a _____ of a k-place relation $L \subseteq X_1 \times ... \times X_k$ is one of the sets X_j, $1 \leq j \leq k$. In the special case where k = 2 and $L \subseteq X_1 \times X_2$ is a function $L : X_1 \to X_2$, it is conventional to refer to X_1 as the _____ of the function and to refer to X_2 as the codomain of the function.
- a. Domain0
- b. Thing
- c. Undefined
- d. Undefined

68. In geometry, a _____ is a surface of revolution generated by revolving a circle in three dimensional space about an axis coplanar with the circle, which does not touch the circle. Examples of tori include the surfaces of doughnuts and inner tubes. A circle rotated about a chord of the circle is called a _____ in some contexts, but this is not a common usage in mathematics. The shape produced when a circle is rotated about a chord resembles a round cushion. _____ was the Latin word for a cushion of this shape.
- a. Torus0
- b. Thing
- c. Undefined
- d. Undefined

69. The _____ of measurement are a globally standardized and modernized form of the metric system.
- a. Thing
- b. Units0
- c. Undefined
- d. Undefined

70. _____ is the middle point of a line segment.
- a. Thing
- b. Midpoint0
- c. Undefined
- d. Undefined

71. The _____ is the distance around a closed curve. _____ is a kind of perimeter.
- a. Thing
- b. Circumference0
- c. Undefined
- d. Undefined

72. In mathematics, a _____ is the result of multiplying, or an expression that identifies factors to be multiplied.
- a. Thing
- b. Product0
- c. Undefined
- d. Undefined

73. A _____ is a symbolic representation denoting a quantity or expression. It often represents an "unknown" quantity that has the potential to change.
- a. Variable0
- b. Thing
- c. Undefined
- d. Undefined

Chapter 6. Applications of Integrals

74. _____ is a means of calculating the volume of a solid of revolution, when integrating along an axis perpendicular to the axis of revolution.
    a. Shell method0
    b. Thing
    c. Undefined
    d. Undefined

75. In mathematics, a _____ is a curve in a Euclidian plane. The most frequently studied types are the smooth _____, and the algebraic _____.
    a. Plane curve0
    b. Thing
    c. Undefined
    d. Undefined

76. A _____ is a function that assigns a number to subsets of a given set.
    a. Thing
    b. Measure0
    c. Undefined
    d. Undefined

77. In mathematics, an _____ is a theorem with a statement beginning 'there exist ...'. That is, in more formal terms of symbolic logic, it is a theorem with a statement involving the existential quantifier.
    a. Existence theorem0
    b. Thing
    c. Undefined
    d. Undefined

78. The _____, the average in everyday English, which is also called the arithmetic _____ (and is distinguished from the geometric _____ or harmonic _____). The average is also called the sample _____. The expected value of a random variable, which is also called the population _____.
    a. Thing
    b. Mean0
    c. Undefined
    d. Undefined

79. The _____ is a measurement of how a function changes when the values of its inputs change.
    a. Derivative0
    b. Thing
    c. Undefined
    d. Undefined

80. In trigonometry, the _____ is a function defined as $\tan x = {\sin x}/{\cos x}$. The function is so-named because it can be defined as the length of a certain segment of a _____ (in the geometric sense) to the unit circle. In plane geometry, a line is _____ to a curve, at some point, if both line and curve pass through the point with the same direction.
    a. Thing
    b. Tangent0
    c. Undefined
    d. Undefined

81. _____ has many meanings, most of which simply .
    a. Power0
    b. Thing
    c. Undefined
    d. Undefined

82. A _____ is traditionally an infinitesimally small change in a variable.
    a. Differential0
    b. Thing
    c. Undefined
    d. Undefined

83. A _____ is a simplified and structured visual representation of concepts, ideas, constructions, relations, statistical data, anatomy etc used in all aspects of human activities to visualize and clarify the topic.

Chapter 6. Applications of Integrals

   a. Thing
   b. Diagram0
   c. Undefined
   d. Undefined

84. Compass and straightedge or ruler-and-compass _____ is the _____ of lengths or angles using only an idealized ruler and compass.
   a. Thing
   b. Construction0
   c. Undefined
   d. Undefined

85. The _____ of a right triangle is the triangle's longest side; the side opposite the right angle.
   a. Thing
   b. Hypotenuse0
   c. Undefined
   d. Undefined

86. In Euclidean geometry, an _____ is a closed segment of a differentiable curve in the two-dimensional plane; for example, a circular _____ is a segment of a circle.
   a. Concept
   b. Arc0
   c. Undefined
   d. Undefined

87. _____ also called rectification of a curve—was historically difficult.
   a. Arc length0
   b. Thing
   c. Undefined
   d. Undefined

88. In mathematics, a _____ is an ordered list of objects. Like a set, it contains members, also called elements or terms, and the number of terms is called the length of the _____. Unlike a set, order matters, and the exact same elements can appear multiple times at different positions in the _____.
   a. Sequence0
   b. Thing
   c. Undefined
   d. Undefined

89. _____ is the state of being greater than any finite real or natural number, however large.
   a. Thing
   b. Infinite0
   c. Undefined
   d. Undefined

90. In geometry, an _____ is a point at which a line segment or ray terminates.
   a. Endpoint0
   b. Thing
   c. Undefined
   d. Undefined

91. _____, is a Franco-American mathematician, best known as the "father of fractal geometry".
   a. Benoit Mandelbrot0
   b. Person
   c. Undefined
   d. Undefined

92. In colloquial usage, a _____ is "a rough or fragmented geometric shape that can be subdivided in parts, each of which is, at least approximately, a reduced-size copy of the whole."
   a. Fractal0
   b. Concept
   c. Undefined
   d. Undefined

93. _____ is a particular type of curve: a hypocycloid with four cusps.

a. Astroid0
b. Thing
c. Undefined
d. Undefined

94. _____ constitutes a broad family of algorithms for calculating the numerical value of a definite integral, and by extension, the term is also sometimes used to describe the numerical solution of differential equations.
   a. Numerical integration0
   b. Thing
   c. Undefined
   d. Undefined

95. An _____, also called a minor planet or planetoid, comes from a class of atsronomical objects.
   a. Thing
   b. Asteroid0
   c. Undefined
   d. Undefined

96. In mathematics, a _____ of a number x is a number r such that r^2 = x, or in words, a number r whose square (the result of multiplying the number by itself) is x.
   a. Square root0
   b. Thing
   c. Undefined
   d. Undefined

97. An _____ of a function f is a function F whose derivative is equal to f, i.e., F' = f.
   a. Antiderivative0
   b. Thing
   c. Undefined
   d. Undefined

98. _____ is a trigonemtric function that is important when studying triangles and modeling periodic phenomena, among other applications.
   a. Thing
   b. Sine0
   c. Undefined
   d. Undefined

99. _____ is the design, analysis, and/or construction of works for practical purposes.
   a. Engineering0
   b. Thing
   c. Undefined
   d. Undefined

100. _____ is the portion of a solid – normally a cone or pyramid – which lies between two parallel planes cutting the solid.
   a. Truncated pyramid0
   b. Thing
   c. Undefined
   d. Undefined

101. In set theory and other branches of mathematics, the _____ of a collection of sets is the set that contains everything that belongs to any of the sets, but nothing else.
   a. Union0
   b. Thing
   c. Undefined
   d. Undefined

102. _____ is a set, with some particular properties and usually some additional structure, such as the operations of addition or multiplication, for instance.
   a. Thing
   b. Space0
   c. Undefined
   d. Undefined

103. The _____ of a right circular cone is the distance from any point on the circle to the apex of the cone.

Chapter 6. Applications of Integrals

    a. Thing
    c. Undefined
    b. Slant height0
    d. Undefined

104. In mathematics, an _____, mean, or central tendency of a data set refers to a measure of the "middle" or "expected" value of the data set.
    a. Concept
    c. Undefined
    b. Average0
    d. Undefined

105. A _____ is a deliberate process for transforming one or more inputs into one or more results.
    a. Thing
    c. Undefined
    b. Calculation0
    d. Undefined

106. A _____ surface is the surface or face of a solid on its sides. It can also be defined as any face or surface that is not a base.
    a. Thing
    c. Undefined
    b. Lateral0
    d. Undefined

107. A _____ is a negotiable instrument instructing a financial institution to pay a specific amount of a specific currency from a specific demand account held in the maker/depositor's name with that institution. Both the maker and payee may be natural persons or legal entities.
    a. Check0
    c. Undefined
    b. Thing
    d. Undefined

108. An _____ or member of a set is an object that when collected together make up the set.
    a. Thing
    c. Undefined
    b. Element0
    d. Undefined

109. An _____ is a combination of numbers, operators, grouping symbols and/or free variables and bound variables arranged in a meaningful way which can be evaluated..
    a. Thing
    c. Undefined
    b. Expression0
    d. Undefined

110. _____ of a polygon is half its perimeter.
    a. Thing
    c. Undefined
    b. Semiperimeter0
    d. Undefined

111. In mathematics, the _____ (or modulus) of a real number is its numerical value without regard to its sign.
    a. Thing
    c. Undefined
    b. Absolute value0
    d. Undefined

112. The _____ (symbol _____) and the millibar (symbol mbar, also mb) are units of pressure.
    a. Bar0
    c. Undefined
    b. Thing
    d. Undefined

113. _____ has two distinct but etymologically-related meanings: one in geometry and one in trigonometry.

Chapter 6. Applications of Integrals

a. Thing
c. Undefined
b. Tangent line0
d. Undefined

114. _____ is the property of a physical object that quantifies the amount of matter and energy it is equivalent to.
a. Thing
c. Undefined
b. Mass0
d. Undefined

115. Sir Isaac _____, was an English physicist, mathematician, astronomer, natural philosopher, and alchemist, regarded by many as the greatest figure in the history of science
a. Person
c. Undefined
b. Newton0
d. Undefined

116. In geometry, the _____ of an object is a point in some sense in the middle of the object.
a. Thing
c. Undefined
b. Center0
d. Undefined

117. In physics, the _____ of a system of particles is a specific point at which, for many purposes, the system's mass behaves as if it were concentrated.
a. Center of mass0
c. Undefined
b. Thing
d. Undefined

118. _____ is defined as the rate of change or derivative with respect to time of velocity.
a. Acceleration0
c. Undefined
b. Thing
d. Undefined

119. A _____ of a number is the product of that number with any integer.
a. Thing
c. Undefined
b. Multiple0
d. Undefined

120. A _____ is an abstract model that uses mathematical language to describe the behavior of a system. Eykhoff defined a _____ as 'a representation of the essential aspects of an existing system which presents knowledge of that system in usable form'.
a. Mathematical model0
c. Undefined
b. Thing
d. Undefined

121. In mathematics, the _____ of a coordinate system is the point where the axes of the system intersect.
a. Thing
c. Undefined
b. Origin0
d. Undefined

122. The _____ of a mathematical object is its size: a property by which it can be larger or smaller than other objects of the same kind; in technical terms, an ordering of the class of objects to which it belongs.
a. Magnitude0
c. Undefined
b. Thing
d. Undefined

123. In physics, _____ can informally be thought of as "rotational force" or "angular force" which causes a change in rotational motion. This force is defined by linear force multiplied by a radius.

Chapter 6. Applications of Integrals

    a. Thing
    c. Undefined
    b. Torque0
    d. Undefined

124. A _____ ratio, also called, Lift-to-drag ratio, _____ number, or finesse, is an aviation term that refers to the distance an aircraft will move forward for any given amount of lost altitude .
    a. Glide0
    c. Undefined
    b. Thing
    d. Undefined

125. A _____, as defined by the International Astronomical Union , is a celestial body orbiting a star or stellar remnant that is massive enough to be rounded by its own gravity, not massive enough to cause thermonuclear fusion in its core, and has cleared its neighboring region of planetesimals.
    a. Planet0
    c. Undefined
    b. Thing
    d. Undefined

126. In geographic information systems, a _____ comprises an entity with a geographic location, typically determined by points, arcs, or polygons. Carriageways and cadastres exemplify _____ data.
    a. Feature0
    c. Undefined
    b. Thing
    d. Undefined

127. In mathematics and the mathematical sciences, a _____ is a fixed, but possibly unspecified, value. This is in contrast to a variable, which is not fixed.
    a. Thing
    c. Undefined
    b. Constant0
    d. Undefined

128. _____ is the eighteenth letter of the Greek alphabet.
    a. Sigma0
    c. Undefined
    b. Thing
    d. Undefined

129. _____ is used as the symbol for summation. Summation is the addition of a set of numbers; the result is their sum. The "numbers" to be summed may be natural numbers, complex numbers, matrices, or still more complicated objects. An infinite sum is a subtle procedure known as a series.
    a. Thing
    c. Undefined
    b. Sigma notation0
    d. Undefined

130. Mathematical _____ is used to represent ideas.
    a. Thing
    c. Undefined
    b. Notation0
    d. Undefined

131. _____ is the addition of a set of numbers; the result is their sum. The "numbers" to be summed may be natural numbers, complex numbers, matrices, or still more complicated objects. An infinite sum is a subtle procedure known as a series.
    a. Summation0
    c. Undefined
    b. Thing
    d. Undefined

132. In mathematical analysis, _____ are objects which generalize functions and probability distributions.

a. Thing
c. Undefined
b. Distribution0
d. Undefined

133. _____ is mass m per unit volume V.
  a. Thing
  c. Undefined
  b. Density0
  d. Undefined

134. A _____ is the part of a fraction that tells how many equal parts make up a whole, and which is used in the name of the fraction: "halves", "thirds", "fourths" or "quarters", "fifths" and so on.
  a. Denominator0
  c. Undefined
  b. Concept
  d. Undefined

135. In mathematics, a set is called _____ if there is a bijection between the set and some set of the form {1, 2, ..., n} where n is a natural number.
  a. Finite0
  c. Undefined
  b. Thing
  d. Undefined

136. In computer science an _____ is a data structure that consists of a group of elements having a single name that are accessed by indexing. In most programming languages each element has the same data type and the _____ occupies a continuous area of storage.
  a. Array0
  c. Undefined
  b. Thing
  d. Undefined

137. _____ Any process by which a specified characteristic usually amplitude of the output of a device is prevented from exceeding a predetermined value.
  a. Thing
  c. Undefined
  b. Limiting0
  d. Undefined

138. _____ means "constancy", i.e. if something retains a certain feature even after we change a way of looking at it, then it is symmetric.
  a. Symmetry0
  c. Undefined
  b. Thing
  d. Undefined

139. _____ of a two-dimensional figure is a line such that, if a perpendicular is constructed, any two points lying on the perpendicular at equal distances from the _____ are identical.
  a. Thing
  c. Undefined
  b. Axis of symmetry0
  d. Undefined

140. In geometry, the _____ or barycenter of an object X in n-dimensional space is the intersection of all hyperplanes that divide X into two parts of equal moment about the hyperplane
  a. Thing
  c. Undefined
  b. Centroid0
  d. Undefined

141. A _____ is a numeral used to indicate a count. The most common use of the word today is to name the part of a fraction that tells the number or count of equal parts.

Chapter 6. Applications of Integrals

a. Numerator0
b. Thing
c. Undefined
d. Undefined

142. In probability theory and statistics, a _____ is a number dividing the higher half of a sample, a population, or a probability distribution from the lower half.
   a. Median0
   b. Concept
   c. Undefined
   d. Undefined

143. In mathematics, the additive inverse, or _____ of a number n is the number that, when added to n, yields zero. The additive inverse of n is denoted −n. For example, 7 is −7, because 7 + (−7) = 0, and the additive inverse of −0.3 is 0.3, because −0.3 + 0.3 = 0.
   a. Opposite0
   b. Thing
   c. Undefined
   d. Undefined

144. In mathematics, the _____ of a number n is the number that, when added to n, yields zero. The _____ of n is denoted −n. For example, 7 is −7, because 7 + (−7) = 0, and the _____ of −0.3 is 0.3, because −0.3 + 0.3 = 0.
   a. Thing
   b. Additive inverse0
   c. Undefined
   d. Undefined

145. In mathematics, science including computer science, linguistics and engineering, an _____ is, generally speaking, an independent variable or input to a function.
   a. Thing
   b. Argument0
   c. Undefined
   d. Undefined

146. In linear algebra, the _____ of an n-by-n square matrix A is defined to be the sum of the elements on the main diagonal of A,
   a. Thing
   b. Trace0
   c. Undefined
   d. Undefined

147. _____ are flexible, elastic objects used to store mechanical energy.
   a. Springs0
   b. Thing
   c. Undefined
   d. Undefined

148. In physics, an _____ is the path that an object makes around another object while under the influence of a source of centripetal force, such as gravity.
   a. Orbit0
   b. Thing
   c. Undefined
   d. Undefined

149. In the context of spaceflight, a _____ are any object which has been placed into orbit by human endeavor.
   a. Satellites0
   b. Thing
   c. Undefined
   d. Undefined

150. _____ is the SI unit of energy.
   a. Joule0
   b. Thing
   c. Undefined
   d. Undefined

Chapter 6. Applications of Integrals

151. _____ are objects, characters, or other concrete representations of ideas, concepts, or other abstractions.
   a. Symbols0
   b. Thing
   c. Undefined
   d. Undefined

152. In combinatorial mathematics, a _____ is an un-ordered collection of unique elements.
   a. Concept
   b. Combination0
   c. Undefined
   d. Undefined

153. Equivalence is the condition of being _____ or essentially equal.
   a. Thing
   b. Equivalent0
   c. Undefined
   d. Undefined

154. In physics, _____ is the amount of energy transferred by a force. Like energy, it is a scalar quantity, with SI units of joules.
   a. Mechanical work0
   b. Thing
   c. Undefined
   d. Undefined

155. A _____ is a special kind of ratio, indicating a relationship between two measurements with different units, such as miles to gallons or cents to pounds.
   a. Thing
   b. Rate0
   c. Undefined
   d. Undefined

156. The _____ of a geographic location is its height above a fixed reference point, often the mean sea level.
   a. Thing
   b. Elevation0
   c. Undefined
   d. Undefined

157. In mathematics, two quantities are called _____ if they vary in such a way that one of the quantities is a constant multiple of the other, or equivalently if they have a constant ratio.
   a. Proportional0
   b. Thing
   c. Undefined
   d. Undefined

158. The _____ of a ring R is defined to be the smallest positive integer n such that $n\,a = 0$, for all a in R.
   a. Characteristic0
   b. Thing
   c. Undefined
   d. Undefined

159. In mathematics and its applications, a _____ is a system for assigning an n-tuple of numbers or scalars to each point in an n-dimensional space.
   a. Concept
   b. Coordinate system0
   c. Undefined
   d. Undefined

160. In mathematics and more specifically set theory, the _____ set is the unique set which contains no elements.
   a. Thing
   b. Empty0
   c. Undefined
   d. Undefined

Chapter 6. Applications of Integrals

161. A _____ is a landform that extends above the surrounding terrain in a limited area. A _____ is generally steeper than a hill, but there is no universally accepted standard definition for the height of a _____ or a hill although a _____ usually has an identifiable summit.
   a. Mountain0
   b. Thing
   c. Undefined
   d. Undefined

162. In mathematics, a _____ or rhodonea curve is a sinusoid plotted in polar coordinates.
   a. Thing
   b. Rose0
   c. Undefined
   d. Undefined

163. The _____ are a set of laws that describe the relationship between thermodynamic temperature T, pressure P and volume V of gases.
   a. Thing
   b. Gas law0
   c. Undefined
   d. Undefined

164. _____ is a synonym for information.
   a. Data0
   b. Thing
   c. Undefined
   d. Undefined

165. The _____ is an imaginary line on the Earth's surface equidistant from the North Pole and South Pole.
   a. Equator0
   b. Thing
   c. Undefined
   d. Undefined

166. _____ is the weakest of the four fundamental forces of bature, as described by Issac Newton
   a. Thing
   b. Gravitational force0
   c. Undefined
   d. Undefined

167. _____ algebra (sometimes called General algebra) is the field of mathematics that studies the ideas common to all algebraic structures.
   a. Universal0
   b. Thing
   c. Undefined
   d. Undefined

168. _____ of an object is its speed in a particular direction.
   a. Velocity0
   b. Thing
   c. Undefined
   d. Undefined

169. In topology and related areas of mathematics a _____ or Moore-Smith sequence is a generalization of a sequence, intended to unify the various notions of limit and generalize them to arbitrary topological spaces.
   a. Thing
   b. Net0
   c. Undefined
   d. Undefined

170. In calculus, the _____ is a formula for the derivative of the composite of two functions.
   a. Concept
   b. Chain rule0
   c. Undefined
   d. Undefined

171. The _____ of an object is the extra energy which it possesses due to its motion.

126   *Chapter 6. Applications of Integrals*

   a. Kinetic energy0   b. Thing
   c. Undefined   d. Undefined

172. _____, Greek for "knowledge of nature," is the branch of science concerned with the discovery and characterization of universal laws which govern matter, energy, space, and time.
   a. Physics0   b. Thing
   c. Undefined   d. Undefined

173. In navigation, a _____ is the clockwise angle between a reference direction and the direction to an object.
   a. Thing   b. Bearing0
   c. Undefined   d. Undefined

174. _____ (or proportionality) are two quantities that vary in such a way that one of the quatities is a constant multiple of the other, or equivalently if they have a constant ratio.
   a. Thing   b. Proportions0
   c. Undefined   d. Undefined

175. In mathematics and its applications, _____ are used for assigning an n-tuple of numbers or scalars to each point in an n-dimensional space.
   a. Concept   b. Coordinate systems0
   c. Undefined   d. Undefined

176. _____ studies and addresses the ways in which individuals, businesses, and organizations raise, allocate, and use monetary resources over time, taking into account the risks entailed in their projects
   a. Finance0   b. Thing
   c. Undefined   d. Undefined

177. _____ is the transport of people on a trip/journey or the process or time involved in a person or object moving from one location to another.
   a. Travel0   b. Thing
   c. Undefined   d. Undefined

178. Initial objects are also called _____, and terminal objects are also called final.
   a. Coterminal0   b. Thing
   c. Undefined   d. Undefined

179. A _____ is a three-dimensional solid object bounded by six square faces, facets, or sides, with three meeting at each vertex.
   a. Cube0   b. Thing
   c. Undefined   d. Undefined

180. _____ is a subset of a population.
   a. Sample0   b. Thing
   c. Undefined   d. Undefined

181. _____ means in succession or back-to-back

Chapter 6. Applications of Integrals

    a. Thing
    b. Consecutive0
    c. Undefined
    d. Undefined

182. _____ is a special mathematical relationship between two quantities. Two quantities are called proportional if they vary in such a way that one of the quantities is a constant multiple of the other, or equivalently if they have a constant ratio.
    a. Proportionality0
    b. Thing
    c. Undefined
    d. Undefined

183. Two mathematical objects are equal if and only if they are precisely the same in every way. This defines a binary relation, _____, denoted by the sign of _____ "=" in such a way that the statement "x = y" means that x and y are equal.
    a. Thing
    b. Equality0
    c. Undefined
    d. Undefined

184. The deductive-nomological model is a formalized view of scientific _____ in natural language.
    a. Explanation0
    b. Thing
    c. Undefined
    d. Undefined

185. _____ is the fee paid on borrowed money.
    a. Interest0
    b. Thing
    c. Undefined
    d. Undefined

186. In mathematics, a _____ of a positive integer n is a way of writing n as a sum of positive integers.
    a. Composition0
    b. Thing
    c. Undefined
    d. Undefined

187. _____ the expected value of a random variable displays the average or central value of the variable. It is a summary value of the distribution of the variable.
    a. Determining0
    b. Thing
    c. Undefined
    d. Undefined

188. A _____ is a quantity that denotes the proportional amount or magnitude of one quantity relative to another.
    a. Thing
    b. Ratio0
    c. Undefined
    d. Undefined

189. Acid _____ ratio measures the ability of a company to use its near cash or quick assets to immediately extinguish its current liabilities.
    a. Test0
    b. Thing
    c. Undefined
    d. Undefined

190. In mathematics, a _____ is a demonstration that, assuming certain axioms, some statement is necessarily true.
    a. Proof0
    b. Thing
    c. Undefined
    d. Undefined

Chapter 6. Applications of Integrals

191. In mathematical analysis, a _____ is a classification of functions according to the properties of their derivatives.
- a. Thing
- b. Smooth surface0
- c. Undefined
- d. Undefined

192. In mathematics, the _____ , or members of a set or more generally a class are all those objects which when collected together make up the set or class.
- a. Elements0
- b. Thing
- c. Undefined
- d. Undefined

193. In mathematics, a _____ is a constant multiplicative factor of a certain object. The object can be such things as a variable, a vector, a function, etc. For example, the _____ of $9x^2$ is 9.
- a. Thing
- b. Coefficient0
- c. Undefined
- d. Undefined

194. An _____ is a type of quadric surface that is a higher dimensional analogue of an ellipse.
- a. Thing
- b. Ellipsoid0
- c. Undefined
- d. Undefined

195. In mathematics, an _____ .
- a. Ellipse0
- b. Thing
- c. Undefined
- d. Undefined

Chapter 7. Transcendental Functions

1. An _____ in policy debate is part of a speech which is flagged as not responding to the line-by-line arguments on the flow.
   - a. Overview0
   - b. Thing
   - c. Undefined
   - d. Undefined

2. The mathematical concept of a _____ expresses the intuitive idea of deterministic dependence between two quantities, one of which is viewed as primary and the other as secondary. A _____ then is a way to associate a unique output for each input of a specified type, for example, a real number or an element of a given set.
   - a. Function0
   - b. Thing
   - c. Undefined
   - d. Undefined

3. _____ element of an element x with respect to a binary operation * with identity element e is an element y such that x * y = y * x = e. In particular,
   - a. Thing
   - b. Inverse0
   - c. Undefined
   - d. Undefined

4. In mathematics, the _____ functions are functions of an angle; they are important when studying triangles and modeling periodic phenomena, among many other applications.
   - a. Thing
   - b. Trigonometric0
   - c. Undefined
   - d. Undefined

5. The _____ are functions of an angle; they are important when studying triangles and modeling periodic phenomena, among many other applications.
   - a. Thing
   - b. Trigonometric functions0
   - c. Undefined
   - d. Undefined

6. In mathematics, the conjugate _____ or adjoint matrix of an m-by-n matrix A with complex entries is the n-by-m matrix A* obtained from A by taking the transpose and then taking the complex conjugate of each entry.
   - a. Pairs0
   - b. Thing
   - c. Undefined
   - d. Undefined

7. In mathematics, _____ growth occurs when the growth rate of a function is always proportional to the function's current size.
   - a. Thing
   - b. Exponential0
   - c. Undefined
   - d. Undefined

8. _____ is one of the most important functions in mathematics. A function commonly used to study growth and decay
   - a. Thing
   - b. Exponential function0
   - c. Undefined
   - d. Undefined

9. A _____ is an analog of an ordinary trigonometric, or circular, function.
   - a. Thing
   - b. Hyperbolic function0
   - c. Undefined
   - d. Undefined

10. _____ is the force that opposes the relative motion or tendency toward such motion of two surfaces in contact.

a. Thing
b. Friction0
c. Undefined
d. Undefined

11. In mathematics, the _____ of a function is the set of all "output" values produced by that function. Given a function $f : A \to B$, the _____ of f, is defined to be the set $\{x \in B : x = f(a) \text{ for some } a \in A\}$.
   a. Range0
   b. Thing
   c. Undefined
   d. Undefined

12. In mathematics, a _____ of a k-place relation $L \subseteq X_1 \times \ldots \times X_k$ is one of the sets X_j, $1 \leq j \leq k$. In the special case where k = 2 and $L \subseteq X_1 \times X_2$ is a function $L : X_1 \to X_2$, it is conventional to refer to X_1 as the _____ of the function and to refer to X_2 as the codomain of the function.
   a. Domain0
   b. Thing
   c. Undefined
   d. Undefined

13. _____ is a trigonemtric function that is important when studying triangles and modeling periodic phenomena, among other applications.
   a. Sine0
   b. Thing
   c. Undefined
   d. Undefined

14. In plane geometry, a _____ is a polygon with four equal sides, four right angles, and parallel opposite sides. In algebra, the _____ of a number is that number multiplied by itself.
   a. Square0
   b. Thing
   c. Undefined
   d. Undefined

15. A _____ is a three-dimensional solid object bounded by six square faces, facets, or sides, with three meeting at each vertex.
   a. Thing
   b. Cube0
   c. Undefined
   d. Undefined

16. _____ are of a number n in its third power-the result of multiplying it by itself three times.
   a. Cubes0
   b. Thing
   c. Undefined
   d. Undefined

17. In mathematics, a _____ of a number x is a number r such that $r^2 = x$, or in words, a number r whose square (the result of multiplying the number by itself) is x.
   a. Thing
   b. Square root0
   c. Undefined
   d. Undefined

18. In mathematics, a _____ of a complex-valued function f is a member x of the domain of f such that f(x) vanishes at x, that is, $x : f(x) = 0$.
   a. Thing
   b. Root0
   c. Undefined
   d. Undefined

19. In mathematics, a _____ number is a real or complex number which is not algebraic, that is, not a solution of a non-zero polynomial equation, with rational coefficients.

Chapter 7. Transcendental Functions

a. Transcendental0
b. Thing
c. Undefined
d. Undefined

20. The _____ integers are all the integers from zero on upwards.
    a. Nonnegative0
    b. Thing
    c. Undefined
    d. Undefined

21. In astronomy, geography, geometry and related sciences and contexts, a plane is said to be _____ at a given point if it is locally perpendicular to the gradient of the gravity field, i.e., with the direction of the gravitational force at that point.
    a. Horizontal0
    b. Thing
    c. Undefined
    d. Undefined

22. _____ is a test used to determine if a function is injective, surjective or bijective.
    a. Thing
    b. Horizontal line test0
    c. Undefined
    d. Undefined

23. Acid _____ ratio measures the ability of a company to use its near cash or quick assets to immediately extinguish its current liabilities.
    a. Thing
    b. Test0
    c. Undefined
    d. Undefined

24. A _____ consists of one quarter of the coordinate plane.
    a. Quadrant0
    b. Thing
    c. Undefined
    d. Undefined

25. In elementary algebra, an _____ is a set that contains every real number between two indicated numbers and may contain the two numbers themselves.
    a. Thing
    b. Interval0
    c. Undefined
    d. Undefined

26. The _____, the average in everyday English, which is also called the arithmetic _____ (and is distinguished from the geometric _____ or harmonic _____). The average is also called the sample _____. The expected value of a random variable, which is also called the population _____.
    a. Mean0
    b. Thing
    c. Undefined
    d. Undefined

27. An _____ is an equality that remains true regardless of the values of any variables that appear within it, to distinguish it from an equality which is true under more particular conditions.
    a. Identity0
    b. Thing
    c. Undefined
    d. Undefined

28. An _____ is a function that does not have any effect: it always returns the same value that was used as its argument.
    a. Thing
    b. Identity function0
    c. Undefined
    d. Undefined

Chapter 7. Transcendental Functions

29. A _____ of a number is a number a such that $a^3 = x$.
    a. Cube root0
    b. Thing
    c. Undefined
    d. Undefined

30. A _____ is a symbolic representation denoting a quantity or expression. It often represents an "unknown" quantity that has the potential to change.
    a. Thing
    b. Variable0
    c. Undefined
    d. Undefined

31. An _____ is a straight line around which a geometric figure can be rotated.
    a. Axis0
    b. Thing
    c. Undefined
    d. Undefined

32. In mathematics, an _____ is any of the arguments, i.e. "inputs", to a function. Thus if we have a function f(x), then x is a _____.
    a. Thing
    b. Independent variable0
    c. Undefined
    d. Undefined

33. In a function the _____, is the variable which is the value, i.e. the "output", of the function.
    a. Dependent variable0
    b. Thing
    c. Undefined
    d. Undefined

34. _____ are the basic objects of study in graph theory. Informally speaking, a graph is a set of objects called points, nodes, or vertices connected by links called lines or edges.
    a. Thing
    b. Graphs0
    c. Undefined
    d. Undefined

35. _____ means "constancy", i.e. if something retains a certain feature even after we change a way of looking at it, then it is symmetric.
    a. Symmetry0
    b. Thing
    c. Undefined
    d. Undefined

36. A _____ is a negotiable instrument instructing a financial institution to pay a specific amount of a specific currency from a specific demand account held in the maker/depositor's name with that institution. Both the maker and payee may be natural persons or legal entities.
    a. Thing
    b. Check0
    c. Undefined
    d. Undefined

37. A _____ number is a positive integer which has a positive divisor other than one or itself.
    a. Thing
    b. Composite0
    c. Undefined
    d. Undefined

38. _____ statistics are statistics that estimate population parameters.
    a. Thing
    b. Parametric0
    c. Undefined
    d. Undefined

Chapter 7. Transcendental Functions

39. In mathematics, the multiplicative inverse of a number x, denoted 1/x or x^{-1}, is the number which, when multiplied by x, yields 1. The multiplicative inverse of x is also called the _____ of x.
   a. Reciprocal0
   b. Thing
   c. Undefined
   d. Undefined

40. _____ is often used to describe the measurement of the steepness, incline, gradient, or grade of a straight line. The _____ is defined as the ratio of the "rise" divided by the "run" between two points on a line, or in other words, the ratio of the altitude change to the horizontal distance between any two points on the line.
   a. Slope0
   b. Thing
   c. Undefined
   d. Undefined

41. An _____ is a function which does the reverse of a given function.
   a. Inverse function0
   b. Thing
   c. Undefined
   d. Undefined

42. The _____ is a measurement of how a function changes when the values of its inputs change.
   a. Thing
   b. Derivative0
   c. Undefined
   d. Undefined

43. In a mathematical proof or a syllogism, a _____ is a statement that is the logical consequence of preceding statements.
   a. Conclusion0
   b. Concept
   c. Undefined
   d. Undefined

44. In mathematics, _____ is a part of the set theoretic notion of function.
   a. Image0
   b. Thing
   c. Undefined
   d. Undefined

45. _____ is a kind of property which exists as magnitude or multitude. It is among the basic classes of things along with quality, substance, change, and relation.
   a. Thing
   b. Amount0
   c. Undefined
   d. Undefined

46. In mathematics, a _____ is a statement that can be proved on the basis of explicitly stated or previously agreed assumptions.
   a. Theorem0
   b. Thing
   c. Undefined
   d. Undefined

47. In mathematics, the _____ f is the collection of all ordered pairs . In particular, graph means the graphical representation of this collection, in the form of a curve or surface, together with axes, etc. Graphing on a Cartesian plane is sometimes referred to as curve sketching.
   a. Graph of a function0
   b. Thing
   c. Undefined
   d. Undefined

48. In mathematics and the mathematical sciences, a _____ is a fixed, but possibly unspecified, value. This is in contrast to a variable, which is not fixed.

Chapter 7. Transcendental Functions

    a. Thing
    b. Constant0
    c. Undefined
    d. Undefined

49. In mathematics, a _____ number is a number which can be expressed as a ratio of two integers. Non-integer _____ numbers (commonly called fractions) are usually written as the vulgar fraction a / b, where b is not zero.
    a. Rational0
    b. Thing
    c. Undefined
    d. Undefined

50. In mathematics, a _____ is any function which can be written as the ratio of two polynomial functions.
    a. Thing
    b. Rational function0
    c. Undefined
    d. Undefined

51. In calculus, the _____ is a formula for the derivative of the composite of two functions.
    a. Chain rule0
    b. Concept
    c. Undefined
    d. Undefined

52. In mathematics, a _____ is the result of multiplying, or an expression that identifies factors to be multiplied.
    a. Thing
    b. Product0
    c. Undefined
    d. Undefined

53. _____ is a means of calculating the volume of a solid of revolution, when integrating along an axis perpendicular to the axis of revolution.
    a. Thing
    b. Shell method0
    c. Undefined
    d. Undefined

54. The _____ of a solid object is the three-dimensional concept of how much space it occupies, often quantified numerically.
    a. Volume0
    b. Thing
    c. Undefined
    d. Undefined

55. There are two simple _____ the greatest common factor and least common multiple: standard factorization and prime factorization.
    a. Methods for finding0
    b. Thing
    c. Undefined
    d. Undefined

56. Two mathematical objects are equal if and only if they are precisely the same in every way. This defines a binary relation, _____, denoted by the sign of _____ "=" in such a way that the statement "x = y" means that x and y are equal.
    a. Thing
    b. Equality0
    c. Undefined
    d. Undefined

57. The word _____ comes from the Latin word linearis, which means created by lines.
    a. Linear0
    b. Thing
    c. Undefined
    d. Undefined

58. _____ is the logarithm to the base e, where e is an irrational constant approximately equal to 2.718281828459.

Chapter 7. Transcendental Functions

a. Natural logarithm0
b. Thing
c. Undefined
d. Undefined

59. In mathematics, a _____ of a number x is the exponent y of the power by such that $x = b^y$. The value used for the base b must be neither 0 nor 1, nor a root of 1 in the case of the extension to complex numbers, and is typically 10, e, or 2.
   a. Thing
   b. Logarithm0
   c. Undefined
   d. Undefined

60. _____ or arithmetics is the oldest and most elementary branch of mathematics, used by almost everyone, for tasks ranging from simple daily counting to advanced science and business calculations.
   a. Arithmetic0
   b. Thing
   c. Undefined
   d. Undefined

61. _____ is the process of planning, recording, and controlling the movement of a craft or vehicle from one place to another.
   a. Thing
   b. Navigation0
   c. Undefined
   d. Undefined

62. A _____ is a deliberate process for transforming one or more inputs into one or more results.
   a. Thing
   b. Calculation0
   c. Undefined
   d. Undefined

63. The _____ of a function is an extension of the concept of a sum, and are identified or found through the use of integration.
   a. Thing
   b. Integral0
   c. Undefined
   d. Undefined

64. In mathematics, the concept of a _____ tries to capture the intuitive idea of a geometrical one-dimensional and continuous object. A simple example is the circle.
   a. Thing
   b. Curve0
   c. Undefined
   d. Undefined

65. _____ is a mathematical subject that includes the study of limits, derivatives, integrals, and power series and constitutes a major part of modern university curriculum.
   a. Calculus0
   b. Thing
   c. Undefined
   d. Undefined

66. In number theory, the _____ of arithmetic (or unique factorization theorem) states that every natural number greater than 1 can be written as a unique product of prime numbers.
   a. Concept
   b. Fundamental theorem0
   c. Undefined
   d. Undefined

67. _____ of calculus is the statement that the two central operations of calculus, differentiation and integration, are inverse operations: if a continuous function is first integrated and then differentiated, the original function is retrieved.

Chapter 7. Transcendental Functions

    a. Thing
    c. Undefined
    b. Fundamental Theorem of Calculus0
    d. Undefined

68. John _____ of Merchistoun, nicknamed Marvellous Merchistoun, was a Scottish mathematician, physicist, astronomer/astrologer and 8th Laird of Merchistoun. He is most remembered as the inventor of logarithms and _____'s bones, and for popularizing the use of the decimal point.
    a. Person
    c. Undefined
    b. Napier0
    d. Undefined

69. A _____ is a unit of length, usually used to measure distance, in a number of different systems, including Imperial units, United States customary units and Norwegian/Swedish mil. Its size can vary from system to system, but in each is between 1 and 10 kilometers. In contemporary English contexts _____ refers to either:
    a. Thing
    c. Undefined
    b. Mile0
    d. Undefined

70. In mathematics, a _____ is a demonstration that, assuming certain axioms, some statement is necessarily true.
    a. Thing
    c. Undefined
    b. Proof0
    d. Undefined

71. In mathematics, science including computer science, linguistics and engineering, an _____ is, generally speaking, an independent variable or input to a function.
    a. Argument0
    c. Undefined
    b. Thing
    d. Undefined

72. _____ has many meanings, most of which simply .
    a. Power0
    c. Undefined
    b. Thing
    d. Undefined

73. In mathematics, a _____ is a countable collection of open covers of a topological space that satisfies certain separation axioms.
    a. Thing
    c. Undefined
    b. Development0
    d. Undefined

74. In mathematics, a _____ may be described informally as a number that can be given by an infinite decimal representation.
    a. Thing
    c. Undefined
    b. Real number0
    d. Undefined

75. In mathematics, a _____ is the end result of a division problem. It can also be expressed as the number of times the divisor divides into the dividend.
    a. Quotient0
    c. Undefined
    b. Thing
    d. Undefined

76. _____, a field in mathematics, is the study of how functions change when their inputs change. The primary object of study in _____ is the derivative.

Chapter 7. Transcendental Functions

    a. Thing
    b. Differential calculus0
    c. Undefined
    d. Undefined

77. An _____ is a combination of numbers, operators, grouping symbols and/or free variables and bound variables arranged in a meaningful way which can be evaluated..
    a. Thing
    b. Expression0
    c. Undefined
    d. Undefined

78. _____ is the ratio of the adjacent to the opposite side of a right-angeled triangle
    a. Thing
    b. Cotangent0
    c. Undefined
    d. Undefined

79. In trigonometry, the _____ is a function defined as $\tan x = \sin x / \cos x$. The function is so-named because it can be defined as the length of a certain segment of a _____ (in the geometric sense) to the unit circle. In plane geometry, a line is _____ to a curve, at some point, if both line and curve pass through the point with the same direction.
    a. Tangent0
    b. Thing
    c. Undefined
    d. Undefined

80. The term _____ refers to the largest and the smallest element of a set.
    a. Extreme value0
    b. Thing
    c. Undefined
    d. Undefined

81. _____ is a process of combining or accumulating. It may also refer to:
    a. Thing
    b. Integration0
    c. Undefined
    d. Undefined

82. A _____ is a set of numbers that designate location in a given reference system, such as x,y in a planar _____ system or an x,y,z in a three-dimensional _____ system.
    a. Coordinate0
    b. Thing
    c. Undefined
    d. Undefined

83. In mathematics, _____ geometry was the traditional name for the geometry of three-dimensional Euclidean space — for practical purposes the kind of space we live in.
    a. Thing
    b. Solid0
    c. Undefined
    d. Undefined

84. In mathematics, _____ are the intuitive idea of a geometrical one-dimensional and continuous object.
    a. Curves0
    b. Thing
    c. Undefined
    d. Undefined

85. An _____ is when two lines intersect somewhere on a plane creating a right angle at intersection
    a. Axes0
    b. Thing
    c. Undefined
    d. Undefined

86. In mathematical analysis and related areas of mathematics, a set is called _____, if it is, in a certain sense, of finite size.

138 *Chapter 7. Transcendental Functions*

a. Bounded0
b. Thing
c. Undefined
d. Undefined

87. In geometry, the _____ of an object is a point in some sense in the middle of the object.
   a. Center0
   b. Thing
   c. Undefined
   d. Undefined

88. In physics, the _____ of a system of particles is a specific point at which, for many purposes, the system's mass behaves as if it were concentrated.
   a. Thing
   b. Center of mass0
   c. Undefined
   d. Undefined

89. Initial objects are also called _____, and terminal objects are also called final.
   a. Thing
   b. Coterminal0
   c. Undefined
   d. Undefined

90. In mathematics and its applications, _____ refers to finding the linear approximation to a function at a given point.
   a. Thing
   b. Linearization0
   c. Undefined
   d. Undefined

91. _____ is a differential equation together with specified value, called the initial condition, of the unknown function at a given point in the domain of the solution.
   a. Thing
   b. Initial value problem0
   c. Undefined
   d. Undefined

92. _____ is the property of a physical object that quantifies the amount of matter and energy it is equivalent to.
   a. Mass0
   b. Thing
   c. Undefined
   d. Undefined

93. _____ is mass m per unit volume V.
   a. Density0
   b. Thing
   c. Undefined
   d. Undefined

94. In mathematics, especially in order theory, an _____ of a subset S of some partially ordered set is an element of P which is greater than or equal to every element of S.
   a. Upper bound0
   b. Thing
   c. Undefined
   d. Undefined

95. The act of _____ is the calculated approximation of a result which is usable even if input data may be incomplete, uncertain, or noisy.
   a. Thing
   b. Estimating0
   c. Undefined
   d. Undefined

96. In mathematics, two quantities are called _____ if they vary in such a way that one of the quantities is a constant multiple of the other, or equivalently if they have a constant ratio.

Chapter 7. Transcendental Functions

a. Thing
b. Proportional0
c. Undefined
d. Undefined

97. A _____ is a special kind of ratio, indicating a relationship between two measurements with different units, such as miles to gallons or cents to pounds.
a. Rate0
b. Thing
c. Undefined
d. Undefined

98. A _____ is traditionally an infinitesimally small change in a variable.
a. Differential0
b. Thing
c. Undefined
d. Undefined

99. A _____ is a mathematical equation for an unknown function of one or several variables which relates the values of the function itself and of its derivatives of various orders.
a. Differential equation0
b. Thing
c. Undefined
d. Undefined

100. In mathematics, a _____ is a number which can be expressed as a ratio of two integers. Non-integer rational numbers (commonly called fractions) are usually written as the vulgar fraction a / b, where b is not zero.
a. Rational Number0
b. Concept
c. Undefined
d. Undefined

101. In mathematics, an _____ number is any real number that is not a rational number- that is, it is a number which cannot be expressed as a fraction m/n, where m and n are integers.
a. Irrational0
b. Thing
c. Undefined
d. Undefined

102. In mathematics, a _____ is a constant multiplicative factor of a certain object. The object can be such things as a variable, a vector, a function, etc. For example, the _____ of $9x^2$ is 9.
a. Thing
b. Coefficient0
c. Undefined
d. Undefined

103. In mathematics, a _____ is an expression that is constructed from one or more variables and constants, using only the operations of addition, subtraction, multiplication, and constant positive whole number exponents. is a _____. Note in particular that division by an expression containing a variable is not in general allowed in polynomials. [1]
a. Thing
b. Polynomial0
c. Undefined
d. Undefined

104. A _____ is the result of the addition of a set of numbers. The numbers may be natural numbers, complex numbers, matrices, or still more complicated objects. An infinite _____ is a subtle procedure known as a series.
a. Sum0
b. Thing
c. Undefined
d. Undefined

105. _____ is informally a function which satisfies a polynomial equation whose coefficients are themselves polynomials.

Chapter 7. Transcendental Functions

    a. Thing
    c. Undefined
    b. Algebraic function0
    d. Undefined

106. One of the three formats applicable to a quadratic function is the _____ which is defined as f = ax^2 + bx + c.
    a. General form0
    c. Undefined
    b. Thing
    d. Undefined

107. Equivalence is the condition of being _____ or essentially equal.
    a. Thing
    c. Undefined
    b. Equivalent0
    d. Undefined

108. In statistics, a _____ measure is one which is measuring what is supposed to measure.
    a. Thing
    c. Undefined
    b. Valid0
    d. Undefined

109. In mathematics, in the field of differential equations, an initial value problem is a differential equation together with specified value, called the _____, of the unknown function at a given point in the domain of the solution.
    a. Thing
    c. Undefined
    b. Initial condition0
    d. Undefined

110. In mathematics, the _____ of a coordinate system is the point where the axes of the system intersect.
    a. Origin0
    c. Undefined
    b. Thing
    d. Undefined

111. In mathematics, an _____, mean, or central tendency of a data set refers to a measure of the "middle" or "expected" value of the data set.
    a. Concept
    c. Undefined
    b. Average0
    d. Undefined

112. _____ is an approximation of a general function using a linear function more precisely, an affine function.
    a. Thing
    c. Undefined
    b. Linear approximation0
    d. Undefined

113. The _____ of a mathematical object is its size: a property by which it can be larger or smaller than other objects of the same kind; in technical terms, an ordering of the class of objects to which it belongs.
    a. Thing
    c. Undefined
    b. Magnitude0
    d. Undefined

114. _____ is a method for differentiating expressions involving exponentiation the power operation.
    a. Thing
    c. Undefined
    b. Power rule0
    d. Undefined

115. A _____ of a number is the product of that number with any integer.
    a. Thing
    c. Undefined
    b. Multiple0
    d. Undefined

Chapter 7. Transcendental Functions

116. In mathematics, the _____ is the logarithm with base 10.
    a. Common logarithm0
    b. Thing
    c. Undefined
    d. Undefined

117. A central concept in science and the scientific method is that all evidence must be _____, or empirically based, that is, dependent on evidence or consequences that are observable by the senses.
    a. Thing
    b. Empirical0
    c. Undefined
    d. Undefined

118. In business, particularly accounting, a _____ is the time intervals that the accounts, statement, payments, or other calculations cover.
    a. Thing
    b. Period0
    c. Undefined
    d. Undefined

119. The _____ is a nonnegative scalar measure of a wave's magnitude of oscillation, that is, the magnitude of the maximum disturbance in the medium during one wave cycle.
    a. Amplitude0
    b. Thing
    c. Undefined
    d. Undefined

120. An _____ is the result from the sudden release of stored energy in the Earth's crust that creates seismic waves.
    a. Thing
    b. Earthquake0
    c. Undefined
    d. Undefined

121. In physics, a _____ may refer to the scalar _____ or to the vector _____.
    a. Potential0
    b. Thing
    c. Undefined
    d. Undefined

122. In Euclidean geometry, a uniform _____ is a linear transformation that enlargers or diminishes objects, and whose _____ factor is the same in all directions. This is also called homothethy.
    a. Thing
    b. Scale0
    c. Undefined
    d. Undefined

123. The _____ relative to a specified or implied reference level.
    a. Thing
    b. Decibel0
    c. Undefined
    d. Undefined

124. The metre (or _____, see spelling differences) is a measure of length. It is the basic unit of length in the metric system and in the International System of Units (SI), used around the world for general and scientific purposes.
    a. Meter0
    b. Concept
    c. Undefined
    d. Undefined

125. A _____ is a quantity that denotes the proportional amount or magnitude of one quantity relative to another.
    a. Ratio0
    b. Thing
    c. Undefined
    d. Undefined

Chapter 7. Transcendental Functions

126. _____ is a concept in traditional logic referring to a "type of immediate inference in which from a given proposition another proposition is inferred which has as its subject the predicate of the original proposition and as its predicate the subject of the original proposition (the quality of the proposition being retained)."
- a. Concept
- b. Conversion0
- c. Undefined
- d. Undefined

127. In mathematics, factorization (British English: factorisation) or factoring is the decomposition of an object (for example, a number, a polynomial, or a matrix) into a product of other objects, or _____, which when multiplied together give the original.
- a. Thing
- b. Factors0
- c. Undefined
- d. Undefined

128. In sociology and biology a _____ is the collection of people or organisms of a particular species living in a given geographic area or space, usually measured by a census.
- a. Thing
- b. Population0
- c. Undefined
- d. Undefined

129. _____ is change in population over time, and can be quantified as the change in the number of individuals in a population per unit time.
- a. Population growth0
- b. Thing
- c. Undefined
- d. Undefined

130. The word _____ comes from the 15th Century Latin word discretus which means separate.
- a. Discrete0
- b. Thing
- c. Undefined
- d. Undefined

131. _____ is a special mathematical relationship between two quantities. Two quantities are called proportional if they vary in such a way that one of the quantities is a constant multiple of the other, or equivalently if they have a constant ratio.
- a. Thing
- b. Proportionality0
- c. Undefined
- d. Undefined

132. _____ of a population is the number of childbirths per 1,000 persons per year
- a. Birth rate0
- b. Thing
- c. Undefined
- d. Undefined

133. _____ of a single or multiple future payments is the nominal amounts of money to change hands at some future date, discounted to account for the time value of money, and other factors such as investment risk.
- a. Present value0
- b. Thing
- c. Undefined
- d. Undefined

134. A _____ is 360° or 2δ radians.
- a. Thing
- b. Turn0
- c. Undefined
- d. Undefined

135. _____ is the fee paid on borrowed money.

Chapter 7. Transcendental Functions

a. Thing
b. Interest0
c. Undefined
d. Undefined

136. An _____ is the fee paid on borrow money.
a. Interest rate0
b. Concept
c. Undefined
d. Undefined

137. A _____ function is a function for which, intuitively, small changes in the input result in small changes in the output.
a. Continuous0
b. Event
c. Undefined
d. Undefined

138. _____ interest refers to the fact that whenever interest is calculated, it is based not only on the original principal, but also on any unpaid interest that has been added to the principal.
a. Compound0
b. Thing
c. Undefined
d. Undefined

139. _____ refers to the fact that whenever interest is calculated, it is based not only on the original principal, but also on any unpaid interest that has been added to the principal. The more frequently interest is compounded, the faster the balance grows.
a. Concept
b. Compound interest0
c. Undefined
d. Undefined

140. An _____ or member of a set is an object that when collected together make up the set.
a. Element0
b. Thing
c. Undefined
d. Undefined

141. A _____ is the part of the dividend that is left over when the dividend is not evenly divisible by the divisor.
a. Thing
b. Remainder0
c. Undefined
d. Undefined

142. In the scientific method, an _____ (Latin: ex-+-periri, "of (or from) trying"), is a set of actions and observations, performed in the context of solving a particular problem or question, in order to support or falsify a hypothesis or research concerning phenomena.
a. Thing
b. Experiment0
c. Undefined
d. Undefined

143. _____ is a subset of a population.
a. Sample0
b. Thing
c. Undefined
d. Undefined

144. In mathematics, the _____, or members of a set or more generally a class are all those objects which when collected together make up the set or class.
a. Thing
b. Elements0
c. Undefined
d. Undefined

Chapter 7. Transcendental Functions

145. In probability theory, _____ are various sets of outcomes (a subset of the sample space) to which a probability is assigned.
 a. Events0
 b. Thing
 c. Undefined
 d. Undefined

146. Sir Isaac _____, was an English physicist, mathematician, astronomer, natural philosopher, and alchemist, regarded by many as the greatest figure in the history of science
 a. Newton0
 b. Person
 c. Undefined
 d. Undefined

147. _____ is a physical property of a system that underlies the common notions of hot and cold; something that is hotter has the greater _____.
 a. Thing
 b. Temperature0
 c. Undefined
 d. Undefined

148. _____ are a measure of time.
 a. Thing
 b. Minutes0
 c. Undefined
 d. Undefined

149. In mathematics, _____ refers to the rewriting of an expression into a simpler form.
 a. Reduction0
 b. Thing
 c. Undefined
 d. Undefined

150. _____ is a synonym for information.
 a. Data0
 b. Thing
 c. Undefined
 d. Undefined

151. In geometry, an _____ of a triangle is a straight line through a vertex and perpendicular to (i.e. forming a right angle with) the opposite side or an extension of the opposite side.
 a. Altitude0
 b. Concept
 c. Undefined
 d. Undefined

152. _____ is electromagnetic radiation with a wavelength that is visible to the eye (visible _____) or, in a technical or scientific context, electromagnetic radiation of any wavelength.
 a. Light0
 b. Thing
 c. Undefined
 d. Undefined

153. The _____ of measurement are a globally standardized and modernized form of the metric system.
 a. Thing
 b. Units0
 c. Undefined
 d. Undefined

154. In finance and economics, _____ is the process of finding the present value of an amount of cash at some future date, and along with compounding cash forms the basis of time value of money calculations.
 a. Discount0
 b. Thing
 c. Undefined
 d. Undefined

Chapter 7. Transcendental Functions

155. _____ is a business term for the amount of money that a company receives from its activities in a given period, mostly from sales of products and/or services to customers
   a. Thing
   b. Revenue0
   c. Undefined
   d. Undefined

156. _____ of Nerchistoun, nicknamed Marvellous Merchistoun, was a Scottish mathematician, physicist, astronomer/astrologer and 8th Laird of Merchistoun.
   a. John Napier0
   b. Person
   c. Undefined
   d. Undefined

157. _____ is the estimation of a physical quantity such as distance, energy, temperature, or time.
   a. Measurement0
   b. Thing
   c. Undefined
   d. Undefined

158. Johann Bernoulli was a Swiss mathematician. He was the brother of Jakob Bernoulli, and the father of Daniel Bernoulli and Nicolaus II Bernoulli. He is also known as Jean or _____. He educated the great mathematician Leonhard Euler in his youth.
   a. Thing
   b. John Bernoulli0
   c. Undefined
   d. Undefined

159. A _____ is a numeral used to indicate a count. The most common use of the word today is to name the part of a fraction that tells the number or count of equal parts.
   a. Numerator0
   b. Thing
   c. Undefined
   d. Undefined

160. A _____ is the part of a fraction that tells how many equal parts make up a whole, and which is used in the name of the fraction: "halves", "thirds", "fourths" or "quarters", "fifths" and so on.
   a. Concept
   b. Denominator0
   c. Undefined
   d. Undefined

161. In calculus and other branches of mathematical analysis, an _____ is an algebraic expression obtained in the context of limits.
   a. Thing
   b. Indeterminate form0
   c. Undefined
   d. Undefined

162. A _____ decimal is a number whose decimal representation eventually becomes periodic (i.e. the same number sequence _____ indefinitely).
   a. Thing
   b. Repeating0
   c. Undefined
   d. Undefined

163. _____ is the state of being greater than any finite number, however large.
   a. Thing
   b. Infinity0
   c. Undefined
   d. Undefined

164. _____ is the state of being greater than any finite real or natural number, however large.

Chapter 7. Transcendental Functions

    a. Infinite0
    b. Thing
    c. Undefined
    d. Undefined

165. In mathematics, a set is called _____ if there is a bijection between the set and some set of the form {1, 2, ..., n} where n is a natural number.
    a. Thing
    b. Finite0
    c. Undefined
    d. Undefined

166. _____ is a branch of mathematics concerning the study of structure, relation and quantity.
    a. Algebra0
    b. Concept
    c. Undefined
    d. Undefined

167. _____ the expected value of a random variable displays the average or central value of the variable. It is a summary value of the distribution of the variable.
    a. Thing
    b. Determining0
    c. Undefined
    d. Undefined

168. _____ (Groups, Algorithms and Programming) is a computer algebra system for computational discrete algebra with particular emphasis on, but not restricted to, computational group theory.
    a. Gap0
    b. Thing
    c. Undefined
    d. Undefined

169. An _____ of a function f is a function F whose derivative is equal to f, i.e., F' = f.
    a. Antiderivative0
    b. Thing
    c. Undefined
    d. Undefined

170. _____ is the transport of people on a trip/journey or the process or time involved in a person or object moving from one location to another.
    a. Thing
    b. Travel0
    c. Undefined
    d. Undefined

171. In _____ algebra, a *-ring is an associative ring with an antilinear, antiautomorphism * : A ¨ A which is an involution.
    a. Star0
    b. Thing
    c. Undefined
    d. Undefined

172. Mathematical _____ is used to represent ideas.
    a. Thing
    b. Notation0
    c. Undefined
    d. Undefined

173. _____ is the mathematical action of repeatedly adding or subtracting one, usually to find out how many objects there are or to set aside a desired number of objects.
    a. Counting0
    b. Thing
    c. Undefined
    d. Undefined

174. A _____ is a function that assigns a number to subsets of a given set.

Chapter 7. Transcendental Functions

a. Thing
b. Measure0
c. Undefined
d. Undefined

175. In mathematics, computing, linguistics, and related disciplines, an _____ is a finite list of well-defined instructions for accomplishing some task which, given an initial state, will terminate in a defined end-state.
a. Algorithm0
b. Concept
c. Undefined
d. Undefined

176. In mathematics, a subset of Euclidean space R^n is called _____ if it is closed and bounded.
a. Compact0
b. Thing
c. Undefined
d. Undefined

177. _____ the American term is a way to approximately calculate the definite integral
a. Thing
b. Trapezoidal Rule0
c. Undefined
d. Undefined

178. _____ is an extension of the concept of a sum.
a. Thing
b. Definite integral0
c. Undefined
d. Undefined

179. A _____ is one of the basic shapes of geometry: a polygon with three vertices and three sides which are straight line segments.
a. Triangle0
b. Thing
c. Undefined
d. Undefined

180. In mathematics, the _____ are the inverse functions of the trigonometric functions.
a. Thing
b. Inverse trigonometric functions0
c. Undefined
d. Undefined

181. In Euclidean geometry, an _____ is a closed segment of a differentiable curve in the two-dimensional plane; for example, a circular _____ is a segment of a circle.
a. Arc0
b. Concept
c. Undefined
d. Undefined

182. The _____ of an angle is the ratio of the length of the adjacent side to the length of the hypotenuse.
a. Cosine0
b. Concept
c. Undefined
d. Undefined

183. In mathematics, a _____ (also spelled reflexion) is a map that transforms an object into its mirror image.
a. Reflection0
b. Concept
c. Undefined
d. Undefined

184. In mathematics, defined and _____ are used to explain whether or not expressions have meaningful, sensible, and unambiguous values.

a. Undefined0
b. Thing
c. Undefined
d. Undefined

185. _____ is a trigonometric function that is the reciprocal of cosine.
   a. Thing
   b. Secant0
   c. Undefined
   d. Undefined

186. The _____ (symbol _____) and the millibar (symbol mbar, also mb) are units of pressure.
   a. Bar0
   b. Thing
   c. Undefined
   d. Undefined

187. In mathematics, the _____ (or modulus) of a real number is its numerical value without regard to its sign.
   a. Thing
   b. Absolute value0
   c. Undefined
   d. Undefined

188. In mathematics, the additive inverse, or _____ of a number n is the number that, when added to n, yields zero. The additive inverse of n is denoted −n. For example, 7 is −7, because 7 + (−7) = 0, and the additive inverse of −0.3 is 0.3, because −0.3 + 0.3 = 0.
   a. Opposite0
   b. Thing
   c. Undefined
   d. Undefined

189. The _____ of a right triangle is the triangle's longest side; the side opposite the right angle.
   a. Hypotenuse0
   b. Thing
   c. Undefined
   d. Undefined

190. _____ has one 90° internal angle a right angle.
   a. Right triangle0
   b. Thing
   c. Undefined
   d. Undefined

191. In mathematics, the _____ of a number n is the number that, when added to n, yields zero. The _____ of n is denoted −n. For example, 7 is −7, because 7 + (−7) = 0, and the _____ of −0.3 is 0.3, because −0.3 + 0.3 = 0.
   a. Additive inverse0
   b. Thing
   c. Undefined
   d. Undefined

192. _____ is a term in Trigonometry used to describe the secant of the complement of a cirlce.
   a. Thing
   b. Cosecant0
   c. Undefined
   d. Undefined

193. _____ is a circle with a unit radius, i.e., a circle whose radius is 1.
   a. Thing
   b. Unit circle0
   c. Undefined
   d. Undefined

194. In Euclidean geometry, a _____ is the set of all points in a plane at a fixed distance, called the radius, from a given point, the center.

a. Thing
b. Circle0
c. Undefined
d. Undefined

195. In mathematics and logic, a _____ proof is a way of showing the truth or falsehood of a given statement by a straightforward combination of established facts, usually existing lemmas and theorems, without making any further assumptions.
  a. Direct0
  b. Thing
  c. Undefined
  d. Undefined

196. A _____, formed by the composition of one function on another, represents the application of the former to the result of the application of the latter to the argument of the composite.
  a. Composite function0
  b. Thing
  c. Undefined
  d. Undefined

197. A frame of _____ is a particular perspective from which the universe is observed.
  a. Reference0
  b. Thing
  c. Undefined
  d. Undefined

198. In elementary algebra, a _____ is a polynomial with two terms: the sum of two monomials. It is the simplest kind of polynomial except for a monomial.
  a. Binomial0
  b. Thing
  c. Undefined
  d. Undefined

199. In geometry, a _____ is the intersection of a body in 2-dimensional space with a line, or of a body in 3-dimensional space with a plane
  a. Cross section0
  b. Thing
  c. Undefined
  d. Undefined

200. In geometry, two lines or planes if one falls on the other in such a way as to create congruent adjacent angles. The term may be used as a noun or adjective. Thus, referring to Figure 1, the line AB is the _____ to CD through the point B.
  a. Thing
  b. Perpendicular0
  c. Undefined
  d. Undefined

201. In mathematics, a _____ is a two-dimensional manifold or surface that is perfectly flat.
  a. Thing
  b. Plane0
  c. Undefined
  d. Undefined

202. In mathematics, _____ are two-dimensional manifolds or surfaces that are perfectly flat.
  a. Planes0
  b. Thing
  c. Undefined
  d. Undefined

203. In geometry, a _____ (Greek words diairo = divide and metro = measure) of a circle is any straight line segment that passes through the centre and whose endpoints are on the circular boundary, or, in more modern usage, the length of such a line segment. When using the word in the more modern sense, one speaks of the _____ rather than a _____, because all diameters of a circle have the same length. This length is twice the radius. The _____ of a circle is also the longest chord that the circle has.

Chapter 7. Transcendental Functions

a. Diameter0
b. Thing
c. Undefined
d. Undefined

204. _____ constitutes a broad family of algorithms for calculating the numerical value of a definite integral, and by extension, the term is also sometimes used to describe the numerical solution of differential equations.
   a. Numerical integration0
   b. Thing
   c. Undefined
   d. Undefined

205. The _____ function (weight function) is a mathematical device used when performing a sum, integral, or average in order to give some elements more of a "weight" than others.
   a. Thing
   b. Weighted0
   c. Undefined
   d. Undefined

206. The Jefferson National Expansion Memorial or _____ is located in St. Louis, Missouri near the start of the Lewis and Clark Expedition. It was designated as a National Memorial by Executive Order 7523, on December 21, 1935, and is maintained by the National Park Service ..
   a. Place
   b. Gateway Arch0
   c. Undefined
   d. Undefined

207. _____ are functions which satisfy particular symmetry relations, with respect to taking additive inverses.
   a. Even function0
   b. Thing
   c. Undefined
   d. Undefined

208. _____ refers to the reduction of the body of a formerly living organism into simpler forms of matter.
   a. Thing
   b. Decomposing0
   c. Undefined
   d. Undefined

209. In mathematics, in the field of group theory, a _____ of a group is a quasisimple subnormal subgroup.
   a. Component0
   b. Concept
   c. Undefined
   d. Undefined

210. _____ is the curve along which a small object moves when pulled on a horizontal plane with a piece of thread by a puller, which moves rectilinearly with infinitesimal speed.
   a. Thing
   b. Tractrix0
   c. Undefined
   d. Undefined

211. The plus and _____ signs are mathematical symbols used to represent the notions of positive and negative as well as the operations of addition and subtraction.
   a. Thing
   b. Minus0
   c. Undefined
   d. Undefined

212. _____ of an object is its speed in a particular direction.
   a. Velocity0
   b. Thing
   c. Undefined
   d. Undefined

213. _____ is defined as the rate of change or derivative with respect to time of velocity.

Chapter 7. Transcendental Functions

    a. Thing
    b. Acceleration0
    c. Undefined
    d. Undefined

214. In geometry, a line _____ is a part of a line that is bounded by two end points, and contains every point on the line between its end points.
    a. Segment0
    b. Concept
    c. Undefined
    d. Undefined

215. In mathematics, suppose C is a collection of mathematical objects . Then we say that C is _____ if every c ⸲ C is uniquely determined by less information about c than one would expect.
    a. Rigid0
    b. Thing
    c. Undefined
    d. Undefined

216. In geometry, the _____ or barycenter of an object X in n-dimensional space is the intersection of all hyperplanes that divide X into two parts of equal moment about the hyperplane
    a. Thing
    b. Centroid0
    c. Undefined
    d. Undefined

217. A circular _____ or circle _____ also known as a pie piece is the portion of a circle enclosed by two radii and an arc.
    a. Thing
    b. Sector0
    c. Undefined
    d. Undefined

218. In mathematics, a _____ is a type of conic section defined as the intersection between a right circular conical surface and a plane which cuts through both halves of the cone.
    a. Hyperbola0
    b. Thing
    c. Undefined
    d. Undefined

219. _____ is bother the congnitive process of transferring information from a particular subject , and a linguistic expression corresponding to such a process.
    a. Thing
    b. Analogy0
    c. Undefined
    d. Undefined

220. In physics and in _____ calculus, a spatial _____, or simply _____, is a concept characterized by a magnitude and a direction.
    a. Vector0
    b. Thing
    c. Undefined
    d. Undefined

221. In mathematics and its applications, a _____ is a system for assigning an n-tuple of numbers or scalars to each point in an n-dimensional space.
    a. Concept
    b. Coordinate system0
    c. Undefined
    d. Undefined

222. _____ is a reaction force applied by a stretched string on the objects which stretch it.

a. Tension0
b. Thing
c. Undefined
d. Undefined

223. In physics, _____ is an influence that may cause an object to accelerate. It may be experienced as a lift, a push, or a pull. The actual acceleration of the body is determined by the vector sum of all forces acting on it, known as net _____ or resultant _____.
   a. Force0
   b. Thing
   c. Undefined
   d. Undefined

224. _____ is the shape of a hanging flexible chain or cable when supported at its ends and acted upon by a uniform gravitational force. The chain is steepest near the points of suspension because this part of the chain has the most weight pulling down on it. Toward the bottom, the slope of the chain decreases because the chain is supporting less weight.
   a. Thing
   b. Catenary0
   c. Undefined
   d. Undefined

225. In mathematics, an _____ is a generalization for the concept of a function in which the dependent variable may not be given explicitly in terms of the independent variable.
   a. Implicit function0
   b. Thing
   c. Undefined
   d. Undefined

226. _____ is a notation for writing numbers that is often used by scientists and mathematicians to make it easier to write large and small numbers.
   a. Thing
   b. Scientific notation0
   c. Undefined
   d. Undefined

227. _____ is the process in which an unstable atomic nucleus loses energy by emitting radiation in the form of particles or electromagnetic waves.
   a. Radioactive decay0
   b. Thing
   c. Undefined
   d. Undefined

228. _____ is process in which two clone daughter cells are produced by the cell division of one bacterium.
   a. Thing
   b. Bacterial growth0
   c. Undefined
   d. Undefined

229. Compass and straightedge or ruler-and-compass _____ is the _____ of lengths or angles using only an idealized ruler and compass.
   a. Construction0
   b. Thing
   c. Undefined
   d. Undefined

230. _____ is a function that is chosen to facilitate the solving of a given ordinary differential equation. Consider an ordinary differential equation of the form
   a. Integrating factor0
   b. Thing
   c. Undefined
   d. Undefined

231. The _____ or kilogramme is the SI base unit of mass. It is defined as being equal to the mass of the international prototype of the _____.

Chapter 7. Transcendental Functions 153

    a. Thing   b. Kilogram0
    c. Undefined   d. Undefined

232. In mathematics a _____ is a function which defines a distance between elements of a set.
    a. Thing   b. Metric0
    c. Undefined   d. Undefined

233. The _____ is a decimalized system of measurement based on the metre and the gram.
    a. Concept   b. Metric system0
    c. Undefined   d. Undefined

234. The _____ refers to a unit in one of a number of systems of units of measurement, some obsolete, and some still in use.
    a. Thing   b. English system0
    c. Undefined   d. Undefined

235. The _____, in practice often shortened to amp, is a unit of electric current, or amount of electric charge per second.
    a. Amperes0   b. Thing
    c. Undefined   d. Undefined

236. For a given gravitational field and a given position, the _____ is the minimum speed an object without propulsion needs to have to move away indefinitely from the source of the field, as opposed to falling back or staying in an orbit within a bounded distance from the source.
    a. Thing   b. Escape velocity0
    c. Undefined   d. Undefined

237. A _____ is a method for fastening or securing linear material such as rope by tying or interweaving. It may consist of a length of one or more segments of rope, string, webbing, twine, strap or even chain interwoven so as to create in the line the ability to bind to itself or to some other object - the "load". Knots have been the subject of interest both for their ancient origins, common use, and the mathematical implications of _____ theory.
    a. Thing   b. Knot0
    c. Undefined   d. Undefined

238. A _____ is a simplified and structured visual representation of concepts, ideas, constructions, relations, statistical data, anatomy etc used in all aspects of human activities to visualize and clarify the topic.
    a. Diagram0   b. Thing
    c. Undefined   d. Undefined

239. _____ is the difference of electrical potential between two points of an electrical or electronic circuit, expressed in volts
    a. Thing   b. Voltage0
    c. Undefined   d. Undefined

240. In economics, economic _____ is simply a state of the world where economic forces are balanced and in the absence of external influences the values of economic variables will not change.

Chapter 7. Transcendental Functions

    a. Thing
    b. Equilibrium0
    c. Undefined
    d. Undefined

241. In chemistry, a _____ is substance made by combining two or more different materials in such a way that no chemical reaction occurs.
    a. Thing
    b. Mixture0
    c. Undefined
    d. Undefined

242. U.S. liquid _____ is legally defined as 231 cubic inches, and is equal to 3.785411784 litres or abotu 0.13368 cubic feet. This is the most common definition of a _____. The U.S. fluid ounce is defined as 1/128 of a U.S. _____.
    a. Thing
    b. Gallon0
    c. Undefined
    d. Undefined

243. In mathematics, the _____ inverse, or opposite, of a number n is the number that, when added to n, yields zero. The _____ inverse of n is denoted −n.
    a. Additive0
    b. Thing
    c. Undefined
    d. Undefined

244. In botany, _____ are above-ground plant organs specialized for photosynthesis. Their characteristics are typically analyzed by using Fiobonacci's sequences.
    a. Leaves0
    b. Thing
    c. Undefined
    d. Undefined

245. Leonhard _____ was a pioneering Swiss mathematician and physicist, who spent most of his life in Russia and Germany.
    a. Euler0
    b. Person
    c. Undefined
    d. Undefined

246. A _____ is a graphical tool to qualitatively visualize, or aid in numerical approximation of, solutions to differential equations.
    a. Thing
    b. Slope field0
    c. Undefined
    d. Undefined

247. An _____ is an increase, either of some fixed amount, for example added regularly, or of a variable amount.
    a. Increment0
    b. Thing
    c. Undefined
    d. Undefined

248. _____ has two distinct but etymologically-related meanings: one in geometry and one in trigonometry.
    a. Thing
    b. Tangent line0
    c. Undefined
    d. Undefined

249. The _____ rule, also known as a slipstick, is a mechanical analog computer, consisting of at least two finely divided scales , most often a fixed outer pair and a movable inner one, with a sliding window called the cursor.

a. Slide0
b. Thing
c. Undefined
d. Undefined

250. _____ is a way of expressing a number as a fraction of 100 per cent meaning "per hundred".
a. Thing
b. Percent0
c. Undefined
d. Undefined

251. _____ is the chance that something is likely to happen or be the case.
a. Probability0
b. Thing
c. Undefined
d. Undefined

252. A _____ is an abstract model that uses mathematical language to describe the behavior of a system. Eykhoff defined a _____ as 'a representation of the essential aspects of an existing system which presents knowledge of that system in usable form'.
a. Mathematical model0
b. Thing
c. Undefined
d. Undefined

1. An _____ in policy debate is part of a speech which is flagged as not responding to the line-by-line arguments on the flow.
   a. Overview0
   b. Thing
   c. Undefined
   d. Undefined

2. The _____ of a function is an extension of the concept of a sum, and are identified or found through the use of integration.
   a. Integral0
   b. Thing
   c. Undefined
   d. Undefined

3. _____ is a process of combining or accumulating. It may also refer to:
   a. Integration0
   b. Thing
   c. Undefined
   d. Undefined

4. An _____ of a function f is a function F whose derivative is equal to f, i.e., F' = f.
   a. Antiderivative0
   b. Thing
   c. Undefined
   d. Undefined

5. _____ is a function that extends the concept of an ordinary sum
   a. Thing
   b. Integrand0
   c. Undefined
   d. Undefined

6. In mathematics and the mathematical sciences, a _____ is a fixed, but possibly unspecified, value. This is in contrast to a variable, which is not fixed.
   a. Constant0
   b. Thing
   c. Undefined
   d. Undefined

7. In mathematics, _____ expressions is used to reduce the expression into the lowest possible term.
   a. Thing
   b. Simplifying0
   c. Undefined
   d. Undefined

8. In plane geometry, a _____ is a polygon with four equal sides, four right angles, and parallel opposite sides. In algebra, the _____ of a number is that number multiplied by itself.
   a. Thing
   b. Square0
   c. Undefined
   d. Undefined

9. In mathematics, a _____ of a number x is a number r such that $r^2 = x$, or in words, a number r whose square (the result of multiplying the number by itself) is x.
   a. Square root0
   b. Thing
   c. Undefined
   d. Undefined

10. An _____ is an equality that remains true regardless of the values of any variables that appear within it, to distinguish it from an equality which is true under more particular conditions.
    a. Thing
    b. Identity0
    c. Undefined
    d. Undefined

Chapter 8. Techniques of Integration

11. In mathematics, a _____ of a complex-valued function f is a member x of the domain of f such that f(x) vanishes at x, that is, x : f (x) = 0.
    a. Root0
    b. Thing
    c. Undefined
    d. Undefined

12. A _____ fraction is a fraction in which the absolute value of the numerator is less than the denominator--hence, the absolute value of the fraction is less than 1.
    a. Proper0
    b. Thing
    c. Undefined
    d. Undefined

13. In mathematics, an inequality is a statement about the relative size or order of two objects. For example 14 > 10, or 14 is _____ 10.
    a. Greater than0
    b. Thing
    c. Undefined
    d. Undefined

14. A _____ is a numeral used to indicate a count. The most common use of the word today is to name the part of a fraction that tells the number or count of equal parts.
    a. Thing
    b. Numerator0
    c. Undefined
    d. Undefined

15. In mathematics, a _____ is the end result of a division problem. It can also be expressed as the number of times the divisor divides into the dividend.
    a. Quotient0
    b. Thing
    c. Undefined
    d. Undefined

16. An _____ is a combination of numbers, operators, grouping symbols and/or free variables and bound variables arranged in a meaningful way which can be evaluated..
    a. Expression0
    b. Thing
    c. Undefined
    d. Undefined

17. In arithmetic, _____ is a procedure for calculating the division of one integer, called the dividend, by another integer called the divisor, to produce a result called the quotient.
    a. Long division0
    b. Thing
    c. Undefined
    d. Undefined

18. A _____ is the part of the dividend that is left over when the dividend is not evenly divisible by the divisor.
    a. Thing
    b. Remainder0
    c. Undefined
    d. Undefined

19. In mathematics, there are several meanings of _____ depending on the subject.
    a. Degree0
    b. Thing
    c. Undefined
    d. Undefined

20. A _____ is the part of a fraction that tells how many equal parts make up a whole, and which is used in the name of the fraction: "halves", "thirds", "fourths" or "quarters", "fifths" and so on.

158 Chapter 8. Techniques of Integration

    a. Denominator0
    b. Concept
    c. Undefined
    d. Undefined

21. _____ is a notation for writing numbers that is often used by scientists and mathematicians to make it easier to write large and small numbers.
    a. Thing
    b. Scientific notation0
    c. Undefined
    d. Undefined

22. _____ is a technique used in algebra to solve quadratic equations, in analytic geometry for determining the shapes of graphs, and in calculus for computing integrals, including, but hardly limited to, the integrals that define Laplace transforms. The essential objective is to reduce a quadratic polynomial in a variable in an equation or expression to a squared polynomial of linear order. This can reduce an equation or integral to one that is more easily solved or evaluated.
    a. Thing
    b. Completing the square0
    c. Undefined
    d. Undefined

23. In mathematics, the _____ functions are functions of an angle; they are important when studying triangles and modeling periodic phenomena, among many other applications.
    a. Thing
    b. Trigonometric0
    c. Undefined
    d. Undefined

24. The _____ of a solid object is the three-dimensional concept of how much space it occupies, often quantified numerically.
    a. Volume0
    b. Thing
    c. Undefined
    d. Undefined

25. In mathematics, _____ geometry was the traditional name for the geometry of three-dimensional Euclidean space — for practical purposes the kind of space we live in.
    a. Thing
    b. Solid0
    c. Undefined
    d. Undefined

26. In geometry, the _____ or barycenter of an object X in n-dimensional space is the intersection of all hyperplanes that divide X into two parts of equal moment about the hyperplane
    a. Thing
    b. Centroid0
    c. Undefined
    d. Undefined

27. In mathematics, the concept of a _____ tries to capture the intuitive idea of a geometrical one-dimensional and continuous object. A simple example is the circle.
    a. Thing
    b. Curve0
    c. Undefined
    d. Undefined

28. In mathematical analysis and related areas of mathematics, a set is called _____, if it is, in a certain sense, of finite size.
    a. Thing
    b. Bounded0
    c. Undefined
    d. Undefined

Chapter 8. Techniques of Integration

29. _____, a field in mathematics, is the study of how functions change when their inputs change. The primary object of study in _____ is the derivative.
    a. Differential calculus0
    b. Thing
    c. Undefined
    d. Undefined

30. _____ is an extension of the concept of a sum.
    a. Thing
    b. Definite integral0
    c. Undefined
    d. Undefined

31. Equivalence is the condition of being _____ or essentially equal.
    a. Thing
    b. Equivalent0
    c. Undefined
    d. Undefined

32. In geometry, a _____ is defined as a quadrilateral where all four of its angles are right angles.
    a. Rectangle0
    b. Thing
    c. Undefined
    d. Undefined

33. The plus and _____ signs are mathematical symbols used to represent the notions of positive and negative as well as the operations of addition and subtraction.
    a. Minus0
    b. Thing
    c. Undefined
    d. Undefined

34. _____ are objects, characters, or other concrete representations of ideas, concepts, or other abstractions.
    a. Thing
    b. Symbols0
    c. Undefined
    d. Undefined

35. In calculus, the indefinite integral of a given function i.e. the set of all antiderivatives of the function is always written with a constant, the _____.
    a. Thing
    b. Constant of integration0
    c. Undefined
    d. Undefined

36. A _____ is a deliberate process for transforming one or more inputs into one or more results.
    a. Thing
    b. Calculation0
    c. Undefined
    d. Undefined

37. A _____ consists of one quarter of the coordinate plane.
    a. Thing
    b. Quadrant0
    c. Undefined
    d. Undefined

38. A _____ is a set of numbers that designate location in a given reference system, such as x,y in a planar _____ system or an x,y,z in a three-dimensional _____ system.
    a. Thing
    b. Coordinate0
    c. Undefined
    d. Undefined

39. An _____ is when two lines intersect somewhere on a plane creating a right angle at intersection

a. Axes0
b. Thing
c. Undefined
d. Undefined

40. _____ is mass m per unit volume V.
   a. Density0
   b. Thing
   c. Undefined
   d. Undefined

41. In geometry, the _____ of an object is a point in some sense in the middle of the object.
   a. Center0
   b. Thing
   c. Undefined
   d. Undefined

42. In physics, the _____ of a system of particles is a specific point at which, for many purposes, the system's mass behaves as if it were concentrated.
   a. Thing
   b. Center of mass0
   c. Undefined
   d. Undefined

43. _____ is the property of a physical object that quantifies the amount of matter and energy it is equivalent to.
   a. Mass0
   b. Thing
   c. Undefined
   d. Undefined

44. The _____ function (weight function) is a mathematical device used when performing a sum, integral, or average in order to give some elements more of a "weight" than others.
   a. Thing
   b. Weighted0
   c. Undefined
   d. Undefined

45. In mathematics, an _____, mean, or central tendency of a data set refers to a measure of the "middle" or "expected" value of the data set.
   a. Concept
   b. Average0
   c. Undefined
   d. Undefined

46. In physics, _____ is an influence that may cause an object to accelerate. It may be experienced as a lift, a push, or a pull. The actual acceleration of the body is determined by the vector sum of all forces acting on it, known as net _____ or resultant _____.
   a. Force0
   b. Thing
   c. Undefined
   d. Undefined

47. In elementary algebra, an _____ is a set that contains every real number between two indicated numbers and may contain the two numbers themselves.
   a. Thing
   b. Interval0
   c. Undefined
   d. Undefined

48. The mathematical concept of a _____ expresses the intuitive idea of deterministic dependence between two quantities, one of which is viewed as primary and the other as secondary. A _____ then is a way to associate a unique output for each input of a specified type, for example, a real number or an element of a given set.

Chapter 8. Techniques of Integration

a. Thing
b. Function0
c. Undefined
d. Undefined

49. _____ element of an element x with respect to a binary operation * with identity element e is an element y such that x * y = y * x = e. In particular,
a. Inverse0
b. Thing
c. Undefined
d. Undefined

50. A _____ is a negotiable instrument instructing a financial institution to pay a specific amount of a specific currency from a specific demand account held in the maker/depositor's name with that institution. Both the maker and payee may be natural persons or legal entities.
a. Check0
b. Thing
c. Undefined
d. Undefined

51. In mathematics, a _____ number is a number which can be expressed as a ratio of two integers. Non-integer _____ numbers (commonly called fractions) are usually written as the vulgar fraction a / b, where b is not zero.
a. Thing
b. Rational0
c. Undefined
d. Undefined

52. In mathematics, a _____ is any function which can be written as the ratio of two polynomial functions.
a. Thing
b. Rational function0
c. Undefined
d. Undefined

53. A _____ is the result of the addition of a set of numbers. The numbers may be natural numbers, complex numbers, matrices, or still more complicated objects. An infinite _____ is a subtle procedure known as a series.
a. Thing
b. Sum0
c. Undefined
d. Undefined

54. In algebra, the _____ decomposition or _____ expansion is used to reduce the degree of either the numerator or the denominator of a rational function.
a. Thing
b. Partial fraction0
c. Undefined
d. Undefined

55. _____ is a branch of mathematics concerning the study of structure, relation and quantity.
a. Algebra0
b. Concept
c. Undefined
d. Undefined

56. In mathematics, a _____ is a statement that can be proved on the basis of explicitly stated or previously agreed assumptions.
a. Thing
b. Theorem0
c. Undefined
d. Undefined

57. In mathematics, a _____ is a constant multiplicative factor of a certain object. The object can be such things as a variable, a vector, a function, etc. For example, the _____ of $9x^2$ is 9.

a. Thing
b. Coefficient0
c. Undefined
d. Undefined

58. In mathematics, factorization (British English: factorisation) or factoring is the decomposition of an object (for example, a number, a polynomial, or a matrix) into a product of other objects, or _____, which when multiplied together give the original.
    a. Factors0
    b. Thing
    c. Undefined
    d. Undefined

59. The word _____ comes from the Latin word linearis, which means created by lines.
    a. Linear0
    b. Thing
    c. Undefined
    d. Undefined

60. _____ has many meanings, most of which simply .
    a. Power0
    b. Thing
    c. Undefined
    d. Undefined

61. In mathematics, a _____ is the result of multiplying, or an expression that identifies factors to be multiplied.
    a. Product0
    b. Thing
    c. Undefined
    d. Undefined

62. In mathematics, a _____ is an expression that is constructed from one or more variables and constants, using only the operations of addition, subtraction, multiplication, and constant positive whole number exponents. is a _____. Note in particular that division by an expression containing a variable is not in general allowed in polynomials. [1]
    a. Thing
    b. Polynomial0
    c. Undefined
    d. Undefined

63. An _____ of a product of sums expresses it as a sum of products by using the fact that multiplication distributes over addition.
    a. Thing
    b. Expansion0
    c. Undefined
    d. Undefined

64. In a mathematical proof or a syllogism, a _____ is a statement that is the logical consequence of preceding statements.
    a. Concept
    b. Conclusion0
    c. Undefined
    d. Undefined

65. Initial objects are also called _____, and terminal objects are also called final.
    a. Thing
    b. Coterminal0
    c. Undefined
    d. Undefined

66. _____ is a differential equation together with specified value, called the initial condition, of the unknown function at a given point in the domain of the solution.
    a. Thing
    b. Initial value problem0
    c. Undefined
    d. Undefined

Chapter 8. Techniques of Integration 163

67. _____ is the net action of matter particles or molecules, heat, momentum, or light whose end is to minimize a concentration gradient
 a. Diffusion0
 b. Thing
 c. Undefined
 d. Undefined

68. In sociology and biology a _____ is the collection of people or organisms of a particular species living in a given geographic area or space, usually measured by a census.
 a. Thing
 b. Population0
 c. Undefined
 d. Undefined

69. In mathematics, two quantities are called _____ if they vary in such a way that one of the quantities is a constant multiple of the other, or equivalently if they have a constant ratio.
 a. Proportional0
 b. Thing
 c. Undefined
 d. Undefined

70. A _____ is a special kind of ratio, indicating a relationship between two measurements with different units, such as miles to gallons or cents to pounds.
 a. Thing
 b. Rate0
 c. Undefined
 d. Undefined

71. The _____ is a measurement of how a function changes when the values of its inputs change.
 a. Thing
 b. Derivative0
 c. Undefined
 d. Undefined

72. _____ is a kind of property which exists as magnitude or multitude. It is among the basic classes of things along with quality, substance, change, and relation.
 a. Amount0
 b. Thing
 c. Undefined
 d. Undefined

73. A _____ is traditionally an infinitesimally small change in a variable.
 a. Thing
 b. Differential0
 c. Undefined
 d. Undefined

74. A _____ is a mathematical equation for an unknown function of one or several variables which relates the values of the function itself and of its derivatives of various orders.
 a. Differential equation0
 b. Thing
 c. Undefined
 d. Undefined

75. In mathematics, a class _____ is a structure used to organize the various Galois groups and modules that appear in class field theory. They were invented by Emil Artin and John Tate.
 a. Formation0
 b. Thing
 c. Undefined
 d. Undefined

76. In mathematics, the _____ of a function is the set of all "output" values produced by that function. Given a function $f : A \to B$, the _____ of f, is defined to be the set $\{x \in B : x = f(a) \text{ for some } a \in A\}$.

164 Chapter 8. Techniques of Integration

   a. Thing
   c. Undefined
   b. Range0
   d. Undefined

77. In the scientific method, an _____ (Latin: ex-+-periri, "of (or from) trying"), is a set of actions and observations, performed in the context of solving a particular problem or question, in order to support or falsify a hypothesis or research concerning phenomena.
   a. Thing
   c. Undefined
   b. Experiment0
   d. Undefined

78. A _____ is one of the basic shapes of geometry: a polygon with three vertices and three sides which are straight line segments.
   a. Triangle0
   c. Undefined
   b. Thing
   d. Undefined

79. A frame of _____ is a particular perspective from which the universe is observed.
   a. Thing
   c. Undefined
   b. Reference0
   d. Undefined

80. _____ has one 90° internal angle a right angle.
   a. Right triangle0
   c. Undefined
   b. Thing
   d. Undefined

81. In mathematics, _____ is the substitution of trigonometric functions for other expressions.
   a. Trigonometric substitution0
   c. Undefined
   b. Thing
   d. Undefined

82. In elementary algebra, a _____ is a polynomial with two terms: the sum of two monomials. It is the simplest kind of polynomial except for a monomial.
   a. Thing
   c. Undefined
   b. Binomial0
   d. Undefined

83. In Euclidean geometry, an _____ is a closed segment of a differentiable curve in the two-dimensional plane; for example, a circular _____ is a segment of a circle.
   a. Arc0
   c. Undefined
   b. Concept
   d. Undefined

84. _____ is a trigonemtric function that is important when studying triangles and modeling periodic phenomena, among other applications.
   a. Thing
   c. Undefined
   b. Sine0
   d. Undefined

85. In trigonometry, the _____ is a function defined as $\tan x = \sin x / \cos x$. The function is so-named because it can be defined as the length of a certain segment of a _____ (in the geometric sense) to the unit circle. In plane geometry, a line is _____ to a curve, at some point, if both line and curve pass through the point with the same direction.

Chapter 8. Techniques of Integration

    a. Tangent0
    b. Thing
    c. Undefined
    d. Undefined

86. _____ is a trigonometric function that is the reciprocal of cosine.
    a. Secant0
    b. Thing
    c. Undefined
    d. Undefined

87. A _____ is a symbolic representation denoting a quantity or expression. It often represents an "unknown" quantity that has the potential to change.
    a. Variable0
    b. Thing
    c. Undefined
    d. Undefined

88. In mathematics, the _____ (or modulus) of a real number is its numerical value without regard to its sign.
    a. Absolute value0
    b. Thing
    c. Undefined
    d. Undefined

89. A _____ is a quantity that denotes the proportional amount or magnitude of one quantity relative to another.
    a. Thing
    b. Ratio0
    c. Undefined
    d. Undefined

90. _____ is the symbol used to indicate the nth root of a number
    a. Thing
    b. Radical0
    c. Undefined
    d. Undefined

91. The _____ is the number or expression underneath the radical sign.
    a. Radicand0
    b. Thing
    c. Undefined
    d. Undefined

92. The _____ are functions of an angle; they are important when studying triangles and modeling periodic phenomena, among many other applications.
    a. Thing
    b. Trigonometric functions0
    c. Undefined
    d. Undefined

93. _____ is a means of calculating the volume of a solid of revolution, when integrating along the axis of revolution. This method models the generated 3 dimensional shape as a "stack" of an infinite number of disks of infinitesimal thickness.
    a. Thing
    b. Disk method0
    c. Undefined
    d. Undefined

94. _____ algebra (sometimes called General algebra) is the field of mathematics that studies the ideas common to all algebraic structures.
    a. Universal0
    b. Thing
    c. Undefined
    d. Undefined

95. _____ of an object is its speed in a particular direction.

Chapter 8. Techniques of Integration

    a. Velocity0
    b. Thing
    c. Undefined
    d. Undefined

96. In physics, the _____ momentum of an object rotating about some reference point is the measure of the extent to which the object will continue to rotate about that point unless acted upon by an external torque.
    a. Angular0
    b. Thing
    c. Undefined
    d. Undefined

97. In physics, the _____ is a vector quantity (more precisely, a pseudovector) which specifies the angular speed at which an object is rotating along with the direction in which it is rotating.
    a. Thing
    b. Angular velocity0
    c. Undefined
    d. Undefined

98. A _____ is a number that is less than zero.
    a. Thing
    b. Negative number0
    c. Undefined
    d. Undefined

99. In mathematics, _____ refers to the rewriting of an expression into a simpler form.
    a. Reduction0
    b. Thing
    c. Undefined
    d. Undefined

100. In combinatorial mathematics, a _____ is an un-ordered collection of unique elements.
    a. Concept
    b. Combination0
    c. Undefined
    d. Undefined

101. In mathematics, a set is called _____ if there is a bijection between the set and some set of the form {1, 2, ..., n} where n is a natural number.
    a. Thing
    b. Finite0
    c. Undefined
    d. Undefined

102. A _____ function is a function for which, intuitively, small changes in the input result in small changes in the output.
    a. Event
    b. Continuous0
    c. Undefined
    d. Undefined

103. _____, in economics and political economy, are the distributions or payments awarded to the various suppliers of the factors of production.
    a. Thing
    b. Returns0
    c. Undefined
    d. Undefined

104. _____ is a list of goods and materials, or those goods and materials themselves, held available in stock by a business
    a. Thing
    b. Inventory0
    c. Undefined
    d. Undefined

105. _____ is a synonym for information.

a. Thing
b. Data0
c. Undefined
d. Undefined

106. _____ is the estimation of a physical quantity such as distance, energy, temperature, or time.
a. Measurement0
b. Thing
c. Undefined
d. Undefined

107. Mathematical _____ is used to represent ideas.
a. Thing
b. Notation0
c. Undefined
d. Undefined

108. _____ is the state of being greater than any finite real or natural number, however large.
a. Infinite0
b. Thing
c. Undefined
d. Undefined

109. An _____ is the limit of a definite integral, as an endpoint of the interval of integration approaches either a specified real number or ‡ or − ‡ or, in some cases, as both endpoints approach limits.
a. Improper integral0
b. Thing
c. Undefined
d. Undefined

110. _____ denotes the approach toward a definite value, as time goes on; or to a definite point, a common view or opinion, or toward a fixed or equilibrium state.
a. Convergence0
b. Thing
c. Undefined
d. Undefined

111. In mathematics, a _____ series is an infinite series that is not convergent, meaning that the infinite sequence of the partial sums of the series does not have a limit.
a. Divergent0
b. Thing
c. Undefined
d. Undefined

112. In geometry, a _____ is the intersection of a body in 2-dimensional space with a line, or of a body in 3-dimensional space with a plane
a. Cross section0
b. Thing
c. Undefined
d. Undefined

113. In geometry, two lines or planes if one falls on the other in such a way as to create congruent adjacent angles. The term may be used as a noun or adjective. Thus, referring to Figure 1, the line AB is the _____ to CD through the point B.
a. Perpendicular0
b. Thing
c. Undefined
d. Undefined

114. In geometry, a _____ (Greek words diairo = divide and metro = measure) of a circle is any straight line segment that passes through the centre and whose endpoints are on the circular boundary, or, in more modern usage, the length of such a line segment. When using the word in the more modern sense, one speaks of the _____ rather than a _____, because all diameters of a circle have the same length. This length is twice the radius. The _____ of a circle is also the longest chord that the circle has.

Chapter 8. Techniques of Integration

    a. Diameter0
    b. Thing
    c. Undefined
    d. Undefined

115. In mathematics, a _____ of a number x is the exponent y of the power by such that $x = b^y$. The value used for the base b must be neither 0 nor 1, nor a root of 1 in the case of the extension to complex numbers, and is typically 10, e, or 2.
    a. Thing
    b. Logarithm0
    c. Undefined
    d. Undefined

116. In calculus and other branches of mathematical analysis, an _____ is an algebraic expression obtained in the context of limits.
    a. Indeterminate form0
    b. Thing
    c. Undefined
    d. Undefined

117. _____ is electromagnetic radiation with a wavelength that is visible to the eye (visible _____) or, in a technical or scientific context, electromagnetic radiation of any wavelength.
    a. Thing
    b. Light0
    c. Undefined
    d. Undefined

118. In mathematics, _____ are the intuitive idea of a geometrical one-dimensional and continuous object.
    a. Thing
    b. Curves0
    c. Undefined
    d. Undefined

119. A _____ is 360° or 2δ radians.
    a. Thing
    b. Turn0
    c. Undefined
    d. Undefined

120. Acid _____ ratio measures the ability of a company to use its near cash or quick assets to immediately extinguish its current liabilities.
    a. Thing
    b. Test0
    c. Undefined
    d. Undefined

121. _____ is an operator that measures the magnitude of a vector field's source or sink at a given point; the _____ of a vector field is a signed scalar.
    a. Thing
    b. Divergence0
    c. Undefined
    d. Undefined

122. _____ is a criterion for convergence or divergence of a series whose terms are real or complex numbers.
    a. Comparison test0
    b. Thing
    c. Undefined
    d. Undefined

123. In mathematics and logic, a _____ proof is a way of showing the truth or falsehood of a given statement by a straightforward combination of established facts, usually existing lemmas and theorems, without making any further assumptions.
    a. Direct0
    b. Thing
    c. Undefined
    d. Undefined

Chapter 8. Techniques of Integration

124. In mathematics, _____ describes an entity with a limit.
    a. Convergent0
    b. Thing
    c. Undefined
    d. Undefined

125. In mathematics, a _____ may be described informally as a number that can be given by an infinite decimal representation.
    a. Thing
    b. Real number0
    c. Undefined
    d. Undefined

126. _____ is the chance that something is likely to happen or be the case.
    a. Thing
    b. Probability0
    c. Undefined
    d. Undefined

127. _____ is a mathematical science pertaining to the collection, analysis, interpretation or explanation, and presentation of data. It is applicable to a wide variety of academic disciplines, from the physical and social sciences to the humanities.
    a. Statistics0
    b. Thing
    c. Undefined
    d. Undefined

128. In mathematics, the _____ also called the Gauss _____ is a non-elementary function which occurs in probability, statistics and partial differential equations.
    a. Error function0
    b. Thing
    c. Undefined
    d. Undefined

129. In mathematics a _____ is a function which defines a distance between elements of a set.
    a. Thing
    b. Metric0
    c. Undefined
    d. Undefined

130. In mathematics, a _____ is a two-dimensional manifold or surface that is perfectly flat.
    a. Plane0
    b. Thing
    c. Undefined
    d. Undefined

131. An _____, also called a minor planet or planetoid, comes from a class of atsronomical objects.
    a. Asteroid0
    b. Thing
    c. Undefined
    d. Undefined

132. _____ is a particular type of curve: a hypocycloid with four cusps.
    a. Thing
    b. Astroid0
    c. Undefined
    d. Undefined

133. In mathematics, the _____ of a coordinate system is the point where the axes of the system intersect.
    a. Origin0
    b. Thing
    c. Undefined
    d. Undefined

134. The _____ integers are all the integers from zero on upwards.

a. Thing
b. Nonnegative0
c. Undefined
d. Undefined

135. Leonhard _____ was a pioneering Swiss mathematician and physicist, who spent most of his life in Russia and Germany.
a. Euler0
b. Person
c. Undefined
d. Undefined

136. _____ of a non-negative integer n is the product of all positive integers less than or equal to n.
a. Factorial0
b. Thing
c. Undefined
d. Undefined

137. The _____ are the only integral domain whose positive elements are well-ordered, and in which order is preserved by addition. Like the natural numbers, the _____ form a countably infinite set. The set of all _____ is usually denoted in mathematics by a boldface Z .
a. Integers0
b. Thing
c. Undefined
d. Undefined

138. _____ is a method of mathematical proof typically used to establish that a given statement is true of all natural numbers
a. Thing
b. Mathematical induction0
c. Undefined
d. Undefined

Chapter 9. Infinite Series

1. A _____ is the sum of the elements of a sequence.
   a. Series0
   b. Thing
   c. Undefined
   d. Undefined

2. _____ is the state of being greater than any finite real or natural number, however large.
   a. Thing
   b. Infinite0
   c. Undefined
   d. Undefined

3. In mathematics, a _____ is an expression that is constructed from one or more variables and constants, using only the operations of addition, subtraction, multiplication, and constant positive whole number exponents. is a _____. Note in particular that division by an expression containing a variable is not in general allowed in polynomials. [1]
   a. Polynomial0
   b. Thing
   c. Undefined
   d. Undefined

4. _____ has many meanings, most of which simply .
   a. Power0
   b. Thing
   c. Undefined
   d. Undefined

5. _____ in one variable is an infinite series of the form
   a. Power series0
   b. Thing
   c. Undefined
   d. Undefined

6. The _____ is a measurement of how a function changes when the values of its inputs change.
   a. Thing
   b. Derivative0
   c. Undefined
   d. Undefined

7. The mathematical concept of a _____ expresses the intuitive idea of deterministic dependence between two quantities, one of which is viewed as primary and the other as secondary. A _____ then is a way to associate a unique output for each input of a specified type, for example, a real number or an element of a given set.
   a. Thing
   b. Function0
   c. Undefined
   d. Undefined

8. A _____ of a number is the product of that number with any integer.
   a. Thing
   b. Multiple0
   c. Undefined
   d. Undefined

9. Mathematical _____ is used to represent ideas.
   a. Thing
   b. Notation0
   c. Undefined
   d. Undefined

10. In mathematics, the _____ of a function is the set of all "output" values produced by that function. Given a function $f : A \to B$, the _____ of f, is defined to be the set $\{x \in B : x = f(a) \text{ for some } a \in A\}$.
    a. Range0
    b. Thing
    c. Undefined
    d. Undefined

11. In mathematics, a _____ of a k-place relation $L \subseteq X_1 \times ... \times X_k$ is one of the sets X_j, $1 \leq j \leq k$. In the special case where k = 2 and $L \subseteq X_1 \times X_2$ is a function $L : X_1 \to X_2$, it is conventional to refer to X_1 as the _____ of the function and to refer to X_2 as the codomain of the function.
   a. Thing
   b. Domain0
   c. Undefined
   d. Undefined

12. In mathematics, a _____ is an ordered list of objects. Like a set, it contains members, also called elements or terms, and the number of terms is called the length of the _____. Unlike a set, order matters, and the exact same elements can appear multiple times at different positions in the _____.
   a. Sequence0
   b. Thing
   c. Undefined
   d. Undefined

13. In mathematics, an inequality is a statement about the relative size or order of two objects. For example 14 > 10, or 14 is _____ 10.
   a. Greater than0
   b. Thing
   c. Undefined
   d. Undefined

14. The _____ are the only integral domain whose positive elements are well-ordered, and in which order is preserved by addition. Like the natural numbers, the _____ form a countably infinite set. The set of all _____ is usually denoted in mathematics by a boldface Z.
   a. Integers0
   b. Thing
   c. Undefined
   d. Undefined

15. _____ is often represented as the sum of a sequence of terms.
   a. Thing
   b. Infinite series0
   c. Undefined
   d. Undefined

16. A _____ is a symbolic representation denoting a quantity or expression. It often represents an "unknown" quantity that has the potential to change.
   a. Variable0
   b. Thing
   c. Undefined
   d. Undefined

17. In mathematics, an _____ is any of the arguments, i.e. "inputs", to a function. Thus if we have a function f(x), then x is a _____.
   a. Thing
   b. Independent variable0
   c. Undefined
   d. Undefined

18. In statistics, a _____ measure is one which is measuring what is supposed to measure.
   a. Valid0
   b. Thing
   c. Undefined
   d. Undefined

19. The word _____ is used in a variety of ways in mathematics.
   a. Thing
   b. Index0
   c. Undefined
   d. Undefined

Chapter 9. Infinite Series

20. A _____ is a number, figure, or indicator that appears below the normal line of type, typically used in a formula, mathematical expression, or description of a chemical compound.
    a. Subscript0
    b. Thing
    c. Undefined
    d. Undefined

21. A _____ is a set of numbers that designate location in a given reference system, such as x,y in a planar _____ system or an x,y,z in a three-dimensional _____ system.
    a. Coordinate0
    b. Thing
    c. Undefined
    d. Undefined

22. An _____ is a straight line around which a geometric figure can be rotated.
    a. Thing
    b. Axis0
    c. Undefined
    d. Undefined

23. In mathematics, a _____ is a two-dimensional manifold or surface that is perfectly flat.
    a. Plane0
    b. Thing
    c. Undefined
    d. Undefined

24. In mathematics and the mathematical sciences, a _____ is a fixed, but possibly unspecified, value. This is in contrast to a variable, which is not fixed.
    a. Thing
    b. Constant0
    c. Undefined
    d. Undefined

25. _____ denotes the approach toward a definite value, as time goes on; or to a definite point, a common view or opinion, or toward a fixed or equilibrium state.
    a. Thing
    b. Convergence0
    c. Undefined
    d. Undefined

26. _____ is an operator that measures the magnitude of a vector field's source or sink at a given point; the _____ of a vector field is a signed scalar.
    a. Thing
    b. Divergence0
    c. Undefined
    d. Undefined

27. _____ Any process by which a specified characteristic usually amplitude of the output of a device is prevented from exceeding a predetermined value.
    a. Thing
    b. Limiting0
    c. Undefined
    d. Undefined

28. An _____ is a straight line or curve A to which another curve B approaches closer and closer as one moves along it. As one moves along B, the space between it and the _____ A becomes smaller and smaller, and can in fact be made as small as one could wish by going far enough along. A curve may or may not touch or cross its _____. In fact, the curve may intersect the _____ an infinite number of times.
    a. Asymptote0
    b. Thing
    c. Undefined
    d. Undefined

29. In astronomy, geography, geometry and related sciences and contexts, a plane is said to be _____ at a given point if it is locally perpendicular to the gradient of the gravity field, i.e., with the direction of the gravitational force at that point.
   a. Horizontal0
   b. Thing
   c. Undefined
   d. Undefined

30. In mathematics, a _____ may be described informally as a number that can be given by an infinite decimal representation.
   a. Thing
   b. Real number0
   c. Undefined
   d. Undefined

31. _____ is the state of being greater than any finite number, however large.
   a. Infinity0
   b. Thing
   c. Undefined
   d. Undefined

32. The _____, the average in everyday English, which is also called the arithmetic _____ (and is distinguished from the geometric _____ or harmonic _____). The average is also called the sample _____. The expected value of a random variable, which is also called the population _____.
   a. Thing
   b. Mean0
   c. Undefined
   d. Undefined

33. In mathematics, when a method of defining functions is utilized, in which the function being defined is applied within its own definition, that pertaining function is called _____.
   a. Thing
   b. Recursive0
   c. Undefined
   d. Undefined

34. Initial objects are also called _____, and terminal objects are also called final.
   a. Coterminal0
   b. Thing
   c. Undefined
   d. Undefined

35. _____ is a method of defining functions in which the function being defined is applied within its own definition. The term is also used more generally to describe a process of repeating objects in a self-similar way.
   a. Thing
   b. Recursion0
   c. Undefined
   d. Undefined

36. In mathematics, the factorial of a non-negative integer n is the product of all positive integers less than or equal to n. This is written as n! and pronounced _____, or colloquially "n shriek", "n bang" or "n crit".
   a. Thing
   b. N factorial0
   c. Undefined
   d. Undefined

37. In mathematics, a _____ is the result of multiplying, or an expression that identifies factors to be multiplied.
   a. Product0
   b. Thing
   c. Undefined
   d. Undefined

38. In common philosophical language, a proposition or _____, is the content of an assertion, that is, it is true-or-false and defined by the meaning of a particular piece of language.

Chapter 9. Infinite Series

a. Concept
b. Statement0
c. Undefined
d. Undefined

39. _____ of a non-negative integer n is the product of all positive integers less than or equal to n.
    a. Factorial0
    b. Thing
    c. Undefined
    d. Undefined

40. In mathematics, a _____ number (or a _____) is a natural number that has exactly two (distinct) natural number divisors, which are 1 and the _____ number itself.
    a. Thing
    b. Prime0
    c. Undefined
    d. Undefined

41. In mathematical analysis and related areas of mathematics, a set is called _____, if it is, in a certain sense, of finite size.
    a. Thing
    b. Bounded0
    c. Undefined
    d. Undefined

42. In mathematics, a _____ can mean either an element of the set {1, 2, 3, ...} (i.e the positive integers or the counting numbers) or an element of the set {0, 1, 2, 3, ...} (i.e. the non-negative integers).
    a. Natural number0
    b. Thing
    c. Undefined
    d. Undefined

43. In mathematics, a set is called _____ if there is a bijection between the set and some set of the form {1, 2, ..., n} where n is a natural number.
    a. Thing
    b. Finite0
    c. Undefined
    d. Undefined

44. In mathematics, especially in order theory, an _____ of a subset S of some partially ordered set is an element of P which is greater than or equal to every element of S.
    a. Thing
    b. Upper bound0
    c. Undefined
    d. Undefined

45. In mathematics, a _____ is a statement that can be proved on the basis of explicitly stated or previously agreed assumptions.
    a. Thing
    b. Theorem0
    c. Undefined
    d. Undefined

46. Sir Isaac _____, was an English physicist, mathematician, astronomer, natural philosopher, and alchemist, regarded by many as the greatest figure in the history of science
    a. Person
    b. Newton0
    c. Undefined
    d. Undefined

47. In mathematics, an _____, mean, or central tendency of a data set refers to a measure of the "middle" or "expected" value of the data set.

a. Average0
b. Concept
c. Undefined
d. Undefined

48. A _____ is a special kind of ratio, indicating a relationship between two measurements with different units, such as miles to gallons or cents to pounds.
   a. Thing
   b. Rate0
   c. Undefined
   d. Undefined

49. In a mathematical proof or a syllogism, a _____ is a statement that is the logical consequence of preceding statements.
   a. Concept
   b. Conclusion0
   c. Undefined
   d. Undefined

50. In mathematics, _____ describes an entity with a limit.
   a. Thing
   b. Convergent0
   c. Undefined
   d. Undefined

51. _____ is the fee paid on borrowed money.
   a. Thing
   b. Interest0
   c. Undefined
   d. Undefined

52. _____ interest refers to the fact that whenever interest is calculated, it is based not only on the original principal, but also on any unpaid interest that has been added to the principal.
   a. Thing
   b. Compound0
   c. Undefined
   d. Undefined

53. _____ refers to the fact that whenever interest is calculated, it is based not only on the original principal, but also on any unpaid interest that has been added to the principal. The more frequently interest is compounded, the faster the balance grows.
   a. Compound interest0
   b. Concept
   c. Undefined
   d. Undefined

54. In business, particularly accounting, a _____ is the time intervals that the accounts, statement, payments, or other calculations cover.
   a. Period0
   b. Thing
   c. Undefined
   d. Undefined

55. _____ is a kind of property which exists as magnitude or multitude. It is among the basic classes of things along with quality, substance, change, and relation.
   a. Thing
   b. Amount0
   c. Undefined
   d. Undefined

56. An _____ is the fee paid on borrow money.
   a. Concept
   b. Interest rate0
   c. Undefined
   d. Undefined

Chapter 9. Infinite Series

57. In elementary algebra, an _____ is a set that contains every real number between two indicated numbers and may contain the two numbers themselves.
 a. Interval0
 b. Thing
 c. Undefined
 d. Undefined

58. In calculus, the _____ is a theorem regarding the limit of a function. The theorem asserts that if two functions approach the same limit at a point, and if a third function is "squeezed" between those functions, then the third function also approaches that limit at that point.
 a. Squeeze Theorem0
 b. Thing
 c. Undefined
 d. Undefined

59. A _____ function is a function for which, intuitively, small changes in the input result in small changes in the output.
 a. Continuous0
 b. Event
 c. Undefined
 d. Undefined

60. In plane geometry, a _____ is a polygon with four equal sides, four right angles, and parallel opposite sides. In algebra, the _____ of a number is that number multiplied by itself.
 a. Square0
 b. Thing
 c. Undefined
 d. Undefined

61. In mathematics, a _____ of a number x is a number r such that r^2 = x, or in words, a number r whose square (the result of multiplying the number by itself) is x.
 a. Thing
 b. Square root0
 c. Undefined
 d. Undefined

62. In mathematics, a _____ of a complex-valued function f is a member x of the domain of f such that f(x) vanishes at x, that is, x : f (x) = 0.
 a. Thing
 b. Root0
 c. Undefined
 d. Undefined

63. _____ is the logarithm to the base e, where e is an irrational constant approximately equal to 2.718281828459.
 a. Natural logarithm0
 b. Thing
 c. Undefined
 d. Undefined

64. Equivalence is the condition of being _____ or essentially equal.
 a. Thing
 b. Equivalent0
 c. Undefined
 d. Undefined

65. In mathematics, a _____ of a number x is the exponent y of the power by such that x = b^y. The value used for the base b must be neither 0 nor 1, nor a root of 1 in the case of the extension to complex numbers, and is typically 10, e, or 2.
 a. Thing
 b. Logarithm0
 c. Undefined
 d. Undefined

66. In calculus and other branches of mathematical analysis, an _____ is an algebraic expression obtained in the context of limits.

Chapter 9. Infinite Series

a. Thing
b. Indeterminate form0
c. Undefined
d. Undefined

67. The easiest _____ prime numbers resides in the use of the Sieve of Eratosthenes, an algorithm that discovers all prime numbers to a specified integer.
a. Method for finding0
b. Thing
c. Undefined
d. Undefined

68. The _____ of a mathematical object is its size: a property by which it can be larger or smaller than other objects of the same kind; in technical terms, an ordering of the class of objects to which it belongs.
a. Thing
b. Magnitude0
c. Undefined
d. Undefined

69. The _____ of an angle is the ratio of the length of the adjacent side to the length of the hypotenuse.
a. Concept
b. Cosine0
c. Undefined
d. Undefined

70. The _____ is a unit of plane angle. It is represented by the symbol "rad" or, more rarely, by the superscript c (for "circular measure"). For example, an angle of 1.2 radians would be written "1.2 rad" or "1.2c" (second symbol can produce confusion with centigrads).
a. Thing
b. Radian0
c. Undefined
d. Undefined

71. In statistics, _____ means the most frequent value assumed by a random variable, or occurring in a sampling of a random variable.
a. Concept
b. Mode0
c. Undefined
d. Undefined

72. In mathematics, a _____ are a curve which emanates from a central point, getting progressively farther away as it revolves around the point.
a. Thing
b. Spirals0
c. Undefined
d. Undefined

73. In mathematics, a _____ series is an infinite series that is not convergent, meaning that the infinite sequence of the partial sums of the series does not have a limit.
a. Thing
b. Divergent0
c. Undefined
d. Undefined

74. _____ is often used to describe the measurement of the steepness, incline, gradient, or grade of a straight line. The _____ is defined as the ratio of the "rise" divided by the "run" between two points on a line, or in other words, the ratio of the altitude change to the horizontal distance between any two points on the line.
a. Thing
b. Slope0
c. Undefined
d. Undefined

75. A _____ is a numeral used to indicate a count. The most common use of the word today is to name the part of a fraction that tells the number or count of equal parts.

Chapter 9. Infinite Series

　　a. Numerator0　　　　　　　　　　　　　　b. Thing
　　c. Undefined　　　　　　　　　　　　　　　d. Undefined

76. A _____ is the part of a fraction that tells how many equal parts make up a whole, and which is used in the name of the fraction: "halves", "thirds", "fourths" or "quarters", "fifths" and so on.
　　a. Concept　　　　　　　　　　　　　　　　b. Denominator0
　　c. Undefined　　　　　　　　　　　　　　　d. Undefined

77. _____ element of an element x with respect to a binary operation * with identity element e is an element y such that x * y = y * x = e. In particular,
　　a. Thing　　　　　　　　　　　　　　　　　b. Inverse0
　　c. Undefined　　　　　　　　　　　　　　　d. Undefined

78. _____ are the basic objects of study in graph theory. Informally speaking, a graph is a set of objects called points, nodes, or vertices connected by links called lines or edges.
　　a. Thing　　　　　　　　　　　　　　　　　b. Graphs0
　　c. Undefined　　　　　　　　　　　　　　　d. Undefined

79. A _____ is the result of the addition of a set of numbers. The numbers may be natural numbers, complex numbers, matrices, or still more complicated objects. An infinite _____ is a subtle procedure known as a series.
　　a. Sum0　　　　　　　　　　　　　　　　　b. Thing
　　c. Undefined　　　　　　　　　　　　　　　d. Undefined

80. An _____ is a combination of numbers, operators, grouping symbols and/or free variables and bound variables arranged in a meaningful way which can be evaluated..
　　a. Expression0　　　　　　　　　　　　　　b. Thing
　　c. Undefined　　　　　　　　　　　　　　　d. Undefined

81. The metre (or _____, see spelling differences) is a measure of length. It is the basic unit of length in the metric system and in the International System of Units (SI), used around the world for general and scientific purposes.
　　a. Concept　　　　　　　　　　　　　　　　b. Meter0
　　c. Undefined　　　　　　　　　　　　　　　d. Undefined

82. _____ is the transport of people on a trip/journey or the process or time involved in a person or object moving from one location to another.
　　a. Thing　　　　　　　　　　　　　　　　　b. Travel0
　　c. Undefined　　　　　　　　　　　　　　　d. Undefined

83. A _____ is a quantity that denotes the proportional amount or magnitude of one quantity relative to another.
　　a. Ratio0　　　　　　　　　　　　　　　　　b. Thing
　　c. Undefined　　　　　　　　　　　　　　　d. Undefined

84. A _____ decimal is a number whose decimal representation eventually becomes periodic (i.e. the same number sequence _____ indefinitely).

a. Thing
b. Repeating0
c. Undefined
d. Undefined

85. Recurring or _____ are numbers which when expressed as decimals have a set of "final" digits which repeat an infinite number of times.
a. Thing
b. Repeating decimals0
c. Undefined
d. Undefined

86. _____ is a process of combining or accumulating. It may also refer to:
a. Integration0
b. Thing
c. Undefined
d. Undefined

87. In algebra, the _____ decomposition or _____ expansion is used to reduce the degree of either the numerator or the denominator of a rational function.
a. Thing
b. Partial fraction0
c. Undefined
d. Undefined

88. In mathematics, the additive inverse, or _____ of a number n is the number that, when added to n, yields zero. The additive inverse of n is denoted −n. For example, 7 is −7, because 7 + (−7) = 0, and the additive inverse of −0.3 is 0.3, because −0.3 + 0.3 = 0.
a. Opposite0
b. Thing
c. Undefined
d. Undefined

89. _____, either of the curved-bracket punctuation marks that together make a set of _____
a. Thing
b. Parentheses0
c. Undefined
d. Undefined

90. In mathematics, the _____ of a number n is the number that, when added to n, yields zero. The _____ of n is denoted −n. For example, 7 is −7, because 7 + (−7) = 0, and the _____ of −0.3 is 0.3, because −0.3 + 0.3 = 0.
a. Thing
b. Additive inverse0
c. Undefined
d. Undefined

91. _____ is an infinite series that is not convergent, meaning that the infinite sequence of the partial sums of the series does not have a limit.
a. Thing
b. Divergent series0
c. Undefined
d. Undefined

92. Acid _____ ratio measures the ability of a company to use its near cash or quick assets to immediately extinguish its current liabilities.
a. Test0
b. Thing
c. Undefined
d. Undefined

93. In mathematics, a _____ is a demonstration that, assuming certain axioms, some statement is necessarily true.
a. Proof0
b. Thing
c. Undefined
d. Undefined

Chapter 9. Infinite Series

94. _____ a series is the sum of the terms of a sequence of numbers.
    a. Convergent series0
    b. Thing
    c. Undefined
    d. Undefined

95. In calculus, the _____ in differentiation is a method of finding the derivative of a function that is the sum of two other functions for which derivatives exist.
    a. Sum Rule0
    b. Thing
    c. Undefined
    d. Undefined

96. A _____ is a mathematical statement which follows easily from a previously proven statement, typically a mathematical theorem.
    a. Thing
    b. Corollary0
    c. Undefined
    d. Undefined

97. The _____ of measurement are a globally standardized and modernized form of the metric system.
    a. Thing
    b. Units0
    c. Undefined
    d. Undefined

98. _____ is the middle point of a line segment.
    a. Midpoint0
    b. Thing
    c. Undefined
    d. Undefined

99. In classical geometry, a _____ of a circle or sphere is any line segment from its center to its boundary. By extension, the _____ of a circle or sphere is the length of any such segment. The _____ is half the diameter. In science and engineering the term _____ of curvature is commonly used as a synonym for _____.
    a. Radius0
    b. Thing
    c. Undefined
    d. Undefined

100. In mathematics, the concept of a _____ tries to capture the intuitive idea of a geometrical one-dimensional and continuous object. A simple example is the circle.
    a. Thing
    b. Curve0
    c. Undefined
    d. Undefined

101. The _____ integers are all the integers from zero on upwards.
    a. Nonnegative0
    b. Thing
    c. Undefined
    d. Undefined

102. In acoustics and telecommunication, the _____ of a wave is a component frequency of the signal that is an integer multiple of the fundamental frequency.
    a. Thing
    b. Harmonic0
    c. Undefined
    d. Undefined

103. The _____ of a function is an extension of the concept of a sum, and are identified or found through the use of integration.

Chapter 9. Infinite Series

    a. Integral0
    c. Undefined
    b. Thing
    d. Undefined

104. _____ is a method used to test infinite series of non-negative terms for convergence.
    a. Thing
    c. Undefined
    b. Integral Test0
    d. Undefined

105. In geometry, a _____ is defined as a quadrilateral where all four of its angles are right angles.
    a. Thing
    c. Undefined
    b. Rectangle0
    d. Undefined

106. In mathematics, science including computer science, linguistics and engineering, an _____ is, generally speaking, an independent variable or input to a function.
    a. Argument0
    c. Undefined
    b. Thing
    d. Undefined

107. Nicole _____, also known as Nicolas _____, Nicholas _____, or Nicolas d'_____ was one of the most famous and influential philosophers of the later Middle Ages. He was an economist, mathematician, physicist, astronomer, philosopher, psychologist, and musicologist, a passionate theologian and Bishop of Lisieux, a competent translator, counselor of King Charles V of France, one of the principal founders and popularizers of modern sciences, and probably one of the most original thinkers of the 14th century.
    a. Oresme0
    c. Undefined
    b. Person
    d. Undefined

108. _____ was a Greek philosopher, a student of Plato and teacher of Alexander the Great. He wrote on diverse subjects, including physics, metaphysics, poetry, biology and zoology, logic, rhetoric, politics, government, and ethics.
    a. Aristotle0
    c. Undefined
    b. Person
    d. Undefined

109. _____ was an Italian physicist, mathematician, astronomer, and philosopher who is closely associated with the scientific revolution.
    a. Person
    c. Undefined
    b. Galileo Galilei0
    d. Undefined

110. In mathematics, an _____ is a statement about the relative size or order of two objects.
    a. Thing
    c. Undefined
    b. Inequality0
    d. Undefined

111. In logic and mathematics, logical _____ is a logical relation that holds between a set T of formulas and a formula B when every model (or interpretation or valuation) of T is also a model of B.
    a. Concept
    c. Undefined
    b. Implication0
    d. Undefined

112. Leonhard _____ was a pioneering Swiss mathematician and physicist, who spent most of his life in Russia and Germany.

Chapter 9. Infinite Series

a. Euler0
b. Person
c. Undefined
d. Undefined

113. _____ is a criterion for convergence or divergence of a series whose terms are real or complex numbers.
   a. Comparison test0
   b. Thing
   c. Undefined
   d. Undefined

114. In mathematics and logic, a _____ proof is a way of showing the truth or falsehood of a given statement by a straightforward combination of established facts, usually existing lemmas and theorems, without making any further assumptions.
   a. Thing
   b. Direct0
   c. Undefined
   d. Undefined

115. _____ is a test or "criterion" for the convergence of a series
   a. Ratio Test0
   b. Thing
   c. Undefined
   d. Undefined

116. A _____ is a function that assigns a number to subsets of a given set.
   a. Thing
   b. Measure0
   c. Undefined
   d. Undefined

117. In mathematics, the _____ (or modulus) of a real number is its numerical value without regard to its sign.
   a. Thing
   b. Absolute value0
   c. Undefined
   d. Undefined

118. _____ is a natural number that has exactly two distinct natural number divisors, which are 1 and the _____ itself.
   a. Prime number0
   b. Thing
   c. Undefined
   d. Undefined

119. _____ is an infinite series of the form
   a. Alternating series0
   b. Thing
   c. Undefined
   d. Undefined

120. The material _____, also known as the material implication or truth functional _____, expresses a property of certain conditionals in logic.
   a. Conditional0
   b. Thing
   c. Undefined
   d. Undefined

121. In mathematics, the _____ of a coordinate system is the point where the axes of the system intersect.
   a. Thing
   b. Origin0
   c. Undefined
   d. Undefined

122. _____ consists either of a suggested explanation for a phenomenon or of a reasoned proposal suggesting a possible correlation between multiple phenomena.

Chapter 9. Infinite Series

    a. Event
    c. Undefined
    b. Hypotheses0
    d. Undefined

123. A _____ is the part of the dividend that is left over when the dividend is not evenly divisible by the divisor.
    a. Remainder0
    c. Undefined
    b. Thing
    d. Undefined

124. _____ or integral is said to converge absolutely if the sum or integral of the absolute value of the summand or integrand is finite.
    a. Thing
    c. Undefined
    b. Absolutely convergent series0
    d. Undefined

125. In mathematics, a series or integral is said to be _____ if the sum or integral of the absolute value of the summand or integrand is finite.
    a. Thing
    c. Undefined
    b. Absolute convergence0
    d. Undefined

126. _____ means in succession or back-to-back
    a. Thing
    c. Undefined
    b. Consecutive0
    d. Undefined

127. _____ is the calculated approximation of a result which is usable even if input data may be incomplete, uncertain, or noisy.
    a. Estimation0
    c. Undefined
    b. Concept
    d. Undefined

128. In geometry, the _____ of an object is a point in some sense in the middle of the object.
    a. Center0
    c. Undefined
    b. Thing
    d. Undefined

129. In mathematics, a _____ is a constant multiplicative factor of a certain object. The object can be such things as a variable, a vector, a function, etc. For example, the _____ of $9x^2$ is 9.
    a. Thing
    c. Undefined
    b. Coefficient0
    d. Undefined

130. In geometry, an _____ is a point at which a line segment or ray terminates.
    a. Thing
    c. Undefined
    b. Endpoint0
    d. Undefined

131. _____ is a mathematical subject that includes the study of limits, derivatives, integrals, and power series and constitutes a major part of modern university curriculum.
    a. Calculus0
    c. Undefined
    b. Thing
    d. Undefined

132. _____, a field in mathematics, is the study of how functions change when their inputs change. The primary object of study in _____ is the derivative.

Chapter 9. Infinite Series

a. Differential calculus0
c. Undefined
b. Thing
d. Undefined

133. An _____ of a function f is a function F whose derivative is equal to f, i.e., F' = f.
a. Thing
b. Antiderivative0
c. Undefined
d. Undefined

134. _____ constitutes a broad family of algorithms for calculating the numerical value of a definite integral, and by extension, the term is also sometimes used to describe the numerical solution of differential equations.
a. Thing
b. Numerical integration0
c. Undefined
d. Undefined

135. _____ is an extension of the concept of a sum.
a. Definite integral0
b. Thing
c. Undefined
d. Undefined

136. _____ is a branch of mathematics concerning the study of structure, relation and quantity.
a. Concept
b. Algebra0
c. Undefined
d. Undefined

137. In mathematics, _____ is an elementary arithmetic operation. When one of the numbers is a whole number, _____ is the repeated sum of the other number.
a. Thing
b. Multiplication0
c. Undefined
d. Undefined

138. In mathematics a _____ is a formal power series whose coefficients encode information about a sequence a_n that is indexed by the natural numbers.
a. Generating function0
b. Thing
c. Undefined
d. Undefined

139. Mathematical _____ are the wide variety of ways to capture an abstract mathematical concept or relationship.
a. Thing
b. Representations0
c. Undefined
d. Undefined

140. Colin _____ was a Scottish mathematician.
a. Maclaurin0
b. Person
c. Undefined
d. Undefined

141. In mathematics, there are several meanings of _____ depending on the subject.
a. Thing
b. Degree0
c. Undefined
d. Undefined

142. The word _____ comes from the Latin word linearis, which means created by lines.
a. Linear0
b. Thing
c. Undefined
d. Undefined

Chapter 9. Infinite Series

143. _____ is an approximation of a general function using a linear function more precisely, an affine function.
   a. Linear approximation0
   b. Thing
   c. Undefined
   d. Undefined

144. In mathematics and its applications, _____ refers to finding the linear approximation to a function at a given point.
   a. Linearization0
   b. Thing
   c. Undefined
   d. Undefined

145. In mathematics, the _____ is a representation of a function as an infinite sum of terms calculated from the values of its derivatives at a single point.
   a. Thing
   b. Taylor series0
   c. Undefined
   d. Undefined

146. _____ was an English mathematician. His is the name that is attached to Taylor's Theorem and the Taylor Series.
   a. Person
   b. Brook Taylor0
   c. Undefined
   d. Undefined

147. _____ was a Scottish mathematician and astronomer.
   a. Person
   b. James Gregory0
   c. Undefined
   d. Undefined

148. _____ are a set of equations containing multiple variables.
   a. Systems of equations0
   b. Thing
   c. Undefined
   d. Undefined

149. In the mathematical field of numerical analysis, the _____ in some data is the discrepancy between an exact value and some approximation to it.
   a. Approximation Error0
   b. Thing
   c. Undefined
   d. Undefined

150. In mathematics, _____ is the term used for reducing the number of digits right of the decimal point, by discarding the least significant ones.
   a. Truncation0
   b. Thing
   c. Undefined
   d. Undefined

151. _____ is a trigonemtric function that is important when studying triangles and modeling periodic phenomena, among other applications.
   a. Sine0
   b. Thing
   c. Undefined
   d. Undefined

152. In mathematics, the _____ of two sets A and B is the set that contains all elements of A that also belong to B (or equivalently, all elements of B that also belong to A), but no other elements.

Chapter 9. Infinite Series

a. Intersection0
b. Thing
c. Undefined
d. Undefined

153. _____ are objects, characters, or other concrete representations of ideas, concepts, or other abstractions.
   a. Thing
   b. Symbols0
   c. Undefined
   d. Undefined

154. An _____ is an equality that remains true regardless of the values of any variables that appear within it, to distinguish it from an equality which is true under more particular conditions.
   a. Identity0
   b. Thing
   c. Undefined
   d. Undefined

155. _____ is a a point on a curve at which the tangent crosses the curve itself.
   a. Thing
   b. Inflection point0
   c. Undefined
   d. Undefined

156. _____ determines whether a given stationary point of a function is a maximum or a minimum.
   a. Thing
   b. Second derivative test0
   c. Undefined
   d. Undefined

157. A real-valued function f defined on the real line is said to have a _____ point at the point x∗, if there exists some ε > 0, such that f when x − x∗ < ε.
   a. Thing
   b. Local maximum0
   c. Undefined
   d. Undefined

158. A _____ is a function that repeats its values after some definite period has been added to its independent variable.
   a. Thing
   b. Periodic function0
   c. Undefined
   d. Undefined

159. In mathematics, _____ are the intuitive idea of a geometrical one-dimensional and continuous object.
   a. Curves0
   b. Thing
   c. Undefined
   d. Undefined

160. In mathematics, a _____ is a number in the form of a + bi where a and b are real numbers, and i is the imaginary unit, with the property i 2 = −1. The real number a is called the real part of the _____, and the real number b is the imaginary part.
   a. Complex number0
   b. Thing
   c. Undefined
   d. Undefined

161. In calculus, the indefinite integral of a given function i.e. the set of all antiderivatives of the function is always written with a constant, the _____.
   a. Thing
   b. Constant of integration0
   c. Undefined
   d. Undefined

Chapter 9. Infinite Series

162. _____ generalizes the purely algebraic formula of the binomial theorem to complex values of "¢. It is also a special case of a Newton series.
   a. Binomial series0
   b. Thing
   c. Undefined
   d. Undefined

163. In elementary algebra, a _____ is a polynomial with two terms: the sum of two monomials. It is the simplest kind of polynomial except for a monomial.
   a. Binomial0
   b. Thing
   c. Undefined
   d. Undefined

164. _____ is a differential equation together with specified value, called the initial condition, of the unknown function at a given point in the domain of the solution.
   a. Thing
   b. Initial value problem0
   c. Undefined
   d. Undefined

165. In mathematics, in the field of differential equations, an initial value problem is a differential equation together with specified value, called the _____, of the unknown function at a given point in the domain of the solution.
   a. Thing
   b. Initial condition0
   c. Undefined
   d. Undefined

166. A _____ is traditionally an infinitesimally small change in a variable.
   a. Differential0
   b. Thing
   c. Undefined
   d. Undefined

167. A _____ is a mathematical equation for an unknown function of one or several variables which relates the values of the function itself and of its derivatives of various orders.
   a. Thing
   b. Differential equation0
   c. Undefined
   d. Undefined

168. A _____ is a negotiable instrument instructing a financial institution to pay a specific amount of a specific currency from a specific demand account held in the maker/depositor's name with that institution. Both the maker and payee may be natural persons or legal entities.
   a. Check0
   b. Thing
   c. Undefined
   d. Undefined

169. _____ is electromagnetic radiation with a wavelength that is visible to the eye (visible _____) or, in a technical or scientific context, electromagnetic radiation of any wavelength.
   a. Light0
   b. Thing
   c. Undefined
   d. Undefined

170. _____ the American term is a way to approximately calculate the definite integral
   a. Trapezoidal Rule0
   b. Thing
   c. Undefined
   d. Undefined

171. _____ is a function that extends the concept of an ordinary sum

Chapter 9. Infinite Series

a. Thing
b. Integrand0
c. Undefined
d. Undefined

172. John Brehaut _____ was born in Ashford, Kent, the third of five children.
a. Wallis0
b. Person
c. Undefined
d. Undefined

173. In trigonometry, the _____ is a function defined as $\tan x = \sin x / \cos x$. The function is so-named because it can be defined as the length of a certain segment of a _____ (in the geometric sense) to the unit circle. In plane geometry, a line is _____ to a curve, at some point, if both line and curve pass through the point with the same direction.
a. Thing
b. Tangent0
c. Undefined
d. Undefined

174. In mathematics, factorization (British English: factorisation) or factoring is the decomposition of an object (for example, a number, a polynomial, or a matrix) into a product of other objects, or _____, which when multiplied together give the original.
a. Factors0
b. Thing
c. Undefined
d. Undefined

175. A _____ is one of the basic shapes of geometry: a polygon with three vertices and three sides which are straight line segments.
a. Triangle0
b. Thing
c. Undefined
d. Undefined

176. In geometry, an _____ polygon is a polygon which has all sides of the same length.
a. Thing
b. Equilateral0
c. Undefined
d. Undefined

177. An _____ is a triangle in which all sides are of equal length.
a. Equilateral triangle0
b. Thing
c. Undefined
d. Undefined

178. _____ is the chance that something is likely to happen or be the case.
a. Thing
b. Probability0
c. Undefined
d. Undefined

179. In probability theory the _____ .
a. Expected value0
b. Thing
c. Undefined
d. Undefined

180. In mathematics, a _____ set is the complement of a meager set. A meager set is one which is the countable union of nowhere dense sets.
a. Thing
b. Residual0
c. Undefined
d. Undefined

Chapter 9. Infinite Series

181. In arithmetic, _____ is a procedure for calculating the division of one integer, called the dividend, by another integer called the divisor, to produce a result called the quotient.
   a. Long division0
   b. Thing
   c. Undefined
   d. Undefined

Chapter 10. Conic Sections, Parametrized Curves, and Polar Coordinates

1. A number that does not change in value in a given situation is a _____.
   - a. 15 theorem
   - b. Constant1
   - c. Undefined
   - d. Undefined

2. _____ is implied when data values are distributed in the same way above and below the middle of the sample.
   - a. Symmetry1
   - b. 15 theorem
   - c. Undefined
   - d. Undefined

3. The same statistical principles apply to the evaluation of observed _____ between sets of data. The field of statistics provides the necessary techniques for making statements of our certainty that there are real as opposed to chance differences.
   - a. 15 theorem
   - b. Differences1
   - c. Undefined
   - d. Undefined

4. A measure of variability, the _____ is the distance from the lowest to the highest score.
   - a. 15 theorem
   - b. Range1
   - c. Undefined
   - d. Undefined

5. In a large distribution of data it is often easier to understand the data if it is grouped into intervals where each _____ can contain more than one data value. Distributions are often reduced to 10 to 20 intervals.
   - a. Interval1
   - b. ACTRAN
   - c. Undefined
   - d. Undefined

6. A _____ is a scheme for the numerical representation of the values of a variable. The interpretation we place upon the numbers of the scale, rather than the numbers themselves, makes the _____ useful. The most common scales are nominal, ordinal, interval
   - a. 15 theorem
   - b. Scale1
   - c. Undefined
   - d. Undefined

7. There are properties of objects that do assume one and only value, and we refer to these characteristics as constants. _____, then, are the invariables that differentiate one class of objects from another.
   - a. Constants1
   - b. 15 theorem
   - c. Undefined
   - d. Undefined

8. The very fact that we are measuring objects with respect to some characteristic implies that the objects differ in that characteristic; or stated in another way, that the characteristic can take on a number of different values. These properties or characteristics of an object that can assume two or more different values are referred to as a _____.
   - a. Variable1
   - b. 15 theorem
   - c. Undefined
   - d. Undefined

9. Another word for independent variables in the analysis of variance is _____.
   - a. Factors1
   - b. 15 theorem
   - c. Undefined
   - d. Undefined

10. A _____ is a value used to represent a certain population characteristic. Because of the impracticality of measuring an entire population to determine this value, parameters are usually estimated.

a. Parameter1
b. 15 theorem
c. Undefined
d. Undefined

11. The number of times a particular score or observation occurs is its _____.
    a. Frequency1
    b. 15 theorem
    c. Undefined
    d. Undefined

12. At times we must contend with variables that assume a large number of values. In this case it is typical to create _____ of values of the variable and then make a frequency tally of the number of observations falling within each interval. As is the case with any data reduction technique, detail is lost.
    a. Intervals1
    b. ACTRAN
    c. Undefined
    d. Undefined

13. The _____ refers to the amount of change in Y for a 1 unit change in X; or in-other-words, the rate of change in the predicted value as a function of a change in the predictor variable.
    a. 15 theorem
    b. Slope1
    c. Undefined
    d. Undefined

14. _____, the height of the curve for a given value of X; closely related to the probability of an observation in an interval around X.
    a. Density1
    b. 15 theorem
    c. Undefined
    d. Undefined

15. In statistics an arrangement of values of a variable showing their observed or theoretical frequency of occurrence is called a _____.
    a. 15 theorem
    b. Distribution1
    c. Undefined
    d. Undefined

16. An _____ is an indication of the value of an unknown quantity based on observed data. More formally, an _____ is the particular value of an estimator that is obtained from a particular sample of data and used to indicate the value of a parameter.
    a. ACTRAN
    b. Estimate1
    c. Undefined
    d. Undefined

17. Horizontal axis of display containing the trailing digits is called _____.
    a. 15 theorem
    b. Leaves1
    c. Undefined
    d. Undefined

18. The _____ in inferential statistics is the variable whose values depend on the relative grouping or categories of the independent variable. A dependent variable, for example, can be scores on a test and the independent variable might have been students with groups male and female.
    a. 15 theorem
    b. Dependent variable1
    c. Undefined
    d. Undefined

Chapter 10. Conic Sections, Parametrized Curves, and Polar Coordinates 193

19. Since the observations in most data distributions tend to cluster heavily about certain values, one logical measure of central tendency would be that value which occurs most frequently; and that value is referred to as the _____ or modal value. For a nominal scale of measurement, the _____ is the best indicator of central tendency.
   a. 15 theorem
   b. Mode1
   c. Undefined
   d. Undefined

20. By _____ we mean collecting observations made upon our environment -- observations, which are the results of measurements using clocks, balances, measuring rods, counting operations, or other objectively defined measuring instruments or procedures. _____ may mean simply counting the number of times a particular property occurs.
   a. Data1
   b. 15 theorem
   c. Undefined
   d. Undefined

21. The _____ in a disttribution or in an interval is the least value.
   a. Lower limit1
   b. 15 theorem
   c. Undefined
   d. Undefined

22. _____ refer to any data source, whether individuals, physical or biological things, geographic locations, time periods, or events; that is, anything upon which observations can be made.
   a. ACTRAN
   b. Objects1
   c. Undefined
   d. Undefined

23. A measure of central tendency, the median, corresponds to the point having 50% of the observations below it when observations are arranged in numerical order. The _____ assumes at least an interval level of measurement. For a symmetric distribution such as the normal distribution, the _____ is the same as the mean. For a distribution which is skewed to the right, the _____ is typically smaller than the mean or when skewed to the left, the _____ is smaller.
   a. Median1
   b. 15 theorem
   c. Undefined
   d. Undefined

24. _____ is used synonymously for variable.
   a. Factor1
   b. 15 theorem
   c. Undefined
   d. Undefined

Chapter 11. Vectors and Analytic Geometry in Space

1. The very fact that we are measuring objects with respect to some characteristic implies that the objects differ in that characteristic; or stated in another way, that the characteristic can take on a number of different values. These properties or characteristics of an object that can assume two or more different values are referred to as a _____.
   - a. Variable1
   - b. 15 theorem
   - c. Undefined
   - d. Undefined

2. _____ are characteristics or properties of an object that can take on one or more different values.
   - a. 15 theorem
   - b. Variables1
   - c. Undefined
   - d. Undefined

3. Another word for independent variables in the analysis of variance is _____.
   - a. 15 theorem
   - b. Factors1
   - c. Undefined
   - d. Undefined

4. The _____ refers to the amount of change in Y for a 1 unit change in X; or in-other-words, the rate of change in the predicted value as a function of a change in the predictor variable.
   - a. Slope1
   - b. 15 theorem
   - c. Undefined
   - d. Undefined

5. The _____ is often confused with the median. The Median is a statistic for the distribution whereas the _____ provides a statistic for an interval; it is the center of the interval; the arithmetic average of the upper and lower limits.
   - a. 15 theorem
   - b. Midpoint1
   - c. Undefined
   - d. Undefined

6. A number that does not change in value in a given situation is a _____.
   - a. 15 theorem
   - b. Constant1
   - c. Undefined
   - d. Undefined

7. _____ refer to any data source, whether individuals, physical or biological things, geographic locations, time periods, or events; that is, anything upon which observations can be made.
   - a. ACTRAN
   - b. Objects1
   - c. Undefined
   - d. Undefined

8. At times we must contend with variables that assume a large number of values. In this case it is typical to create _____ of values of the variable and then make a frequency tally of the number of observations falling within each interval. As is the case with any data reduction technique, detail is lost.
   - a. ACTRAN
   - b. Intervals1
   - c. Undefined
   - d. Undefined

9. _____, the height of the curve for a given value of X; closely related to the probability of an observation in an interval around X.
   - a. Density1
   - b. 15 theorem
   - c. Undefined
   - d. Undefined

Chapter 11. Vectors and Analytic Geometry in Space

10. A measure of central tendency, the median, corresponds to the point having 50% of the observations below it when observations are arranged in numerical order. The _____ assumes at least an interval level of measurement. For a symmetric distribution such as the normal distribution, the _____ is the same as the mean. For a distribution which is skewed to the right, the _____ is typically smaller than the mean or when skewed to the left, the _____ is smaller.
    a. Median1
    b. 15 theorem
    c. Undefined
    d. Undefined

11. The same statistical principles apply to the evaluation of observed _____ between sets of data. The field of statistics provides the necessary techniques for making statements of our certainty that there are real as opposed to chance differences.
    a. 15 theorem
    b. Differences1
    c. Undefined
    d. Undefined

12. A _____ is a value used to represent a certain population characteristic. Because of the impracticality of measuring an entire population to determine this value, parameters are usually estimated.
    a. 15 theorem
    b. Parameter1
    c. Undefined
    d. Undefined

13. In a large distribution of data it is often easier to understand the data if it is grouped into intervals where each _____ can contain more than one data value. Distributions are often reduced to 10 to 20 intervals.
    a. ACTRAN
    b. Interval1
    c. Undefined
    d. Undefined

14. There are properties of objects that do assume one and only value, and we refer to these characteristics as constants. _____, then, are the invariables that differentiate one class of objects from another.
    a. Constants1
    b. 15 theorem
    c. Undefined
    d. Undefined

15. The value of Y when X is 0 is the _____.
    a. ACTRAN
    b. Intercept1
    c. Undefined
    d. Undefined

16. _____ is implied when data values are distributed in the same way above and below the middle of the sample.
    a. 15 theorem
    b. Symmetry1
    c. Undefined
    d. Undefined

17. A _____ is a scheme for the numerical representation of the values of a variable. The interpretation we place upon the numbers of the scale, rather than the numbers themselves, makes the _____ useful. The most common scales are nominal, ordinal, interval
    a. Scale1
    b. 15 theorem
    c. Undefined
    d. Undefined

18. The probability of correctly rejecting a false Ho is referred to as _____.
    a. 15 theorem
    b. Power1
    c. Undefined
    d. Undefined

Chapter 11. Vectors and Analytic Geometry in Space

19. An _____ is any process or study, which results in the collection of data, the outcome of which is unknown. In statistics, the term is usually restricted to situations in which the researcher has control over some of the conditions under which the _____ takes place.
   a. Experiment1
   b. ACTRAN
   c. Undefined
   d. Undefined

20. An _____ is an indication of the value of an unknown quantity based on observed data. More formally, an _____ is the particular value of an estimator that is obtained from a particular sample of data and used to indicate the value of a parameter.
   a. Estimate1
   b. ACTRAN
   c. Undefined
   d. Undefined

Chapter 12. Vector-Valued Functions and Motion in Space 197

1. In a large distribution of data it is often easier to understand the data if it is grouped into intervals where each _____ can contain more than one data value. Distributions are often reduced to 10 to 20 intervals.
   a. Interval1
   b. ACTRAN
   c. Undefined
   d. Undefined

2. The very fact that we are measuring objects with respect to some characteristic implies that the objects differ in that characteristic; or stated in another way, that the characteristic can take on a number of different values. These properties or characteristics of an object that can assume two or more different values are referred to as a _____.
   a. Variable1
   b. 15 theorem
   c. Undefined
   d. Undefined

3. At times we must contend with variables that assume a large number of values. In this case it is typical to create _____ of values of the variable and then make a frequency tally of the number of observations falling within each interval. As is the case with any data reduction technique, detail is lost.
   a. Intervals1
   b. ACTRAN
   c. Undefined
   d. Undefined

4. A number that does not change in value in a given situation is a _____.
   a. Constant1
   b. 15 theorem
   c. Undefined
   d. Undefined

5. Another word for independent variables in the analysis of variance is _____.
   a. 15 theorem
   b. Factors1
   c. Undefined
   d. Undefined

6. There are properties of objects that do assume one and only value, and we refer to these characteristics as constants. _____, then, are the invariables that differentiate one class of objects from another.
   a. 15 theorem
   b. Constants1
   c. Undefined
   d. Undefined

7. The same statistical principles apply to the evaluation of observed _____ between sets of data. The field of statistics provides the necessary techniques for making statements of our certainty that there are real as opposed to chance differences.
   a. 15 theorem
   b. Differences1
   c. Undefined
   d. Undefined

8. A _____ is a value used to represent a certain population characteristic. Because of the impracticality of measuring an entire population to determine this value, parameters are usually estimated.
   a. Parameter1
   b. 15 theorem
   c. Undefined
   d. Undefined

9. The most important measure of central tendency, and one of the basic building blocks of all statistical analysis, is the arithmetic _____. It is simply the sum of all the set of values divided by the number of values involved. As a measure of central tendency, it is affected by extreme scores, and it assumes a ratio scale of measurement.
   a. 15 theorem
   b. Mean1
   c. Undefined
   d. Undefined

10. A measure of variability, the _____ is the distance from the lowest to the highest score.
   a. Range1
   b. 15 theorem
   c. Undefined
   d. Undefined

11. A _____ is a scheme for the numerical representation of the values of a variable. The interpretation we place upon the numbers of the scale, rather than the numbers themselves, makes the _____ useful. The most common scales are nominal, ordinal, interval
   a. Scale1
   b. 15 theorem
   c. Undefined
   d. Undefined

12. Horizontal axis of display containing the trailing digits is called _____.
   a. Leaves1
   b. 15 theorem
   c. Undefined
   d. Undefined

13. _____ is implied when data values are distributed in the same way above and below the middle of the sample.
   a. 15 theorem
   b. Symmetry1
   c. Undefined
   d. Undefined

14. An _____ is any process or study, which results in the collection of data, the outcome of which is unknown. In statistics, the term is usually restricted to situations in which the researcher has control over some of the conditions under which the _____ takes place.
   a. Experiment1
   b. ACTRAN
   c. Undefined
   d. Undefined

15. _____ is used synonymously for variable.
   a. Factor1
   b. 15 theorem
   c. Undefined
   d. Undefined

16. The defining characteristics of populations are called _____. Observations must be made on every single member of the population in question in order to precisely state the value of _____.
   a. 15 theorem
   b. Parameters1
   c. Undefined
   d. Undefined

17. In a distribution of data or in an interval of data, the _____ is the greatest value.
   a. Upper limit1
   b. ACTRAN
   c. Undefined
   d. Undefined

18. An _____ is an indication of the value of an unknown quantity based on observed data. More formally, an _____ is the particular value of an estimator that is obtained from a particular sample of data and used to indicate the value of a parameter.
   a. ACTRAN
   b. Estimate1
   c. Undefined
   d. Undefined

19. By _____ we mean collecting observations made upon our environment -- observations, which are the results of measurements using clocks, balances, measuring rods, counting operations, or other objectively defined measuring instruments or procedures. _____ may mean simply counting the number of times a particular property occurs.

a. 15 theorem
b. Data1
c. Undefined
d. Undefined

20. Since the observations in most data distributions tend to cluster heavily about certain values, one logical measure of central tendency would be that value which occurs most frequently; and that value is referred to as the _____ or modal value. For a nominal scale of measurement, the _____ is the best indicator of central tendency.
   a. Mode1
   b. 15 theorem
   c. Undefined
   d. Undefined

Chapter 13. Multivariable Functions and Dervatives

1. _____ are those factors controlled by the experimenter.
   a. Independent variables1
   b. ACTRAN
   c. Undefined
   d. Undefined

2. _____ are characteristics or properties of an object that can take on one or more different values.
   a. 15 theorem
   b. Variables1
   c. Undefined
   d. Undefined

3. The very fact that we are measuring objects with respect to some characteristic implies that the objects differ in that characteristic; or stated in another way, that the characteristic can take on a number of different values. These properties or characteristics of an object that can assume two or more different values are referred to as a _____.
   a. 15 theorem
   b. Variable1
   c. Undefined
   d. Undefined

4. A _____ provides a quantitative description of the likely occurrence of a particular event. _____ is conventionally expressed on a scale from 0 to 1; a rare event has a _____ close to 0, a very common event has a _____ close to 1. _____ is calculated as the ratio of the number of favorable events to the total number of possible events.
   a. 15 theorem
   b. Probability1
   c. Undefined
   d. Undefined

5. Statistical analysis, sometimes referred to simply as _____, is concerned with the definition and collection, organization, and interpretation of data according to well-defined procedures. The term itself, _____, is a defining characteristic of a sample, such as a sample mean, or sample standard deviation.
   a. Statistics1
   b. 15 theorem
   c. Undefined
   d. Undefined

6. In inferential statistics where we are using a statistic to infer differences we need at least two different variables typically called an _____ and a dependent variable. The _____ represents the variable of interest, that is, the variable in which an inference is being made as to whether categories of that variable should be considered the same or different. There must be at least two categories or groupings for this variable in order to make comparisons. The variable is said to be independent since the categories are arbitrarily assigned by the investigator.
   a. ACTRAN
   b. Independent variable1
   c. Undefined
   d. Undefined

7. A measure of variability, the _____ is the distance from the lowest to the highest score.
   a. 15 theorem
   b. Range1
   c. Undefined
   d. Undefined

8. The _____ in inferential statistics is the variable whose values depend on the relative grouping or categories of the independent variable. A dependent variable, for example, can be scores on a test and the independent variable might have been students with groups male and female.
   a. Dependent variable1
   b. 15 theorem
   c. Undefined
   d. Undefined

Chapter 13. Multivariable Functions and Dervatives

9. At times we must contend with variables that assume a large number of values. In this case it is typical to create _____ of values of the variable and then make a frequency tally of the number of observations falling within each interval. As is the case with any data reduction technique, detail is lost.
   a. ACTRAN
   b. Intervals1
   c. Undefined
   d. Undefined

10. A number that does not change in value in a given situation is a _____.
    a. 15 theorem
    b. Constant1
    c. Undefined
    d. Undefined

11. By _____ we mean the cumulative frequency, counting in from the nearer end.
    a. Depth1
    b. 15 theorem
    c. Undefined
    d. Undefined

12. A _____ is a value used to represent a certain population characteristic. Because of the impracticality of measuring an entire population to determine this value, parameters are usually estimated.
    a. Parameter1
    b. 15 theorem
    c. Undefined
    d. Undefined

13. Since the observations in most data distributions tend to cluster heavily about certain values, one logical measure of central tendency would be that value which occurs most frequently; and that value is referred to as the _____ or modal value. For a nominal scale of measurement, the _____ is the best indicator of central tendency.
    a. Mode1
    b. 15 theorem
    c. Undefined
    d. Undefined

14. In a large distribution of data it is often easier to understand the data if it is grouped into intervals where each _____ can contain more than one data value. Distributions are often reduced to 10 to 20 intervals.
    a. Interval1
    b. ACTRAN
    c. Undefined
    d. Undefined

15. The same statistical principles apply to the evaluation of observed _____ between sets of data. The field of statistics provides the necessary techniques for making statements of our certainty that there are real as opposed to chance differences.
    a. 15 theorem
    b. Differences1
    c. Undefined
    d. Undefined

16. The probability of correctly rejecting a false Ho is referred to as _____.
    a. 15 theorem
    b. Power1
    c. Undefined
    d. Undefined

17. _____ is used synonymously for variable.
    a. Factor1
    b. 15 theorem
    c. Undefined
    d. Undefined

Chapter 13. Multivariable Functions and Partial Dervatives

18. The most important measure of central tendency, and one of the basic building blocks of all statistical analysis, is the arithmetic _____. It is simply the sum of all the set of values divided by the number of values involved. As a measure of central tendency, it is affected by extreme scores, and it assumes a ratio scale of measurement.
   a. 15 theorem
   b. Mean1
   c. Undefined
   d. Undefined

19. The _____ refers to the amount of change in Y for a 1 unit change in X; or in-other-words, the rate of change in the predicted value as a function of a change in the predictor variable.
   a. Slope1
   b. 15 theorem
   c. Undefined
   d. Undefined

20. There are properties of objects that do assume one and only value, and we refer to these characteristics as constants. _____, then, are the invariables that differentiate one class of objects from another.
   a. Constants1
   b. 15 theorem
   c. Undefined
   d. Undefined

21. _____ is implied when data values are distributed in the same way above and below the middle of the sample.
   a. 15 theorem
   b. Symmetry1
   c. Undefined
   d. Undefined

22. Vertical axis of display containing the leading digits is referred to as _____.
   a. Stem1
   b. 15 theorem
   c. Undefined
   d. Undefined

23. An _____ is an indication of the value of an unknown quantity based on observed data. More formally, an _____ is the particular value of an estimator that is obtained from a particular sample of data and used to indicate the value of a parameter.
   a. Estimate1
   b. ACTRAN
   c. Undefined
   d. Undefined

24. _____ is the result of assigning numbers to objects to abstractly represent the objects or characteristics of the objects.
   a. 15 theorem
   b. Measurement1
   c. Undefined
   d. Undefined

25. _____, the height of the curve for a given value of X; closely related to the probability of an observation in an interval around X.
   a. Density1
   b. 15 theorem
   c. Undefined
   d. Undefined

26. An _____ is the result of an experiment or other situation involving uncertainty.
   a. Outcome1
   b. ACTRAN
   c. Undefined
   d. Undefined

27. The defining characteristics of populations are called _____. Observations must be made on every single member of the population in question in order to precisely state the value of _____.

a. Parameters1
c. Undefined
b. 15 theorem
d. Undefined

28. The method of _____ is a criterion for fitting a specified model to observed data.
   a. Least Squares1
   b. 15 theorem
   c. Undefined
   d. Undefined

29. _____ describes the phenomenon where the values of distribution tend to move towards the summary statistic. For example, values in a distribution tend to cluster about the mean, and in a linear _____ equation, they tend to cluster about the linear _____ equation.
   a. 15 theorem
   b. Regression1
   c. Undefined
   d. Undefined

30. By _____ we mean collecting observations made upon our environment -- observations, which are the results of measurements using clocks, balances, measuring rods, counting operations, or other objectively defined measuring instruments or procedures. _____ may mean simply counting the number of times a particular property occurs.
   a. 15 theorem
   b. Data1
   c. Undefined
   d. Undefined

31. The 'line of best fit' that represents a straight line drawn through the data points is the _____. .
   a. 15 theorem
   b. Regression line1
   c. Undefined
   d. Undefined

32. The number of times a particular score or observation occurs is its _____.
   a. Frequency1
   b. 15 theorem
   c. Undefined
   d. Undefined

33. A statistic calculated by multiplying the data values together and taking the N-th root of the result., the _____ is often used as a measure of central tendency for skewed distributions.
   a. 15 theorem
   b. Geometric mean1
   c. Undefined
   d. Undefined

34. A _____ is simply a polynomial with two terms.
   a. Binomial1
   b. 15 theorem
   c. Undefined
   d. Undefined

Chapter 14. Multiple Integrals

1. _____ are characteristics or properties of an object that can take on one or more different values.
   a. Variables1
   b. 15 theorem
   c. Undefined
   d. Undefined

2. The very fact that we are measuring objects with respect to some characteristic implies that the objects differ in that characteristic; or stated in another way, that the characteristic can take on a number of different values. These properties or characteristics of an object that can assume two or more different values are referred to as a _____.
   a. 15 theorem
   b. Variable1
   c. Undefined
   d. Undefined

3. At times we must contend with variables that assume a large number of values. In this case it is typical to create _____ of values of the variable and then make a frequency tally of the number of observations falling within each interval. As is the case with any data reduction technique, detail is lost.
   a. ACTRAN
   b. Intervals1
   c. Undefined
   d. Undefined

4. Horizontal axis of display containing the trailing digits is called _____.
   a. Leaves1
   b. 15 theorem
   c. Undefined
   d. Undefined

5. An _____ is an indication of the value of an unknown quantity based on observed data. More formally, an _____ is the particular value of an estimator that is obtained from a particular sample of data and used to indicate the value of a parameter.
   a. Estimate1
   b. ACTRAN
   c. Undefined
   d. Undefined

6. A number that does not change in value in a given situation is a _____.
   a. 15 theorem
   b. Constant1
   c. Undefined
   d. Undefined

7. In a large distribution of data it is often easier to understand the data if it is grouped into intervals where each _____ can contain more than one data value. Distributions are often reduced to 10 to 20 intervals.
   a. ACTRAN
   b. Interval1
   c. Undefined
   d. Undefined

8. _____, the height of the curve for a given value of X; closely related to the probability of an observation in an interval around X.
   a. 15 theorem
   b. Density1
   c. Undefined
   d. Undefined

9. _____ is used synonymously for variable.
   a. 15 theorem
   b. Factor1
   c. Undefined
   d. Undefined

10. In statistics an arrangement of values of a variable showing their observed or theoretical frequency of occurrence is called a _____.

a. Distribution1
c. Undefined
b. 15 theorem
d. Undefined

11. An _____ is any process or study, which results in the collection of data, the outcome of which is unknown. In statistics, the term is usually restricted to situations in which the researcher has control over some of the conditions under which the _____ takes place.
   a. ACTRAN
   b. Experiment1
   c. Undefined
   d. Undefined

12. A population, also referred to as a universe, is any well-defined collection of things. By well-defined we mean that the members of the _____ are spelled out, or an unequivocal statement is made as to which things belong in it and which do not.
   a. Population1
   b. 15 theorem
   c. Undefined
   d. Undefined

13. The most important measure of central tendency, and one of the basic building blocks of all statistical analysis, is the arithmetic _____. It is simply the sum of all the set of values divided by the number of values involved. As a measure of central tendency, it is affected by extreme scores, and it assumes a ratio scale of measurement.
   a. Mean1
   b. 15 theorem
   c. Undefined
   d. Undefined

14. There are properties of objects that do assume one and only value, and we refer to these characteristics as constants. _____, then, are the invariables that differentiate one class of objects from another.
   a. Constants1
   b. 15 theorem
   c. Undefined
   d. Undefined

15. Statistical analysis, sometimes referred to simply as _____, is concerned with the definition and collection, organization, and interpretation of data according to well-defined procedures. The term itself, _____, is a defining characteristic of a sample, such as a sample mean, or sample standard deviation.
   a. 15 theorem
   b. Statistics1
   c. Undefined
   d. Undefined

16. The combination of a particular row and column; the set of observations obtained under identical treatment conditions is simply a _____.
   a. 15 theorem
   b. Cell1
   c. Undefined
   d. Undefined

17. _____ refer to any data source, whether individuals, physical or biological things, geographic locations, time periods, or events; that is, anything upon which observations can be made.
   a. ACTRAN
   b. Objects1
   c. Undefined
   d. Undefined

18. _____ is implied when data values are distributed in the same way above and below the middle of the sample.
   a. Symmetry1
   b. 15 theorem
   c. Undefined
   d. Undefined

Chapter 14. Multiple Integrals

19. A _____ is a subset or portion of a population. Samples are extremely important in the field of statistical analysis, since due to economic and practical constraints we usually cannot make measurements on every single member of the particular population.
    a. 15 theorem
    b. Sample1
    c. Undefined
    d. Undefined

20. The symbol for the effect size is _____.
    a. 15 theorem
    b. Gamma1
    c. Undefined
    d. Undefined

Chapter 15. Integration in Vector Fields

1. In a large distribution of data it is often easier to understand the data if it is grouped into intervals where each _____ can contain more than one data value. Distributions are often reduced to 10 to 20 intervals.
   - a. Interval1
   - b. ACTRAN
   - c. Undefined
   - d. Undefined

2. The very fact that we are measuring objects with respect to some characteristic implies that the objects differ in that characteristic; or stated in another way, that the characteristic can take on a number of different values. These properties or characteristics of an object that can assume two or more different values are referred to as a _____.
   - a. 15 theorem
   - b. Variable1
   - c. Undefined
   - d. Undefined

3. A number that does not change in value in a given situation is a _____.
   - a. 15 theorem
   - b. Constant1
   - c. Undefined
   - d. Undefined

4. In statistics an arrangement of values of a variable showing their observed or theoretical frequency of occurrence is called a _____.
   - a. 15 theorem
   - b. Distribution1
   - c. Undefined
   - d. Undefined

5. _____, the height of the curve for a given value of X; closely related to the probability of an observation in an interval around X.
   - a. Density1
   - b. 15 theorem
   - c. Undefined
   - d. Undefined

6. A _____ is a value used to represent a certain population characteristic. Because of the impracticality of measuring an entire population to determine this value, parameters are usually estimated.
   - a. Parameter1
   - b. 15 theorem
   - c. Undefined
   - d. Undefined

7. At times we must contend with variables that assume a large number of values. In this case it is typical to create _____ of values of the variable and then make a frequency tally of the number of observations falling within each interval. As is the case with any data reduction technique, detail is lost.
   - a. ACTRAN
   - b. Intervals1
   - c. Undefined
   - d. Undefined

8. _____ are characteristics or properties of an object that can take on one or more different values.
   - a. 15 theorem
   - b. Variables1
   - c. Undefined
   - d. Undefined

9. There are properties of objects that do assume one and only value, and we refer to these characteristics as constants. _____, then, are the invariables that differentiate one class of objects from another.
   - a. Constants1
   - b. 15 theorem
   - c. Undefined
   - d. Undefined

10. An _____ is any process or study, which results in the collection of data, the outcome of which is unknown. In statistics, the term is usually restricted to situations in which the researcher has control over some of the conditions under which the _____ takes place.
   a. Experiment1
   b. ACTRAN
   c. Undefined
   d. Undefined

11. Horizontal axis of display containing the trailing digits is called _____.
   a. 15 theorem
   b. Leaves1
   c. Undefined
   d. Undefined

12. An _____ is an indication of the value of an unknown quantity based on observed data. More formally, an _____ is the particular value of an estimator that is obtained from a particular sample of data and used to indicate the value of a parameter.
   a. Estimate1
   b. ACTRAN
   c. Undefined
   d. Undefined

13. _____ is implied when data values are distributed in the same way above and below the middle of the sample.
   a. Symmetry1
   b. 15 theorem
   c. Undefined
   d. Undefined

14. A measure of variability, the _____ is the distance from the lowest to the highest score.
   a. 15 theorem
   b. Range1
   c. Undefined
   d. Undefined

15. The defining characteristics of populations are called _____. Observations must be made on every single member of the population in question in order to precisely state the value of _____.
   a. Parameters1
   b. 15 theorem
   c. Undefined
   d. Undefined

16. The goal of most inferential statistical analyses is to be able to generalize or apply the findings to the entire population and not just to the sample. The concept of _____ requires that the researcher determine some level of probability that the findings were due to chance or that they actually describe the population. The value of the probability that the findings were due to chance is usually reported when the findings of an analysis is reported.
   a. 15 theorem
   b. Generalization1
   c. Undefined
   d. Undefined

17. One major objective of statistical analysis is the identification of associations or _____ that exist between and among sets of observations. In other words, does knowledge about about one set of data allow us to infer or predict characteristics about another set or sets of data.
   a. 15 theorem
   b. Relationships1
   c. Undefined
   d. Undefined

18. The most important measure of central tendency, and one of the basic building blocks of all statistical analysis, is the arithmetic _____. It is simply the sum of all the set of values divided by the number of values involved. As a measure of central tendency, it is affected by extreme scores, and it assumes a ratio scale of measurement.

a. Mean1
c. Undefined
b. 15 theorem
d. Undefined

Chapter 1

1. a	2. b	3. b	4. a	5. a	6. a	7. b	8. b	9. a	10. b
11. a	12. a	13. a	14. a	15. b	16. a	17. a	18. a	19. a	20. b
21. a	22. b	23. b	24. a	25. b	26. a	27. a	28. a	29. a	30. b
31. a	32. b	33. a	34. b	35. a	36. a	37. a	38. a	39. a	40. b
41. a	42. a	43. b	44. a	45. a	46. b	47. a	48. a	49. a	50. b
51. b	52. b	53. a	54. b	55. b	56. a	57. a	58. b	59. b	60. b
61. a	62. b	63. b	64. b	65. b	66. b	67. b	68. a	69. b	70. b
71. b	72. b	73. a	74. a	75. b	76. b	77. b	78. a	79. a	80. a
81. a	82. a	83. a	84. b	85. a	86. b	87. a	88. b	89. b	90. a
91. b	92. a	93. a	94. a	95. b	96. b	97. a	98. a	99. a	100. b
101. a	102. a	103. b	104. b	105. b	106. b	107. a	108. b	109. a	110. a
111. b	112. b	113. a	114. b	115. a	116. a	117. a	118. b	119. b	120. a
121. b	122. b	123. b	124. b	125. b	126. a	127. b	128. a	129. b	130. a
131. a	132. a	133. b	134. a	135. a	136. a	137. a	138. a	139. a	140. a
141. a	142. a	143. b	144. b	145. b	146. a	147. a	148. a	149. a	150. a
151. a	152. a	153. b	154. a	155. b	156. b	157. a	158. a	159. b	160. b
161. b	162. b	163. a	164. a	165. a	166. a	167. a	168. b	169. b	170. a
171. b	172. b	173. a	174. b	175. a	176. b	177. a	178. a	179. a	180. b
181. a	182. b	183. a	184. a	185. a	186. b	187. b			

Chapter 2

1. b	2. b	3. b	4. a	5. a	6. b	7. b	8. b	9. a	10. a
11. b	12. b	13. b	14. a	15. a	16. a	17. b	18. b	19. a	20. b
21. a	22. a	23. a	24. b	25. a	26. b	27. b	28. a	29. a	30. b
31. a	32. a	33. a	34. b	35. a	36. b	37. a	38. a	39. a	40. b
41. b	42. b	43. a	44. a	45. b	46. a	47. b	48. b	49. a	50. b
51. b	52. b	53. b	54. a	55. a	56. b	57. a	58. a	59. b	60. a
61. a	62. b	63. b	64. b	65. a	66. a	67. a	68. b	69. a	70. a
71. a	72. b	73. a	74. a	75. b	76. b	77. b	78. a	79. b	80. b
81. b	82. a	83. a	84. a	85. b	86. b	87. a	88. b	89. b	90. a
91. b	92. b	93. a	94. b	95. b	96. b	97. b	98. a	99. b	100. b
101. b	102. b	103. b	104. b	105. a	106. a	107. b	108. b	109. a	110. a
111. b	112. a	113. b	114. a	115. a	116. b	117. b	118. a	119. b	120. b
121. b	122. a	123. a	124. b	125. b	126. b	127. b	128. b	129. a	130. b
131. b	132. a	133. b	134. a	135. a	136. a	137. a	138. a	139. b	140. b
141. a	142. a	143. b	144. b	145. a	146. b	147. b	148. a	149. b	150. a
151. b	152. a	153. b	154. a	155. b	156. a	157. b	158. b	159. a	

ANSWER KEY

Chapter 3

1. a	2. b	3. b	4. b	5. b	6. a	7. a	8. b	9. b	10. b
11. b	12. b	13. a	14. b	15. b	16. a	17. b	18. b	19. a	20. a
21. b	22. a	23. b	24. a	25. b	26. b	27. b	28. b	29. a	30. b
31. a	32. a	33. b	34. a	35. a	36. a	37. a	38. b	39. a	40. b
41. b	42. b	43. a	44. a	45. b	46. a	47. a	48. a	49. a	50. b
51. b	52. b	53. a	54. b	55. b	56. a	57. b	58. b	59. b	60. b
61. b	62. a	63. b	64. a	65. a	66. a	67. b	68. b	69. b	70. b
71. b	72. a	73. a	74. b	75. a	76. a	77. b	78. a	79. a	80. a
81. b	82. b	83. a	84. b	85. b	86. b	87. b	88. b	89. a	90. b
91. a	92. b	93. b	94. a	95. a	96. a	97. a	98. b	99. b	100. a
101. b	102. a	103. b	104. b	105. b	106. a	107. b	108. a	109. b	110. a
111. b	112. b	113. a	114. a	115. b	116. a	117. b	118. b	119. a	120. a
121. a	122. b	123. a	124. b	125. b	126. a	127. a	128. a	129. b	130. a
131. a	132. a	133. b	134. a	135. a	136. b	137. b	138. a	139. b	140. b
141. b	142. a	143. b	144. a	145. b	146. a	147. b	148. a	149. a	150. a
151. a	152. b	153. a	154. a	155. a	156. b	157. a	158. b	159. a	160. b
161. a	162. b	163. b	164. a	165. b	166. a	167. a	168. b	169. a	170. a
171. b	172. b	173. a	174. a	175. a	176. b	177. b	178. b	179. b	180. a
181. b	182. b	183. b	184. a	185. b	186. b	187. a	188. a	189. b	190. b
191. a	192. a	193. b	194. b	195. b	196. b	197. a	198. b	199. a	200. b
201. a	202. a	203. a	204. a	205. a	206. a	207. a	208. b	209. b	210. b
211. a	212. b	213. b	214. a	215. a	216. a	217. a	218. b	219. b	220. b
221. b	222. a	223. a	224. a	225. b	226. b	227. a	228. b	229. b	230. b
231. b	232. a	233. a	234. a	235. b	236. b	237. a	238. a		

Chapter 4

1. b	2. a	3. a	4. b	5. b	6. a	7. a	8. b	9. b	10. b
11. b	12. b	13. b	14. a	15. b	16. a	17. b	18. a	19. a	20. a
21. a	22. a	23. b	24. a	25. a	26. a	27. b	28. b	29. b	30. b
31. a	32. a	33. a	34. b	35. a	36. a	37. a	38. b	39. b	40. a
41. a	42. b	43. a	44. b	45. a	46. b	47. b	48. a	49. b	50. b
51. a	52. b	53. b	54. b	55. b	56. a	57. a	58. a	59. b	60. a
61. a	62. b	63. b	64. a	65. b	66. a	67. a	68. b	69. b	70. b
71. b	72. b	73. a	74. b	75. a	76. b	77. b	78. a	79. a	80. a
81. b	82. a	83. b	84. b	85. a	86. b	87. b	88. a	89. b	90. a
91. b	92. b	93. a	94. b	95. b	96. a	97. b	98. a	99. b	100. b
101. a	102. a	103. b	104. b	105. b	106. a	107. b	108. a	109. a	110. b
111. a	112. a	113. b	114. a	115. b	116. a	117. a	118. a	119. a	120. b
121. b	122. a	123. b	124. a	125. a	126. a	127. b	128. b	129. a	130. a
131. a	132. a	133. a	134. b	135. b	136. a	137. a	138. a	139. b	140. a
141. b	142. a	143. b	144. b	145. a	146. a	147. b	148. a	149. b	150. b
151. b	152. b	153. b	154. a	155. a	156. b	157. a	158. a	159. a	160. b
161. b	162. a	163. b	164. b	165. a	166. b	167. a	168. b	169. b	170. a
171. a	172. b	173. b	174. a	175. a	176. a	177. b	178. b	179. b	180. b
181. b	182. b	183. b	184. a	185. a	186. a	187. b	188. a	189. a	190. a
191. b	192. a	193. a	194. b	195. a	196. a	197. b	198. a	199. b	200. a
201. b	202. a								

Chapter 5

1. a	2. a	3. b	4. b	5. b	6. b	7. b	8. b	9. b	10. a
11. a	12. b	13. b	14. b	15. a	16. b	17. b	18. b	19. a	20. a
21. b	22. a	23. b	24. a	25. a	26. b	27. b	28. b	29. b	30. a
31. b	32. a	33. a	34. b	35. a	36. a	37. b	38. b	39. a	40. a
41. b	42. a	43. a	44. b	45. b	46. b	47. a	48. a	49. a	50. a
51. b	52. b	53. b	54. a	55. b	56. a	57. b	58. b	59. b	60. b
61. a	62. b	63. a	64. b	65. b	66. b	67. b	68. b	69. a	70. b
71. b	72. a	73. a	74. b	75. a	76. a	77. a	78. a	79. b	80. a
81. a	82. b	83. a	84. b	85. b	86. b	87. b	88. b	89. b	90. a
91. b	92. b	93. b	94. b	95. b	96. a	97. a	98. b	99. b	100. a
101. a	102. b	103. b	104. b	105. b	106. a	107. a	108. b	109. b	110. a
111. a	112. a	113. a	114. b	115. a	116. a	117. a	118. b	119. b	120. b
121. a	122. b	123. b	124. a	125. b	126. b	127. b	128. b	129. a	130. a
131. b	132. a	133. a	134. b	135. a	136. b	137. a	138. a	139. a	140. b
141. a	142. a	143. b	144. b	145. b	146. b	147. a	148. b	149. b	150. a
151. b	152. a	153. b	154. b	155. b	156. a	157. a	158. a	159. a	160. b
161. a	162. a	163. b	164. a	165. b	166. a	167. a	168. b	169. b	170. a
171. a	172. a	173. a	174. b	175. b	176. a	177. b	178. a	179. b	180. a
181. a	182. a	183. a	184. a	185. b	186. a	187. b	188. b	189. b	190. a
191. a	192. b	193. b	194. a	195. a	196. b	197. a	198. b		

ANSWER KEY

Chapter 6

1. b	2. b	3. b	4. a	5. a	6. b	7. a	8. a	9. b	10. b
11. b	12. b	13. a	14. a	15. b	16. a	17. a	18. a	19. b	20. b
21. b	22. a	23. b	24. a	25. a	26. a	27. a	28. a	29. b	30. b
31. a	32. a	33. a	34. a	35. b	36. b	37. b	38. a	39. b	40. b
41. a	42. a	43. a	44. b	45. a	46. a	47. a	48. b	49. a	50. b
51. a	52. a	53. b	54. b	55. a	56. a	57. b	58. a	59. b	60. a
61. a	62. a	63. a	64. b	65. a	66. a	67. a	68. a	69. b	70. b
71. b	72. b	73. a	74. a	75. a	76. b	77. a	78. b	79. a	80. b
81. a	82. a	83. b	84. b	85. b	86. b	87. a	88. a	89. b	90. a
91. a	92. a	93. a	94. a	95. b	96. a	97. a	98. b	99. a	100. a
101. a	102. b	103. b	104. b	105. b	106. b	107. a	108. b	109. b	110. b
111. b	112. a	113. b	114. b	115. b	116. b	117. a	118. a	119. b	120. a
121. b	122. a	123. b	124. a	125. a	126. a	127. b	128. a	129. b	130. b
131. a	132. b	133. b	134. a	135. a	136. a	137. b	138. a	139. b	140. b
141. a	142. a	143. a	144. b	145. b	146. b	147. a	148. a	149. a	150. a
151. a	152. b	153. b	154. a	155. b	156. b	157. a	158. a	159. b	160. b
161. a	162. b	163. b	164. a	165. a	166. b	167. a	168. a	169. b	170. b
171. a	172. a	173. b	174. b	175. b	176. a	177. a	178. a	179. a	180. a
181. b	182. a	183. b	184. a	185. a	186. a	187. a	188. b	189. a	190. a
191. b	192. a	193. b	194. b	195. a					

Chapter 7

1. a	2. a	3. b	4. b	5. b	6. a	7. b	8. b	9. b	10. b
11. a	12. a	13. a	14. a	15. b	16. a	17. b	18. b	19. a	20. a
21. a	22. b	23. b	24. a	25. b	26. a	27. a	28. b	29. a	30. b
31. a	32. b	33. a	34. b	35. a	36. b	37. b	38. b	39. a	40. a
41. a	42. b	43. a	44. a	45. b	46. a	47. a	48. b	49. a	50. b
51. a	52. b	53. b	54. a	55. a	56. b	57. a	58. a	59. b	60. a
61. b	62. b	63. b	64. b	65. a	66. b	67. b	68. b	69. b	70. b
71. a	72. a	73. b	74. b	75. a	76. b	77. b	78. b	79. a	80. a
81. b	82. a	83. b	84. a	85. a	86. a	87. a	88. b	89. b	90. b
91. b	92. a	93. a	94. a	95. b	96. b	97. a	98. a	99. a	100. a
101. a	102. b	103. b	104. a	105. b	106. a	107. b	108. b	109. b	110. a
111. b	112. b	113. b	114. b	115. b	116. a	117. b	118. b	119. a	120. b
121. a	122. b	123. b	124. a	125. a	126. b	127. b	128. b	129. a	130. a
131. b	132. a	133. a	134. b	135. b	136. a	137. a	138. a	139. b	140. a
141. b	142. b	143. a	144. b	145. a	146. a	147. b	148. b	149. a	150. a
151. a	152. a	153. b	154. a	155. a	156. b	157. a	158. b	159. a	160. b
161. b	162. b	163. b	164. a	165. a	166. a	167. b	168. a	169. a	170. a
171. a	172. b	173. a	174. b	175. a	176. a	177. b	178. b	179. a	180. b
181. a	182. a	183. a	184. a	185. b	186. a	187. b	188. a	189. a	190. a
191. a	192. b	193. b	194. b	195. a	196. a	197. a	198. a	199. a	200. b
201. b	202. a	203. a	204. a	205. b	206. b	207. a	208. b	209. a	210. a
211. b	212. a	213. b	214. a	215. a	216. b	217. b	218. a	219. b	220. a
221. b	222. a	223. a	224. b	225. a	226. b	227. a	228. b	229. a	230. a
231. b	232. b	233. b	234. b	235. a	236. b	237. b	238. a	239. b	240. b
241. b	242. b	243. a	244. a	245. a	246. b	247. a	248. b	249. a	250. b
251. a	252. a								

Chapter 8

1. a	2. a	3. a	4. a	5. b	6. a	7. b	8. b	9. a	10. b
11. a	12. a	13. a	14. b	15. a	16. a	17. a	18. b	19. a	20. a
21. b	22. b	23. b	24. a	25. b	26. b	27. a	28. b	29. a	30. b
31. b	32. a	33. a	34. b	35. b	36. b	37. b	38. b	39. a	40. a
41. a	42. b	43. a	44. b	45. b	46. a	47. b	48. b	49. a	50. a
51. b	52. b	53. b	54. b	55. a	56. b	57. b	58. a	59. a	60. a
61. a	62. b	63. b	64. b	65. b	66. b	67. a	68. b	69. a	70. b
71. b	72. a	73. b	74. a	75. a	76. b	77. b	78. a	79. b	80. a
81. a	82. b	83. a	84. b	85. a	86. a	87. a	88. a	89. b	90. b
91. a	92. b	93. b	94. a	95. a	96. a	97. b	98. b	99. a	100. b
101. b	102. b	103. b	104. b	105. b	106. a	107. b	108. a	109. a	110. a
111. a	112. a	113. a	114. a	115. b	116. a	117. b	118. b	119. b	120. b
121. b	122. a	123. a	124. a	125. b	126. b	127. a	128. a	129. b	130. a
131. a	132. b	133. a	134. b	135. a	136. a	137. a	138. b		

ANSWER KEY

Chapter 9

1. a	2. b	3. a	4. a	5. a	6. b	7. b	8. b	9. b	10. a
11. b	12. a	13. a	14. a	15. b	16. a	17. b	18. a	19. b	20. a
21. a	22. b	23. a	24. b	25. b	26. b	27. b	28. a	29. a	30. b
31. a	32. b	33. b	34. a	35. b	36. b	37. a	38. b	39. a	40. b
41. b	42. a	43. b	44. b	45. b	46. b	47. a	48. b	49. b	50. b
51. b	52. b	53. a	54. a	55. b	56. b	57. a	58. a	59. a	60. a
61. b	62. b	63. a	64. b	65. b	66. b	67. a	68. b	69. b	70. b
71. b	72. b	73. b	74. b	75. a	76. b	77. b	78. b	79. a	80. a
81. b	82. b	83. a	84. b	85. b	86. a	87. b	88. a	89. b	90. b
91. b	92. a	93. a	94. a	95. a	96. b	97. b	98. a	99. a	100. b
101. a	102. b	103. a	104. b	105. b	106. a	107. a	108. a	109. b	110. b
111. b	112. a	113. a	114. b	115. a	116. b	117. b	118. a	119. a	120. a
121. b	122. b	123. a	124. b	125. b	126. b	127. a	128. a	129. b	130. b
131. a	132. a	133. b	134. b	135. a	136. b	137. b	138. a	139. b	140. a
141. b	142. a	143. a	144. a	145. b	146. b	147. b	148. a	149. a	150. a
151. a	152. a	153. b	154. a	155. b	156. b	157. b	158. b	159. a	160. a
161. b	162. a	163. a	164. b	165. b	166. a	167. b	168. a	169. a	170. a
171. b	172. a	173. b	174. a	175. a	176. b	177. a	178. b	179. a	180. b
181. a									

Chapter 10

1. b	2. a	3. b	4. b	5. a	6. b	7. a	8. a	9. a	10. a
11. a	12. a	13. b	14. a	15. b	16. b	17. b	18. b	19. b	20. a
21. a	22. b	23. a	24. a						

Chapter 11

1. a	2. b	3. b	4. a	5. b	6. b	7. b	8. b	9. a	10. a
11. b	12. b	13. b	14. a	15. b	16. b	17. a	18. b	19. a	20. a

Chapter 12

1. a	2. a	3. a	4. a	5. b	6. b	7. b	8. a	9. b	10. a
11. a	12. a	13. b	14. a	15. a	16. b	17. a	18. b	19. b	20. a

Chapter 13

1. a	2. b	3. b	4. b	5. a	6. b	7. b	8. a	9. b	10. b
11. a	12. a	13. a	14. a	15. b	16. b	17. a	18. b	19. a	20. a
21. b	22. a	23. a	24. b	25. a	26. a	27. a	28. a	29. b	30. b
31. b	32. a	33. b	34. a						

Chapter 14

1. a	2. b	3. b	4. a	5. a	6. b	7. b	8. b	9. b	10. a
11. b	12. a	13. a	14. a	15. b	16. b	17. b	18. a	19. b	20. b

Chapter 15

1. a 2. b 3. b 4. b 5. a 6. a 7. b 8. b 9. a 10. a
11. b 12. a 13. a 14. b 15. a 16. b 17. b 18. a

www.ingramcontent.com/pod-product-compliance
Lightning Source LLC
Chambersburg PA
CBHW081351230426
43667CB00017B/2792